08-4 ✓

TEACH YOURSELF BOOKS

439
Gle

Glende

D1003041

Icelan

WITHDRAWN

$16.95

ICELANDIC

P. J. T. Glendening

TEACH YOURSELF BOOKS

Long-renowned as the authoritative source for self-guided learning – with more than 30 million copies sold worldwide – the *Teach Yourself* series includes over 200 titles in the fields of languages, crafts, hobbies, sports, and other leisure activities.

British Library Cataloguing in Publication Data

A CIP catalogue record for this title is available from the British Library

Library of Congress Catalog Card Number: 93-83156

First published in UK 1961 by Hodder Headline Plc, 338 Euston Road, London NW1 3BH

First published in US 1993 by NTC Publishing Group, 4255 West Touhy Avenue, Lincolnwood (Chicago), Illinois 60646 – 1975 U.S.A.

Copyright © Hodder & Stoughton Ltd   6/96   493 GLE

Printed in England by Cox & Wyman Ltd, Reading, Berkshire.

Second impression (with revisions) 1966
Impression number   26   25   24   23   22   21   20   19   18
Year   1999   1998   1997   1996   1995

PREFACE

CONSIDERING that Icelandic is one of the few languages in the same category as English, namely a Germanic language, and that it can moreover be regarded as one of the parent languages of English, the study of either its ancient or modern form is singularly neglected.

The surviving members of the Germanic branch of the Indo-European family of languages are: of the Western branch, German on the one hand and Dutch and English on the other; and of the Northern branch, Swedish, Danish, Norwegian, Icelandic and Faroese. The development of certain differences which made it possible to divide this Germanic branch into Western and Northern (the Eastern being Gothic and related languages, all long since dead) occurred about 400 B.C. to 100 B.C., while the emergence of significant differences in the Northern branch became decisive about the year A.D. 800. At this time the Scandinavian dialects were but variations on an original theme, while English, or rather the Anglo-Saxon dialects, were not far removed from Norse in structure, sounds or vocabulary.

Icelandic today is much as it was when Iceland was first colonized, mainly from Norway, in and after A.D. 874. It has in large measure marked time for a thousand years. The great store of literature of the early periods is readily understandable to all speakers of present-day Icelandic. Thus a study of modern Icelandic brings within our grasp the great poetic and prose Eddas as also the great number of sagas of all types. Note also that this early language, called Old Norse, is that of the Runic inscriptions, the stone carvings of the Vikings, and is therefore the oldest form of any Germanic language of which records exist.

To expand the point about Icelandic being one of the parent languages of English. Britain was subjected to two centuries or so of strong Norse influence, from about A.D. 800 to about A.D. 1050. Remember that at the time a strong similarity existed between the Anglo-Saxon dialects and the Norse tongue. Contact with Scandinavians settled in Britain led to many case-endings becoming confused—and confusion leads to discarding

—and to the taking of hundreds of words from Norse, not to mention the copying of the Norse system of forming new expressions by adding a prefix to a common verb to modify the meaning. Clearly the Norse word is often impossible to recognize from the native one, in view of the already existing similarity, while in some cases both words survived with different meanings (e.g. ship and skiff, shirt and skirt). In short, the Norse language had a profound effect on the shaping of English, and its influence is to be seen not in any wealth of literary additions but in its effects on the very heart of the language, on the words we most use in conversation, on the structure of our language. Generalizations are often suspect, but it is pretty near the mark to say that while the Latin element in English is elegant, the Icelandic element is down-to-earth and matter-of-fact.

Naturally, since the time of this close contact English has undergone tremendous changes, while Icelandic, as pointed out, has not. English has dropped its flexions, while Icelandic has retained all hers. Icelandic is thus a highly inflected language. There are three genders, and nouns, adjectives and verbs have considerable variation of endings. This luggage of the language is no doubt unfortunate, but must not bog us down, as inflections often tend to do. To tackle Icelandic it is necessary not to lose sight of the wood for the trees. Here is a case, *par excellence*, for first taking a bird's-eye view of the language before concentrating on the various points of grammar. Realize that the article is attached to the end of the noun, that prepositions govern cases, that many verbs are used impersonally, that there is a middle voice apart from active and passive. Realize these things at the outset, and do not be surprised by them as they crop up in the course of more detailed study. Then—you must read a lot. You cannot hear Icelandic radio programmes, and you seldom meet Icelanders, so the printed page must needs be the main medium of instruction. Bear in mind, too, that the unit of language is the sentence, not the isolated word. Drill yourself with many sentences using any given construction, and do not be content just to learn lists of words.

Iceland is the only country said to have one hundred per cent literacy, and this does not indicate merely that all can

read and write. Writing is a sort of national pastime, and many
people write with no thought of obtaining wide sales for their
works. There is a high standard of literary appreciation, and
many authors achieve a high level of writing, even by world
standards. The obvious name to mention is that of the Nobel
Prize winner, Halldór Kiljan Laxness. This mention of writing
brings us to the last point. In the lessons, the texts have been
chosen on account of their common, everyday language. The
basic, everyday language comes first, and then we may study
style and different literary effects. The idea here is first to study
the language in its general form, leaving further study to
explore the rich fields of Icelandic writing.

CONTENTS

PRONUNCIATION

The Icelandic Alphabet

There are thirty-three letters in the Icelandic alphabet: *a, á, b, d, ð, e, é, f, g, h, i, í, j, k, l, m, n, o, ó, p, r, s, t, u, ú, v, x, y, ý, z, þ, æ, ö*. Apart from these letters, *c, q* and *w* are to be found in foreign words only. These letters are either vowels or conconants (*sérhljóð eða samhljóð*). The following are the vowels: *a, á, e, é, i, í, o, ó, u, ú, y, ý, æ, ö*. In the following, be careful to differentiate between phonetic symbol and ordinary letter.

Vowels

In Icelandic there may be distinguished twelve different pure vowel sounds and six diphthongs. Not in every case does one single letter represent one single sound, although there is far more regularity than in English in this respect.

Single Vowels

Phonetic Symbol

[aɪ]   this is the long *a*-sound, and is pronounced further forward in the mouth than is the corresponding long *a*-sound in Standard English. This sound is heard in such words as *maður, það, dalur, lag*—that is, in words in which the *a* is followed by a single consonant.

[a]   this is the short version of the above long *a*-sound, and is heard in these words: *kalla, hrafn, hattur, aftur*—that is, where there are two consonants following the *a*-sound.

[eɪ]   this long sound is the open ɛ-sound, found in such words as *vel, gleðja, telja*—that is, before a single consonant (the *j* not being reckoned as a true consonant sound). Note that this long *e*-sound tends to become diphthongized, being sounded as *ea*.

[e]   this sound corresponds to the sound found in English "get", and is encountered in such words as: *detta, hestur, gestur*.

[ī] the long *i*-sound is a sort of protracted vowel of the type
     heard in the English "pin". This sound has no equi-
     valent in English (or in the better-known European
     languages). It is found in such words as: *bit, tin, rit*.

[i] this sound is that heard in English "pin", and in Icelandic
     occurs in such words as: *hitta, hilla, rimma*. Note the
     double consonant following.

[iː] this sound is like the vowel in English "been", and is
     found in such words as: *ríkur, líka, fingur, stigi, stígl*.

[oi] this sound resembles the vowel heard in the English "all".
     Note that Icelandic speakers sometimes tend to pro-
     nounce this sound as *oa*, and even as *uo*. It may be
     heard in: *vor, gol, gor, kol*.

[o] this resembles the sound heard in English "pot". Ex-
     amples are: *kobbi, koddi, norska, tollur*.

[uː] this is the long *oo*-sound, as in English "moon". One may
     in fact distinguish two variations of this: the ordinary
     one and the somewhat shorter one in the written com-
     binations -*ung*- and -*unk*-. Words with this sound
     include: *munkur, þungur* (shorter sound), and *stúfur,
     stúka, stúlka*. This is the written *ú*, or unaccented *u*
     before a single consonant.

[u] this resembles the vowel sound of English "earn" or of
     French "*peur*", but is a shorter sound. It is heard in
     such words as: *skurður* (first vowel), *hurð, grunnur*.

[ö] in this sound the position of the tongue is somewhat lower
     in the mouth than it is for the preceding vowel. Other-
     wise it resembles the vowel in English "turn". Ex-
     amples: *börn, röð, rök*.

Diphthongs

[au] this is the sound of the Icelandic letter *á*. Examples are:
     fá, hjá, nál, skrá.

[ei] this sound resembles the Standard English vowel sound
     in "came", and is normally written as *ei, ey*, or *eng* or
     enk. Examples are: *steik, veiki, drengur*.

[je] this is the sound represented by the written symbol *é*, and is pronounced as short Icelandic *í* followed by short *e*. Examples are: *ég, mér, tré, sér, lét*.

[ou] this is like the English sound in "so". It is written as *ó*. Examples are: *hót, ljóð, ljón, ljós*.

[ai] this is the sound of the written symbol *æ*, sounded as in English "eye". Examples are: *hlæja, kær, mæla*.

[öi] this is the sound of the written symbol *au*, being composed of the Icelandic *ö*-sound followed by the long *í*-sound. Words having this sound are: *Haukur, laun, laus, þröngur* (note that the written combinations *-öng-* and *-önk-* also have this sound).

Notes

(1) *Vowel Length*

Vowel length has been mentioned already. The difference between the *i* in tin and the *i* in *finna* is one of length. It is well at this stage to point out the rules governing vowel length. Firstly, a written accent denotes a long vowel (or a diphthong, as seen). Note that *í* and *ý* are equal, as are *i* and *y*, *y* and *ý* being employed only to show mutations of original *u* and *ú*. Secondly, unaccented vowels are long, as pointed out, when followed by a single vowel (see *gul, hafa, koma*). Thirdly, unaccented vowels are long if followed by *-kr, -pr, -tr, -gð* and *-gr*, as in the words *akrar, skopra, slitna, sigð, digran*. Again, unaccented vowels are long before *-kl, -kn, -pn, -tl* and *tn*, but here "aspiration" takes place (see below). Examples include *Hekla, blikna, glapna, kitla, vatna*. In other cases, vowel length is short.

(2) *Aspiration*

By this is meant a characteristic very typical of Icelandic, and having no counterpart in other European languages. The last part of an ordinary vowel or diphthong is aspirated—that is, the vowel is cut short or interrupted, and continued as a sort of whisper, which gives the impression of the introduction of an *h*-sound. The word *"uppi"*, for example, sounds like *u(h)pi*. Note that this aspiration leads to the following double consonant being sounded as a single one. Aspiration occurs

when a vowel comes before *-kl, -kn, -pn, -tl, -tn, -kk, -pp, -tt.*
Examples are: *gutla, líkna, opna, mikla, batna, klakkur, klippa, klettur.*

(3) *-ang* and *-ank* are pronounced as if written *áng, -ánk*—
(that is, *aung, -aunk*). See the words *langur* (*laungur*), *banga*
(*baunga*) and *banki* (*baunki*).

(4) The dative plural of nouns, before the suffixed article,
normally has the pronunciation *-onum* instead of *-unum.*

Consonants

[b] this has the same quality as the English *b*-sound, and is
     silent before *-d, -s* and *-t* when preceded by *m-*. Thus
     the *b* is silent in *lambsins*. Note that the combination
     bb loses its voiced quality to a certain extent, tending
     towards *pp*.

[d] this resembles the English *d*-sound, but most often is
     silent before *-s* of the genitive case of nouns. Lands (of
     the land) is therefore generally pronounced *lans*. Note
     that *dd* also loses something of its voiced quality,
     tending towards *tt*.

[ð] this is the symbol for the *th*-sound as in "the".

[f] this is the sound of the English *f*. Confusion can easily
     arise here, as the written symbol, *f*, represents four
     different sounds. Firstly there is the phonetic *f*, as
     above. This sound occurs when *f* is the first letter of a
     word and when followed by *k* or *s*. (For instance, in
     rífka, hafs.) Secondly, the written *f* stands for the
     phonetic *v*-sound when between vowels or when at the
     end of a word; for example, *hafa* and *haf*. In the com-
     binations *-lft* and *-lfs* it is very common to drop the *f*
     entirely, as in the word *kálfskjöt*. Note that this *v*-sound
     is not used when the *f* stands between two vowels that
     belong to different elements making up a compound
     word. Thirdly, the written *f* represents a phonetic *b*-
     sound when followed by *l* or *n*, as in the words *kefli* and
     stofna. Lastly, the combinations *-fnd* and *-fnt* contain
     an *m*-sound instead of the *-fn*, as in *nefnd*.

[g] this is the hard sound as heard in English "good". The phonetic *g* corresponds to the written Icelandic *g* when initial, and when followed by *a, á, o, ó, u, ú* and *ð*: moreover, when following a consonant, as in *langur*, or when followed by *g, l* or *n*, as in *vagn* (note modifications later).

[x] this is the guttural sound as in Scottish "loch", and is heard in Icelandic when a written *g* is followed by *t*, as in *sagt*.

[ɣ] this is the voiced version of the guttural above, and occurs when the written *g* stands between vowels or before *r* or *ð*. Examples are: *draga, saga, hægð* [draɪɣa—saɪɣa—haɪɣð]. Also at the ends of words, as in *lag* and *lög*. Note, however, that when the *g* comes after *á, ó* or *ú*, the sound almost disappears, as in *bági, lóg, múgur*. The consonant group *-gld-* is pronounced as [ɣld].

[h] this is sounded as in English. The *h* of *hann* and *hún* is often dropped after a consonant.

[k] pronounced as in English "ark". A following *e, i, í, y, ý,* or *æ* results in a slight *y*-sound being added after the *k*, as in *kengur, kisa, kíta, kýta* and *kær*. In the combination *-skt* the pronunciation is *-st*, as in *spanskt, enskt*.

[l] this is the sound that occurs in English "steal", except that the *l* in *-lk, -lp, -lt* is palatalized (resembling the Welsh *ll*). *Stúlka* is an example.

[m] as in English; *nema, heim*.

[n] normally as in English; however, in the combinations *ánn, ínn, ýnn, ónn, ænn, aunn, einn* and *eynn* the first *n* is sounded as a *d* (or *t*), while the second *n* is merely breathed. For instance, *Spánn, finn, sónn, kænn, hreinn*. This does not apply, however, when the *-nn* forms part of the article. Note that in the combination *-ns* the *n* drops out and causes the preceding vowel to become nasalized, as in *dansa*.

[p] as in English. The written *-ps* and *-pt* are pronounced *-fs* and *-ft* respectively, as in *gips, skips*.

[r]   the Icelandic sound is a trilled -r.

[s]   this has the voiceless sound as in English mouse. The
      written z also has this voiceless sound, as in *gizka*, *unz*.

[t]   as in English. In the combinations -*sts* and -*tns* the *t* (and
      n) are not usually sounded. Thus *gests* and *hests* are
      pronounced *gess* and *hess*. Note that this applies only to
      genitive endings, and is not absolutely one hundred per
      cent.

[v]   approximately as in English. Note the spelling with *v* or
      f (see the notes on *f*).

[θ]   this is written *þ*, and is the sound heard in English "think".

Note the following table of combined forms, when an
imperative is followed by *þú*:

ð and *þ*	become	*dd*	:	*bíð· þú*	becomes	*bíddu*
d and *þ*	„	*t*	:	*vind þú*	„	*vintu*
f and *þ*	„	*fð*	:	*klíf þú*	„	*klífðu*
hard *g* and *þ*	„	*gd*	:	*fylg þú*	„	*fylgdu*
soft *g* (*ch*) and *þ*	„	*gð*	:	*seg þú*	„	*segðu*
k and *þ*	„	*kt*	:	*leik þú*	„	*leiktu*
p and *þ*	„	*pt*	:	*drep þú*	„	*dreptu*
t and *þ*	„	*tt*	:	*slít þú*	„	*slíttu*

Note at the same time that the *ú* becomes unaccented *u*.

Notes

(1) All double consonants are really sounded double. Thus
bb, *dd*, *gg*, *kk*, *mm*, *pp*, *rr*, *ss*, *tt* are pronounced double. Special
cases, as seen, are *ll* and *nn*.

(2) The letter *g* has the voiced guttural sound in the combinations: -*gld*, -*glt*, -*glst*, -*gnd*, -*gnt*, -*gnst*. Example: *rigndi*
(rained).

(3) *Guð* is pronounced as though there were a soft *v* after the
g [gvœð]. This holds for all compounds using this word.

(4) *G* has the phonetic *j*-sound when a short vowel is followed
by *gi* or *gj*. Example: *kragi* (collar), pronounced *kraji*.

(5) When beginning a word or preceded by another consonant, and followed by *e, i, í, y, ý* and *æ*, the letter *g* has the phonetic *g*-sound followed by a faint phonetic *j*-sound. Thus in the word *gefa* (give), the pronunciation is *g(j)eva*.

(6) The letters *k, p* and *t* are often voiced, i.e. they are pronounced as *g, b* and *d* respectively. This occurs:

(i) between vowels (e.g. *taka* [taɪga];
(ii) before a vowel or voiceless ð (e.g. *bliðka* [bliːθga];
(iii) after initial *s*, or between *s* and *a* voiced sound (e.g. *spá* [sbau]).

Similarly, *p* and *t* may be sounded as *b* and *d* respectively when they occur before a *j* (e.g. *lepja* [lɛbja]).

(7) Note that the written *j* in Icelandic corresponds to the phonetic *j*-sound, as for example the *y* in the English *yes* and *yacht*.

(8) When the word "*það*" is not the first word of a sentence, and is followed by a vowel sound, normally only the ð is sounded in ordinary colloquial Icelandic. For example, in the sentence: *hún skilur það ekki*, the spoken form would be: *hún skilur 'ð ekki*.

(9) The combination *hv* in *hvað, hvernig*, etc., is usually pronounced [kv], less usually [xw] (i.e. [kvaɪð] or [xwuð]).

(10) Metathesis. This is the changing of the position of two sounds within a word. It sometimes occurs in Icelandic in the consonant group *-gld-*, so that *sigldi* may be pronounced [silʏdi] or [siʏldi]; also in the word *siglt* [sixlt] or [silxt]; and in the combination *gn*, which follows the process with *ng* when there is a following consonant (except *j* or *v*). The sound then becomes [ŋ]. E.g. *hegndi* [hɛŋdi]; *kringla* [kriŋla].

(11) In a number of short words, the *v* is dropped altogether; also in longer words between *á, ó* and *a* following *a, i* or *u*. Thus *því* is pronounced [θiː] and *sljóvan* becomes [sljouan].

(12) Stress. This is very regular in Icelandic, nearly always falling on the first syllable. Occasionally there may be even

stress on the first two syllables, in which case the change from the usual pattern makes it appear that the second syllable actually receives greater emphasis than the first. This even stress occurs in certain words beginning *all-*, and when the negative prefix *ó-* (*un-*) is placed before a word not normally taking any prefix. Examples: *allgóður* (pretty good) and *óítalskur* (un-Italian). However, the important point to remember is the *general regularity of Icelandic stress*.

LESSON 1

Nouns

IT is sometimes said of Icelandic that "it has a lot of grammar". By this is meant that there is a great deal of so-called "formal grammar", the form of words and their endings being changed according to circumstances. In the case of Icelandic nouns, for example, we are up against division according to gender (masculine, feminine and neuter), sub-division according to whether the noun is of the weak or strong variety, and further sub-division into various types (not forgetting the exceptions). This dividing up of nouns is important owing to the fact that noun endings differ (however slightly) according to their category. In English, the only endings we add to nouns are -s and -es in forming plurals (with a few exceptions such as oasis—oases, fly—flies, radius—radii). The process does not stop with mere plural formation in Icelandic, by any manner of means. There exist four cases: the subject or nominative case, the object or accusative case, the dative case and the genitive or possessive case.

Icelandic nouns have, then, four cases: nominative, accusative, dative and genitive. In order to show these endings it is convenient to use the following system, taking as our example the noun *hestur* (horse):

nom.	*hér er hestur* (here is (a) horse)
acc.	*um hest* (about a horse)
dat.	*frá hesti* (from a horse)
gen.	*til hests* (to a horse)
nom.	*hér eru hestar* (here are horses)
acc.	*um hesta* (about some horses)
dat.	*frá hestum* (from some horses)
gen	*til hesta* (to some horses)

Notice that the prepositions *um*, *frá* and *til* take the accusative case, the dative case and the genitive case respectively.

To manipulate these cases requires long practice, extensive reading being of great importance here. However, a large number of the sub-divisions referred to show remarkable similarity in many of their cases, and at all events many are of quite limited occurrence, and they must not be allowed to become a stumbling-block right at the outset. The most important point is to realize that certain differences do exist within the main divisions, but to concentrate on becoming familiar with these main ones only, in the first instance.

Strong nouns end in a consonant in the genitive singular, while weak nouns end in a vowel in every case in the singular; for example: *gestur* (guest)—strong masc. gen. sing.: *gests*; *tími* (time)—weak masc. *tíma* (acc. dat. and gen.).

Strong Masculine Nouns

These are divided into three categories, which have four, three and three sub-divisions respectively. The differences between the main divisions, however, are not great, and are summed up conveniently in the following form:

> *heim/ur-s-ar* (world)
> *gest/ur-s-ir* (guest)
> *fund/ur-ar-ir* (meeting)

The forms given here are the nominative singular (e.g., *heimur*), the genitive singular (e.g., *heims*), and the nominative plural (e.g., *heimar*). These are the parts given in dictionaries against the noun to enable you to see to which group it belongs.

Declension of Strong Masculine Noun, Group 1a (SM 1a).

	Singular	*Plural*
nom.	heimur	heimar
acc.	heim	heima
dat.	heimi	heimum
gen.	heims	heima

Within this declension we note these variations, which may be looked up in the section called Appendixes: SM 1c, SM 1d; SM 2a, SM 2b, SM 2c; SM 3a, SM 3b, SM 3c. Remember that the differences are generally quite small. Here we shall give the declension of one further type, so-called SM 1b, Strong masculine, group 1b. The noun chosen is *drottinn* (king, master, ruler).

	Singular	Plural
nom.	drottinn	drottnar
acc.	drottin	drottna
dat.	drottni	drottnum
gen.	drottins	drottna

It is worth while including here the six irregular nouns of this declension, as they are so frequently used. They are *faðir* (father), *bróðir* (brother), *vetur* (winter), *fótur* (foot), *fingur* (finger), *maður* (man, person).

Singular

nom.	faðir	bróðir	vetur	fótur	fingur	maður
acc.	föður	bróður	vetur	fót	fingur	mann
dat.	föður	bróður	vetri	fæti	fingri	manni
gen.	föður	bróður	vetrar	fótar	fingurs	manns

Plural

nom.	feður	bræður	vetur	fætur	fingur	menn
acc.	feður	bræður	vetur	fætur	fingur	menn
dat.	feðrum	bræðrum	vetrum	fótum	fingrum	mönnum
gen.	feðra	bræðra	vetra	fóta.	fingra	manna

Strong Feminine Nouns

These may be referred to as types SF 1a, 1b, 1c; 2a, 2b, 2c; 3a, 3b and 3c. The essential changes are summed up, as with the strong masculine nouns, in the following way:

borg—borgar—borgir (city, town)
skál—skálar—skálar (bowl)
bók—bókar—bækur (book) (note the radical vowel change)

The majority of strong feminine nouns are of the first type, and therefore the declension of one of these, *borg*, is given.

	Singular		*Plural*
nom.	borg	*nom.*	borgir
acc.	borg	*acc.*	borgir
dat.	borg	*dat.*	borgum
gen.	borgar	*gen.*	borga

The irregular nouns *móðir* (mother), *dóttir* (daughter) and *systir* (sister) are declined like the masculine *bróðir*, except that *systir* retains its root vowel -*y*- all through.

Strong Neuter Nouns

The types here may be referred to as SN 1a, 1b; 2, 3, 4 and 5. Here are examples of types 1a and 3, using the words *blóm* (flower) and *snæri* (line, string).

	Singular			*Plural*	
nom.	blóm	snæri	*nom.*	blóm	snæri
acc	blóm	snæri	*acc.*	blóm	snæri
dat.	blómi	snæri	*dat.*	blómum	snærum
gen.	blóms	snæris	*gen.*	blóma	snæra

Exercise 1

Decline the following nouns, first arranging them in their respective categories (e.g., *hestur*, SM 1a).

lest	öxull	bátur	munnur	drengur
hæll	lax	selur	fiskur	leikur
garður	hross	lengd	djöfull	hús
bíll	haf	tungl	stafur	hundur
gaffall	borg	sjónvarp	hestur	fjall
karl	jökull	haukur	hrafn	skáld
ást	skrækur	gestur	skip	hurð
staður	rúm	ljós	háls	foss
blóm	regn			

It should be pointed out that there are here examples of nouns from the most important categories of the strong declensions. They are namely SM 1a, SM 1b, SM 2a, SF 1a and SN 1a.

LESSON 2

Weak Nouns

Masculine nouns of this category end in a vowel in the singular nominative, as do feminine and neuter nouns also; masculine nouns end in -*i* in the nominative singular, but in -*a* (-*ja*) in the other cases of the singular. Here is the example of the noun *tími* (time):

	Singular	Plural
nom.	tími	tímar
acc.	tíma	tíma
dat.	tíma	tímum
gen.	tíma	tíma

The variations of this type are given in the appendix on declensions.

Feminine weak nouns end either in -*a* in the nominative singular and in -*u* in other cases of the singular, or in -*i* in all cases of the singular. Here is the example of the type *tunga* (tongue):

	Singular	Plural
nom.	tunga	tungur
acc.	tungu	tungur
dat.	tungu	tungum
gen.	tungu	tungna

Note that the feminine noun *kona* (woman, wife) takes the form *kvenna* in the genitive plural.

Neuter nouns of the weak type end in -*a* in all cases of the singular. Here is the noun *auga* (eye):

	Singular	Plural
nom.	auga	augu
acc.	auga	augu
dat.	auga	augum
gen.	auga	augna

The Definite Article

This is the only article used in Icelandic. If you wish to say, for example, "the boy has a little sister", the Icelandic is literally "boy-the has little sister". Here you see also that the usual way of employing the definite article in Icelandic is to affix it to the noun AFTER the noun. This is known technically as having a post-positive article, and is one of the distinguishing features of the Scandinavian languages. The article is placed after the noun in the following instances:

(1) When the noun has no adjective, and
(2) When the adjective follows the noun.

As an example, the translation of "Here is the horse" is:

Hér er hesturinn, here is horse/the.

Similarly in the plural:

Hér eru hestar/nir, here are horses/the.

The definite article is used as in English when there is an adjective before the noun:

The strong horse, hinn sterki hestur
The deep river, hin djúpa á
The rich land, hið ríka land

Note the different forms of the article according to the gender: *hinn* is masculine, *hin* is feminine and *hið* is neuter.
The adjective following the article is always weak, the case ending being that corresponding to the noun.

Declension of the Definite Article

	Singular			*Plural*		
	masc.	*fem.*	*neuter*	*masc.*	*fem.*	*neuter*
nom.	hinn	hin	hið	hinir	hinar	hin
acc	hinn	hina	hið	hina	hinar	hin
dat.	hinum	hinni	hinu	hinum	hinum	hinum
gen.	hins	hinnar	hins	hinna	hinna	hinna

When used after the noun (post-positively) it is as follows:

Masculine:

	Singular	*Plural*
nom.	hestur/inn	hestar/nir
acc.	hest/inn	hesta/na
dat.	hesti/num	hestu/num
gen.	hests/ins	hesta/nna

Feminine:

	Singular	*Plural*
nom.	borg/in	borgir/nar
acc.	borg/ina	borgir/nar
dat.	borg/inni	borgu/num
gen.	borgar/innar	borga/nna

Neuter:

	Singular	*Plural*
nom.	skip/ið	skip/in
acc.	skip/ið	skip/in
dat.	skipi/nu	skipu/num
gen.	skips/ins	skipa/nna

Notice that the three genders share the same endings for the dative and genitive cases in the plural. This applies to both the form without the article and the form with it. Notice, too, that there are slight modifications to the endings in these cases: you say, not *skipa/hinna* but *skipa/nna*, for instance.

Examples of Usage

Drengurinn tók hnífinn minn. (The boy took my knife; lit. boy/the took knife/the mine.)

Sólin skín. (The sun shines; lit. sun/the shines.)

Maðurinn kom hlaupandi. (The man came running up; lit. man/the came running.)

Þetta er maðurinn, sem ég sá í gær. (That is the man I saw yesterday; lit. that is man/the that I saw yesterday.)

Ég set stólinn fyrir dyrnar. (I put the chair in front of the door; lit. I set chair/the before door/the.)

Hann greip sverðið. (He grasped the sword; lit. he grasped sword/the.)

Drengurinn talar ensku mjög vel. (The boy speaks English very well.)
Hundurinn bítur. (The dog bites.)
Fuglinn flaug. (The bird *flew*.)
Stúlkan þvær sér. (The girl is washing herself.)
Barnið er veikt. (The child is ill.)

Exercise 2

Vocabulary

ég tek, I take
ég læt, I put
á (with acc. case where there is motion)
hundur (-s, -ar), dog
drengur (-s, -ar), boy
bók (-ar bækur), *f.* book
borð, *n.* table
ég keypti, I bought
hún, she
köttur (kattar, kettir), *m.* cat
bátur (-s, -ar), *m.* boat

skip, *n.* ship
kona (gen. pl. *kvenna*), *f.* woman, wife
togari, *wm.* trawler
garður -s, -ar), *m.* garden
karl (-s, -ar), *m.* man
þeir eru, they are
hann er hér, he is here
hvar er?, where is?
hann sækir, he is fetching
nýr/nýtt, new

Translate:

(1) The dog and the boy.
(2) I take the book.
(3) I put the book on the table.
(4) I bought the horse.
(5) She bought a cat.
(6) Where is the book?
(7) The boy is here.
(8) The boat is new.
(9) The woman and the man are from Reykjavík.
(10) The boy is from the trawler.
(11) In the garden.
(12) The man is fetching the horses.

Translate into English:

(1) Hún hefur penna og pappír.
(2) Skipið er ekki hér.
(3) Orðabókin er á borðinu.
(4) Hann keypti skipin í Reykjavík.
(5) Bókin liggur á borðinu.
(6) Húsið er nýtt.
(7) Ég les bókina í garðinum.
(8) Karlinn er ekki hér.
(9) Hér eru drengur og stúlka.
(10) Ég á hníf og skeið.
(11) Stúlkan hefur hund.
(12) Hann keypti bækurnar.

LESSON 3

Prepositions

Prepositions govern noun cases (viz. after prepositions, the noun must be given a case ending: accusative, genitive or dative). This is an unfortunate complication in Icelandic grammar, but it is of prime importance to become fully conversant with the prepositions, as they are of such frequent occurrence. Some of them govern the accusative case only, some the genitive case only, some the dative case only, others again the dative case and the accusative case, according, mainly, to whether motion or change is indicated, on the one hand, or rest or position on the other hand. Remember particularly that it is often difficult to give a *general* translation of a preposition; the word "til", for example, corresponds to "till", "to", "for", and other words according to the noun it governs. The translation given must, in many cases, be understood to be approximate.

Prepositions Governing the Accusative:

 um, of, about; around, round; across, over; during, by
 gegnum, through
 kringum, round, around
 umfram, above, beyond
 umhverfis, around
 fyrir ofan, above

Prepositions Governing the Dative:

 að, towards, against, up to, to, at
 af, of, off, by, from, with
 frá, from
 hjá, with, by, near
 úr, from
 andspænis, right opposite
 ásamt, together with
 gagnvart, opposite
 gagn, against
 nálægt, near to
 gegnt, opposite to
 handa, for, to

meðfram, along
mót, against, opposite (also *móti*)
undan, from under

Prepositions Governing the Genitive:
til, to till, for
án, without
auk, besides
meðal, among
megin, on the side of
milli, *millum*, between
sakir, on account of
sökum, on account of
vegna, on account of
innan, within
utan, outside
ofan, above
neðan, below
sunnan, south of
vestan, west of
norðan, north of
austan, east of
í staö, instead of

Note that then the common construction with *fyrir* before a preposition is used (e.g. *fyrir neðan, fyrir ofan, fyrir utan*), the accusative case is required.

Prepositions Governing both Accusative and Dative:

A rough-and-ready guide is to use the accusative case when change or motion is indicated, and to use the dative case when rest or position is indicated.

á, on, upon, in, of, at
eftir, after, by, behind
fyrir, in front of, before, for, because of
í, in, at
með, with
undir, under
við, at, against, by, near
yfir, above, over

Notes

The words that follow are never used as prepositions in Icelandic: *fram, heim, inn, út, upp, niður.*

Examples of Prepositional Usage:

Karlinn reiddi mig yfir ána. (The man took me across the river.) The accusative case after *yfir* because of motion.

6 pör af skóm. (6 pairs of shoes.) Dative case after *af.*

Ekki alls fyrir löngu. (Not very long ago.) Note that this corresponds to the adverbial expression *ago.*

Niður eftir hæðinni. (Down the hill.) Dative after *eftir* in expressions of space.

Hún sat milli trjánna. (She sat among the trees.) Genitive after *milli.*

Hann gekk kringum húsið. (He went round the house.) Accusative after *kringum.*

Á þessum stað. (In this place.)

Það kemur í sama stað niður. (It makes no odds.)

Togaramenn hafa fengið samband við umboðsmann sinn hér á staðnum. (The trawlermen have got into contact with their agent in these parts.)

Fyrir engan mun. (By no means.)

Hún er alltaf góð við mig. (She is always good to me.)

Hann er þrútinn um augun. (He is swollen about the eyes.)

Hárið glóir í sólskininu. (The (her) hair shines in the sunshine.)

Ég vil læra hjá prestinum. (I want to study with the priest.)

Ég mun fara suður í haust og vera hjá ömmu. (I shall go south in the autumn and stay with grandmother.)

Orðin í þessu kvæði. (The words of this poem.)

Hann klappar hundinum á kollinn. (He pats the dog on the head.)

Pabbi brosir til mömmu. (Dad smiles at Mother.)

Ég gríp um hönd hans. (I grasp his hand.)

Það hefur snjóað æði mikið í fjöllin í nótt. (It snowed quite a lot in the mountains last night.)

Exercise 3

Vocabulary

ég fer, I go
hann reis, he rose
hann gekk, he walked
hann talaði um, he spoke about
geturðu vaðið, can you wade?
láttu mig, leave me, or let me
hann féll, he went down on
   (fell)
hún býr, she lives
hann fór, he went
þaðan, from there
í gær, yesterday
sunnudagur, Sunday

á(-r, -r), f. river, stream
bær (-jar, -ir), m. town, farm
dæmi, n. example.
frið (-ar), m. peace
gull, n. gold
kirkja (gen. pl. *kirkna*), *wf.*
   church
kné, n. knee
leikhús, n. theatre
stúlka, wf. girl
tún, n. field, homefield
úr, n. watch, clock
vegur (-s, -ar), m. road, way

Translate into English:

(1) Hann kom til bæjarins í gær.
(2) Hestarnir eru í túninu.
(3) Úrið er úr gulli.
(4) Geturðu vaðið yfir ána?
(5) Þaðan fer ég til Englands.
(6) Til dæmis.
(7) Hann féll á kné.
(8) Hann reis á fætur.
(9) Meðfram veginum eru tré.
(10) Drengurinn er frá Reykjavík.

Translate into Icelandic:

(1) He spoke about the book.
(2) Have you come to Reykjavik?
(3) She bought the book for the girl.
(4) Leave me in peace.
(5) On Sunday.
(6) He sat opposite me.
(7) He went to church (use "í").
(8) She lives in Keflavik.
(9) I often go to the theatre.
(10) The boy went round the house.

LESSON 4

YOU

There is by no means such a straightforward choice in Icelandic as there is in English regarding the addressing of persons. In English we have just the word "you", from which we form "your" and "yours". In Icelandic there are the following forms:

> *þú* (familiar singular);
> *þið* (familiar plural);
> *þér* (polite singular and plural).

The accusative form of *þú* is *þig*, the dative form is *þér*, and the genitive form is *þín*. The corresponding forms of the other words are:

> *þið—ykkur* (acc.)—*ykkur* (dat.)—*ykkar* (gen.).
> *þér—yður* (acc.)—*yður* (dat.)—*yðar* (gen.).

In Iceland, when speaking to a stranger you say "*þér*", but "*þú*" when speaking to a friend. You should say "*þér*" to older persons and to persons of high rank. In certain cases this question of which form of "you" to employ may be of great importance. It must be noted that among a large section of the Icelanders themselves there is a reaction against this polite, formal form of address, which they avoid in almost every case.

For the learner it is naturally best to use "*þér*" at all times, unless you are fortunate enough to have an Icelandic friend with whom you can use the "*þú*" form.

Personal Pronouns

These are declined as follows:

Singular

	1st person	2nd person	3rd person masc.	fem.	neuter
nom.	ég	þú	hann	hún	það
acc.	mig	þig	hann	hana	það
dat.	mér	þér	honum	henni	því
gen.	mín	þín	hans	hennar	þess

Plural

nom.	við (vér)	þið (þér)	þeir	þær	þau
acc.	okkur (oss)	ykkur (yður)	þá	þær	þau
dat.	okkur (oss)	ykkur (yður)	þeim	þeim	þeim
gen.	okkar (vor)	ykkar (yðar)	þeirra	þeirra	þeirra

Note that the forms given in brackets were originally the true ones for the plurals of the first and second persons, and that the forms given first, the ones in general use today, were originally the so-called Dual Forms, that is, the forms used when there were only two persons in question. Also the form *þér* is the polite form of address in the singular; e.g., Hvert farið þér; komið þér sælir.

Reflexives

These do not exist in the nominative case, and there is no difference for gender and number:

nom.	...	dat.	sér
acc.	sig	gen.	sín

Only when the third person is both the subject and the object of the sentence is it possible to use the reflexives; e.g., *hann talar um sig* (he talks about himself); *hún sér sig í spegli* (she looks at herself in the mirror); *stúlkan flýtti sér heim* (the girl hurries home); *barnið naut sín ekki* (the child did not enjoy itself).

Possessive Pronouns

There are four possessive pronouns in modern Icelandic, namely:

minn (my, mine); *þinn* (your); *sinn* (his, her, its, their); *vor* (our).

Declension of *minn* (*þinn* and *sinn* are declined likewise).

	masc.	fem.	neuter
		Singular	
nom.	minn	mín	mitt
acc.	minn	mína	mitt
dat.	mínum	minni	mínu
gen.	míns	minnar	míns
		Plural	
nom.	mínir	mínar	mín
acc.	mína	mínar	mín
dat.	mínum	mínum	mínum
gen.	mínna	mínna	mínna

Note that *vor* (our) is used only in writing in modern Icelandic, the spoken word being *okkar*. *Vor* is declined thus:

	masc.	fem.	neuter
		Singular	
nom.	vor	vor	vort
acc.	vorn	vora	vort
dat.	vorum	vorri	voru
gen.	vors	vorrar	vors
		Plural	
nom.	vorir	vorar	vor
acc.	vora	vorar	vor
dat.	vorum	vorum	vorum
gen.	vorra	vorra	vorra

Note also the following:

hans, his	*ykkar*, your (the familiar
hennar, her	plural)
þess, its	*yðar*, your (polite singular)
okkar, our	*þeirra*, their

These forms are not declined; they are in fact genitives of the personal pronouns.

Relative Pronouns

The two relatives are *sem* and *er*, the latter being used only in the written language. *Sem* is therefore used for "who", "that", "which": e.g., *þarna er drengurinn, sem ég sá í gær* (there is the boy that I saw yesterday). Note that the comma is necessary in such cases before the relative.

Note: *Ég geri hvað ég get—ég geri það sem ég get* (I do what I can—I do that which I can). *Hvað* is used in this way as is *what* in English.

Word Order

In English, the fundamental word order is: subject, verb, object (or, subject, predicate). This is basically the same in Icelandic, but there are some very common variations, which strike the eye at once when you glance at written Icelandic. Notice first that it is important in Icelandic to keep the verb as the second idea, as in all Germanic languages originally, and as we retain in modern English when we have a sentence that is introduced by a negative or restrictive adverb (never have I seen such a thing; rarely do I visit the place). Thus in Icelandic you must say, for instance, "When we arrived at the meeting-place, *were they* already there": or, "If I saw him do that, *should I* be quite surprised".

Another important point to notice here is the occasional use of the adjective and the common use of the possessive pronoun *after* the noun: for example, *þá þagnar Imba gamla, og vill ekki hjálpa mér* (then becomes silent Imba-old one, and will not help me). In this sentence there is another point to note, the common use of the word að. *Þú þarft að fara að læra að lesa, Þóra mín, segir hann* (You ought to go and learn to read, Thora-mine, says he.)

The other important point at this stage is one already made, the use of the article suffixed to the noun and declined with it.

Further Notes on Prepositions

You will find that certain of the prepositions come up again and again. The eleven principal ones are: *um, af, að, frá, til, á, eftir, fyrir, í, með* and *við*. You should notice that the last six of these are prepositions that take both the dative and accusative cases. It is of great importance to be able to manage these words with a reasonable amount of skill, so here are fuller notes on them: firstly *á, að* and *af*.

(1) *á* may be variously translated as—on, upon; in, of, at, by,

about. Remember that an indication of motion means that the accusative case is used, as in *að leggja á borðið*, whereas the idea of position or rest indicates the dative case, as in *að liggja á borðinu* (the first sentence is "to put on the table", and the second "to be lying on the table").

á götunni, in the street
á þessum stað, in this place
á ensku, in English
á sænsku, in Swedish
á morgnana, in the mornings
á kvöldin, in the evenings, of an evening
á veturna, in the winter
á miðnætti, at midnight
á jólunum, at Christmas
á sunnudag, on Sunday
á sunnudagskvöldið, on Sunday evening
á þennan hátt, in this way
á dansleik, at a dance
á minn kostnað, at my expense

á þeim tíma, at that time
tvisvar á dag, twice a day
mér er kalt á fótunum, I have cold feet
mér er kalt á höndunum, I have cold hands
á leið, on the way
á beit, grazing
á sundi, swimming
á lífi, alive
á laun, in secret
á sama stað og, in the same place as . . .
gizka á, to guess at
þreifa (taka) á, to touch
bragða á, to taste

(2) *að*, as a preposition, may be translated thus: to, up to, towards, against, at. The dative case is required after *að*.

að vera að + *verb*, to be (busy) doing something. E.g., *hún er að tala við mig*, she is talking to me.
að lokum, at last
að eilífu, for ever (and ever)
að sumri, in the summer—next summer
að vetri, next winter
að vori, next spring
að hausti, next autumn
að láni, as a loan
tvítugur að aldri, twenty years of age
að lögum, by law, in law
spyrja að . . ., ask for . . .
hlæja að . . ., laugh at . . .

3. *af,* (with dative) of, off, from, by, with.

10 *þör af skóm,* ten pairs of shoes
af hendingu, by chance, accidentally
af öllu afli, with all one's might
hver af öðrum, one after the other
mynd af manni, mér, picture of a person, of me
hvað hefur þú gert af bókinni?, what have you done with the book?
hvað er orðið af honum?, what has become of him?
fljúga af stað, to take off
bera af sér (högg), to ward off (a blow)
detta af baki, to fall off a horse
af því, because
láta peningana af hendi, to shell out
virtur af öllum, respected by everyone
vera af sér kominn (af þreytu), to be worn out (with fatigue)
koma af stað, to get away
deyja af, to die of
af heilum hug, with all one's heart
koma ... af sér, to get rid of ...

Exercise 4

Vocabulary

hann fór, he went
han gekk út, he went out
hann hefur beðið, he has asked (with gen.)
ég gleymi (with dat.), I forget
þetta gladdi, that pleased
ég efni, I keep
ég þekki, I know (person)
hún þvær, she washes
hittuð þið? did you (pl.) find?
beit, bit (past, sing.)
elskar, loves (3rd pers. sing.)
situr, sit (2nd pers. sing.)
stend, stand (1st pers. sing.)
tefur, hinder (2nd pers. sing.)
ég skil, I understand

hneigði (reflex.), bowed (3rd pers. sing. past)
heilsa (with dat.), greet
brenna sig (past: *brenndi*), burn oneself
jafna sig, steady oneself
anza (with dat.), answer
móðga, offend
drekkja sér, drown oneself
klæddi, dressed (3rd pers. sing.)
heima, at home
fljótt, quickly
aldrei, never
sannarlega, really
loforð, promise
í brunninum, in the well

(a) *Translate into Icelandic:*

   (1) Your brother Sigurður is at home.
   (2) He went out with his wife.
   (3) She dressed.
   (4) That is your father.
   (5) He went with me to (see) my sister.
   (6) He has asked her.
   (7) You are sitting and I am standing.
   (8) The dog bit me.
   (9) She loves him.
  (10) You are hindering me.
  (11) She quickly steadies herself.
  (12) He bowed and went out.

(b) *Translate into English:*

   (1) Hann heilsar mér.
   (2) Ég brenndi mig.
   (3) Hún drekkti sér í brunninum.
   (4) Ég skil hann.
   (5) Þú móðgar mig.
   (6) Ég gleymi þér aldrei.
   (7) Þetta gladdi mig sannarlega.
   (8) Ég efni loforð mín.
   (9) Ég þekki þig.
  (10) Hittuð þið bróður minn?
  (11) Ég anza þér.
  (12) Stúlkan þvær hár sitt.

LESSON 5

Special Verbs

THERE are seventeen so-called special verbs in Icelandic. It is of great importance to know these verbs extremely well, in all their forms. The four basic auxiliary verbs are:

        vera, to be   *munu,* shall/will
        hafa, to have   *skulu,* shall/will

Another auxiliary verb is:

verða, to become, get

The following three verbs share the peculiarity of governing the supine, instead of the infinitive:

geta, to be able, can
eiga, ought to (also, to have—possess)
fá, to be able, be allowed, have something done (also, obtain, etc.).

Here are examples of their usage; *ég get ekki* farið (I am not able to go); *ég á þetta ekki* skilið (I do not deserve that); *ég fékk ekki* náð *honum* (I was not able to catch him).

fara means to go, travel, leave. Note especially the construction:

að fara að gjöra (*gera*), to be just going to do something, to go and do something: e.g., *þú þarft að fara að læra að lesa* (you must go and learn to read).

Other auxiliary verbs are:

mega, may, be allowed
þurfa, need, have to

Non-auxiliary anomalous verbs are:

unna, to love, grant, not grudge (someone something)
kunna, to know
muna, to remember
vita, to know
vilja, to want to, will

The last verb is the only regular one of the seventeen; that is to say, it is included in the category of weak verbs, Group 1a, the principal group. This verb is *að ætla*, and means to intend, to mean. The importance of this verb derives from its use in the construction:

að ætla að gera . . ., to be going to do something: e.g., *ég ætla að fara á morgun* (I am going to leave tomorrow, I am thinking of leaving tomorrow, I shall leave tomorrow, I'll be leaving tomorrow).

Here are the conjugations of the four basic tenses (present and past indicative, present and past subjunctive) of these seventeen verbs:

hafa; supine *haft*; pres. part. *hafandi*

	pres. indic.	*pres. subj.*	*past indic.*	*past subj.*
ég	hefi (hef)	hafi	hafði	hefði
þú	hefur	hafir	hafðir	hefðir
hann	hefur	hafi	hafði	hefði
við	höfum	höfum	höfðum	hefðum
þið (þér)	hafið	hafið	höfðuð	hefðuð
þeir	hafa	hafi	höfðu	hefðu

vera; supine *verið*; pres. part. *verandi*

ég	er	sé (veri)	var	væri
þú	ert	sért (verir)	varst	værir
hann	er	sé (veri)	var	væri
við	erum	séum (verum)	vorum	værum
þið (þér)	eruð	séuð (verið)	voruð	væruð
þeir	eru	séu (veri)	voru	væru

munu; supine and participles do not exist.

ég	mun	muni	mundi	myndi
þú	munt	munir	mundir	myndir
hann	mun	muni	mundi	myndi
við	munum	munum	mundum	myndum
þið (þér)	munuð	munið	munduð	mynduð (-ið)
þeir	munu	muni	mundu	myndu (-i)

skulu; supine and participles do not exist.

ég	skal	skuli	(does	skyldi
þú	skalt	skulir	not	skyldir
hann	skal	skuli	exist)	skyldi
við	skulum	skulum		skyldum
þið (þér)	skuluð	skulið		skylduð
þeir	skulu	skuli		skyldu

verða; past part. *orðinn*; supine *orðið*; pres. part. *verðandi*

	pres. indic.	pres. subj.	past. indic.	past subj.
ég	verð	verði	varð	yrði
þú	verður	verðir	varðst	yrðir
hann	verður	verði	varð	yrði
við	verðum	verðum	urðum	yrðum
þið (þér)	verðið	verðið	urðuð	yrðuð
þeir	verða	verði	urðu	yrðu

geta; past part. *getinn*; supine *getið, getað*; pres. part. *getandi*

ég	get	geti	gat	gæti
þú	getur	getir	gatst	gætir
hann	getur	geti	gat	gæti
við	getum	getum	gátum	gætum
þið (þér)	getið	getið	gátuð	gætuð
þeir	geta	geti	gátu	gætu

eiga; supine *átt*; pres. part. *eigandi*

ég	á	eigi	átti	ætti
þú	átt	eigir	áttir	ættir
hann	á	eigi	átti	ætti
við	eigum	eigum	áttum	ættum
þið (þér)	eigið	eigið	áttuð	ættuð
þeir	eiga	eigi	áttu	ættu

fá; past part. *fenginn*; supine *fengið*; pres. part. *fáandi*

ég	fæ	fái	fékk	fengi
þú	færð	fáir	fékkst	fengir
hann	fær	fái	fékk	fengi
við	fáum	fáum	fengum	fengum
þið (þér)	fáið	fáið	fenguð	fenguð
þeir	fá	fái	fengu	fengu

fara; past part. *farinn*; supine *farið*; pres. part. *farandi*

ég	fer	fari	fór	færi
þú	ferð	farir	fórst	færir
hann	fer	fari	fór	færi
við	förum	förum	fórum	færum
þið (þér)	farið	farið	fóruð	færuð
þeir	fara	fari	fóru	færu

mega; supine *mátt*; pres. part. *megandi*

	pres. indic.	pres. subj.	past. indic.	past. subj.
ég	má	megi	mátti	mætti
þú	mátt	megir	máttir	mættir
hann	má	megi	mátti	mætti
við	megum	megum	máttum	mættum
þið (þér)	megið	megið	máttuð	mættuð
þeir	mega	megi	máttu	mættu

þurfa; supine *þurft*; pres. part. *þurfandi*

ég	þarf	þurfi	þurfti	þyrfti
þú	þarft	þurfir	þurftir	þyrftir
hann	þarf	þurfi	þurfti	þyrfti
við	þurfum	þurfum	þurftum	þyrftum
þið (þér)	þurfið	þurfið	þurftuð	þyrftuð
þeir	þurfa	þurfi	þurftu	þyrfti

unna; supine *unnað*; pres. part. *unnandi*

ég	ann	unni	unni	ynni
þú	annt	unnir	unnir	ynnir
hann	ann	unni	unni	ynni
við	unnum	unnum	unnum	ynnum
þið (þér)	unnið	unnið	unnuð	ynnuð
þeir	unna	unni	unnu	ynni

kunna; supine *kunnað*; pres. part. *kunnandi*

ég	kann	kunni	kunni	kynni
þú	kannt	kunnir	kunnir	kynnir
hann	kann	kunni	kunni	kynni
við	kunnum	kunnum	kunnum	kynnum
þið (þér)	kunnið	kunnið	kunnuð	kynnuð
þeir	kunna	kunni	kunnu	kynni

muna; supine *munað*; pres. part. *munandi*

ég	man	muni	mundi	myndi
þú	manst	munir	mundir	myndir
hann	man	muni	mundi	myndi
við	munum	munum	mundum	myndum
þið (þér)	munið	munið	munduð	mynduð
þeir	muna	muni	mundu	myndi

vita; supine *vitað*; pres. part. *vitandi*

	pres. indic.	pres. subj.	past. indic.	past. subj.
ég	veit	viti	vissi	vissi
þú	veizt	vitir	vissir	vissir
hann	veit	viti	vissi	vissi
við	vitum	vitum	vissum	vissum
þið (þér)	vitið	vitið	vissuð	vissuð
þeir	vita	viti	vissu	vissu

vilja; supine *viljað*; pres. part. *viljandi*

ég	vil	vilji	vildi	vildi
þú	vilt	viljir	vildir	vildir
hann	vill	vilji	vildi	vildi
við	viljum	viljum	vildum	vildum
þið (þér)	viljið	viljið	vilduð	vilduð
þeir	vilja	vilji	vildu	vildu

ætla; supine *ætlað*; pres. part. *ætlandi*; past part. *ætlaður*

ég	ætla	ætli	ætlaði	ætlaði
þú	ætlar	ætlir	ætlaðir	ætlaðir
hann	ætlar	ætli	ætlaði	ætlaði
við	ætlum	ætlum	ætluðum	ætluðum
þið (þér)	ætlið	ætlið	ætluðuð	ætluðuð
þeir	ætla	ætli	ætluðu	ætluðu

Remember that this verb is of the regular weak conjugation.

Note. The verb *munu* really indicates the pure future, while *skulu* gives an idea of determination, desire, and so on; but you will find that the verb *skulu* is of more frequent occurrence in modern Icelandic than is *munu*.

Exercise 5a

Vocabulary

sýna (with dat.), to show
búa, to live
fara í bíó, to go to the pictures
hjálpa, to help
kaupa, to buy
ná í, to catch or fetch
rifja upp, to brush up

segja, to say
sjá, to see
skýra e-um frá e-u, to tell someone about something
sofa, to sleep
spila, to play
svara, to answer

vilja fá að, to want (to be permitted) to
vaka, to stay awake
séð, seen
talað um, spoken about
hefurðu?, have you?
hvað?, where?
hérna, here
neitt, nothing at all
í gær, yesterday
í kvöld, this evening
miklu fremur, far sooner

nokkuð merkilegt, something remarkable
nákvæmlega, exactly, precisely
saman, together
án þess að, without
allan þennan tíma, all this time
allar óreglulega sagnirnar í ensku, all the irregular verbs in English
fréttir, news
lest, train
skurðlæknir, surgeon

Translate into Icelandic:

(1) I will show you something remarkable.
(2) I have never seen that.
(3) Have you spoken about this to father?
(4) He intends to live here.
(5) I will stay up tonight and brush up all the irregular verbs in English.
(6) Have you never seen the sea?
(7) Where have you been all this time?
(8) She wants to help her sister.
(9) You ought to buy that.
(10) We wanted to (be permitted to) speak to her.
(11) I'm never allowed to sleep at all (to get any sleep).
(12) I can tell you exactly what he will say.

(b) *Translate into English:*

(1) Nú vil ég fá að vita, hvar Jón er.
(2) Ég hefi skýrt þér frá öllu sem ég veit um hann.
(3) Ég þarf að ná í lest.
(4) Við viljum miklu fremur spila bridge en sofa.
(5) Hann er maðurinn, sem vill tala við yður.
(6) Hún hafði komið í gær.
(7) Ég ætla að svara fyrri spurningunni fyrst.
(8) Hefur þú lesið þessa bók?
(9) Hann vildi ekki fara án þess að sjá þig.
(10) Þeir hafa haft fréttir af Jóni.
(11) Ég ætla að verða skurðlæknir.
(12) Við skulum fara í bíó saman.

LESSON 6

Weak Verbs

In the previous lesson we saw the conjugation of the present and past tenses, indicative and subjunctive, of the verb *ætla*. This verb is, as stated, in the main group of the weak verbs. Icelandic verbs are divided, as are English verbs, into strong and weak types, or into irregular and regular types, if you prefer to put it this way. Among the weak verbs it is possible to distinguish four groups.

Group 1 { *ætla*; pres. indic. *ætla*; past indic. *ætlaði*.
{ *kalla*; pres. indic. *kalla*; past indic. *kallaði*.

Group 2 { *una*; pres. indic. *uni*; past indic. *undi*.
{ *vaka*; pres. indic. *vaki*; past indic. *vakti*.

Group 3 { *deila*; pres. indic. *deili*; past indic. *deildi*.
{ *hengja*; pres. indic. *hengi*; past indic. *hengdi*.

Group 4 { *dvelja*; pres. indic. *dvel*; past indic. *dvaldi*.
{ *spyrja*; pres. indic. *spyr*; past indic. *spurði*.

Of these groups, the second one is of relatively little importance, as there are not very many verbs belonging to it. The full differences between the different groups cannot be realized from the above table, however. In the first group, for example, the root vowel of the verb *ætla* does not change, whereas the root vowel of the verb *kalla* changes when there is a following *u* in the termination (*við kölluðum* instead of *kalluðum*). In the second group, the verb shown first undergoes a root vowel change in the past subjunctive (*ég yndi*), while the verb *vaka* changes its root vowel to *ö* when there is a *u* in the ending, and changes it to *e* in the past subjunctive.

In the third group, an important one, there is no change of root vowel. The *j* in the ending of such verbs as *hengja* appears only before *a* and *u*. The ending of the past is variously *di* and *ti*, according to whether the end consonant is of the voiced or unvoiced variety, *di* being used after a voiced sound and *ti* after an unvoiced sound.

There are several verbs in the fourth group, and here it is

necessary to learn the past indicative forms, as these undergo vowel changes. *Dvelja* becomes *dvaldi*, for instance, and *setja* becomes *setti*. For a list of these verbs, see Appendix 3.

Before giving examples of the conjugations of a model verb, there are certain points to be noted. It must not be thought that the vowel modifications indicated above are mere haphazard changes. There is in Icelandic a regular system of vowel mutation (*hljóðvörp*); here we distinguish between *i*-mutation and *u*-mutation. In mutation, a following *i* (*j*) can cause the root vowel to change, as also can a following *u*. Here is a table of such changes:

a	becomes	*e*	as in	*vanur/venja*
á	,,	*æ*	as in	*þráður/þræðir*
e	,,	*i*	as in	*verð/virði*
o	,,	*e*	as in	*koma/kemur*
o	,,	*y*	as in	*sonur/synir*
ó	,,	*æ*	as in	*fórum/færi*
u	,,	*y*	as in	*fullur/fyllri*
ú	,,	*ý*	as in	*hús/hýsa*
ju	,,	*y*	as in	*jukum/yki*
jó	,,	*ý*	as in	*ljós/lýsa*
jú	,,	*ý*	as in	*djúpur/dýpi*
au	,,	*ey*	as in	*hraustur/hreysti*

Here is the table of *u*-mutations. The most common one is from *a* to *ö*.

a	becomes	*ö*	*kalla/köllum*
a	,,	*u*	*sumar/sumur*
i	,,	*y*	*singva/syngja*
vi	,,	*y*	*kvirr/kyrr*

There also exist two further mutations, the *r*-mutation and the *g/k*-mutation. These are relatively unimportant; examples are:

glas	becomes	*gler*
dagur	,,	*degi*
taka	,,	*tekinn*

Other regular sound changes in Icelandic come under the categories of gradation (*hljóðskipti*) and fracture (*klofning*), for which see the Appendix section. The modifications given will prove useful in helping to conjugate verbs with root vowels as in the tables above.

	Singular	*Plural*
nom.	land	lönd (old -u ending)
acc.	land	lönd
dat.	landi	löndum
gen.	lands	landa
nom.	fjall	fjöll
acc.	fjall	fjöli
dat.	fjalli	fjöllum
gen.	fjalls	fjalla
nom.	haf	höf (old -u ending)
acc.	haf	höf
dat.	hafi	höfum
gen.	hafs	hafa

ég kalla
þú kallar
hann kallar
við köllum
þið kallið
þeir kalla

Formation of the Negative

To make a verb negative you have only to add *"ekki"* (a) after the auxiliary verb; (b) after the principal verb if there is no auxiliary; (c) after the direct pronoun object. Examples:

(a) *ég get ekki sagt þér það* (I cannot tell you that).
　　ég hefi ekki skilið (I have not understood).
(b) *ég skil ekki* (I don't understand).
(c) *ég þekki þig ekki* (I don't recognize (or know) you).

List of Tenses

In Icelandic there are Active and Passive tenses, as in English, but there exists also a so-called Middle Voice, much used especially in writing. Each of these three categories have fourteen tenses, and here we have examples of the fourteen *Active Tenses*.

að tala (to speak)

	pres. indic.	pres. subj.	past indic.	past subj.
ég	tala	tali	talaði	talaði
þú	talar	talir	talaðir	talaðir
hann	talar	tali	talaði	talaði
við	tölum	tölum	töluðum	töluðum
þið (þér)	talið	talið	töluðuð	töluðuð
þeir	tala	tali	töluðu	töluðu

perfect tense	ég hefi talað
perfect subj.	ég hafi talað
past perfect indic.	ég hafði talað
past perfect subj.	ég hefði talað
future indic.	ég mun tala
future subj.	ég muni tala
future perf. indic.	ég mun hafa talað
future perf. subj.	ég muni hafa talað
conditional	ég mundi tala
conditional perfect	ég mundi hafa talað

From this you can see that there are four basic tenses, the other ten being composed of the auxiliary verbs *hafa* and *munu* together with the supine or the infinitive; these are the compound tenses. However, it must be pointed out that there are a number of verbs that form their tenses with the auxiliary *vera*, to be. Here it is a question of verbs of motion, and in this Icelandic shares a process common to several languages. They say, for instance, "to be jumped" instead of "to have jumped". Common verbs in this category are the following:

byrja, begin	*koma*, come
detta, fall	*róa*, row
falla, fall	*sigla*, sail
fljúga, fly	*stökkva*, jump
ganga, walk	*þjóta*, rush
hlaupa, run	*fara*, go

Example of Verb conjugated using vera (or verða): **að fara**

present indic.	ég er farinn
present subj.	ég sé farinn
past indic.	ég var farinn

past subj.	ég væri farinn
perfect indic.	ég hefi verið farinn
perfect subj.	ég hafi verið farinn
past perfect indic.	ég hafði verið farinn
past perfect subj.	ég hefði verið farinn
future indic.	ég mun verða (vera) farinn
future subj.	ég muni verða (vera) farinn
future perfect indic.	ég mun hafa verið farinn
future perfect subj.	ég muni hafa verið farinn
conditional	ég mundi verða (vera) farinn
conditional perfect	ég mundi hafa verið farinn

Note that this method is sometimes an alternative to the common way of forming the various tenses; you can say, for example, *"ég hefi farið"* just as we have shown above that you can say *"ég hefi verið farinn"*. (Compare the English in "I shall have gone" and "I shall be gone".)

Now we may take this a step further. In the future and conditional, the auxiliary *verða (vera)* is commonly dropped, so that, for instance, *mun verða (vera) farinn* becomes *mun farinn*, and *mundi verða (vera) farinn* becomes *mundi farinn*.

Examples

Hann mun nú farinn til kirkju. (He will (have) gone to church now.)

Jón mundi nú kominn alla leið, ef hann hefði lagt af stað með birtu í morgun. (John would now (have) come the whole way, if he had set off at daybreak.)

Note that the future and the conditional are sometimes formed by using *verða* with the past participle, so that *verð farinn* means *mun verða (vera) farinn*, and *yrði farinn* means *mundi verða (vera) farinn*. (Observe in this last example that the subjunctive form *yrði* of the verb *verða* is used.)

Examples

Ég verð farinn þegar þú kemur. (I shall have gone when you come.)

Hann bjóst við, að þú yrðir kominn fyrir háttatíma. (He expected you to have come before bedtime—he expected that you would have (be) come before . . .)

In conclusion, it would be as well to compare the following forms:

ég fer, often denotes the future
ég er farinn, denotes "just gone"
ég hefi farið, denotes occasionally "just gone", but usually 'have been" at some more distant time in the past.

Examples

Ég fer til Noregs í haust. (I am going to Norway this autumn.)
Báturinn er kominn til eyjarinnar. (The boat has (just) reached the island.)
Ég hefi farið til Englands. (I have been to England.)

Vocabulary

borða (a), to eat
duglegur, clever
ekki . . . nema, only, not but.
blanda (a) *sér*, enter, mix one-
　self up
heyra (i), hear
hlýna (a), get warmer
hönd (*handar, hendur*), f. hand
í vetur, this winter
kalsi, m. cold weather
kinka (a) with dat., to nod

kollur (-s, -ar), m. head
mála (a), paint
prestur (-s, -ar), m. clergyman
rödd (*raddar, raddir*), f. voice
samtal, n. conversation
sími, m. telephone
skál (ar), f. bowl
smámsaman, gradually
telpa, f. girl, lass.
verða reiður, become angry
vor, n. spring (time)

Exercise 6a

Translate into Icelandic:

(1) Now the clergyman has come to find father.
(2) She clapped her hands together.
(3) He nodded his head.
(4) I wrote a letter yesterday.
(5) She became angry when she saw what was in the bowl.
(6) The ship has reached (come to) land.
(7) He has become clever at writing.
(8) She rang (to) him, and heard his voice over (in) the telephone.

(9) Now I must be going.
(10) I spoke to her yesterday.
(11) The girl now entered the conversation.
(12) That is from (out of) a letter which you wrote.

Exercise 6b

Translate into English:

(1) Hún ætlar ekki að vera nema í nokkra daga.
(2) Það veit ég ekki.
(3) Drengurinn fór til Noregs fyrir sex árum.
(4) Inga er orðin tólf ára.
(5) Við förum til Íslands í vetur.
(6) Stúlkan verður farin þegar hann kemur (mun verða farin).
(7) Hann gat ekki talað.
(8) Vorið byrjaði með kalsa, en veðrið hlýnaði smámsaman.
(9) Hún hafði ekki skilið.
(10) Þeir töluðu um að gera það.
(11) Drengurinn málaði togarann í dag.
(12) Fólkið er komið heim að borða.

LESSON 7

Three Common Constructions

(1) *fara* plus infinitive, e.g., *ég fer að skrifa* (I am going to write).

(2) *vera (verða)* plus infinitive, e.g., *ég er að skrifa* (I am writing).

(3) *vera (verða)* plus *búinn* plus infinitive, e.g., *ég er búinn að skrifa* (I have just written).

As can be seen from the translations given, these three constructions refer respectively to the near future, the present moment, and the recently-completed past. Each construction is very important owing to the frequency of its use.

Table of Forms of the Above-mentioned Constructions

present	*ég fer að skrifa,* I am going to write
past	*ég fór að skrifa,* I was going to write
pres. perf.	*ég hefi farið að skrifa,* I have been going to write
past perf.	*ég hafði farið að skrifa,* I had been going to write
future	*ég mun fara að skrifa,* I shall be writing
future perf.	*ég mun hafa farið að skrifa,* I'll have been going to write
conditional	*ég mundi fara að skrifa,* I should be going to write
cond. perf.	*ég mundi hafa farið að skrifa,* I should have been going to write
present	*ég er að skrifa,* I am writing
past	*ég var að skrifa,* I was writing
pres. perf.	*ég hefi verið að skrifa,* I've been writing
past perf.	*éf hafði verið að skrifa,* I had been writing.
future	*ég mun verða (vera) að skrifa/verð að skrifa,* I'll be writing
future perf.	*ég mun hafa verið að skrifa,* I'll have been writing
conditional	*ég mundi verða (vera) að skrifa/yrði að skrifa,* I should be writing
cond. perf.	*ég mundi hafa verið að skrifa,* I should have been writing
present	*ég er búinn að skrifa,* I have just written
past	*ég var búinn að skrifa,* I had just written
pres. perf.	*ég hefi verið að skrifa,* I have written
past perf.	*ég hafði verið að skrifa,* I had been writing/had written
future	*ég mun verða (vera) búinn að skrifa,* I'll have just written
future perf.	*ég mun hafa verið búinn að skrifa,* I'll have just been writing
conditional	*ég mundi verða (vera) búinn að skrifa,* I should have just written
cond. perf.	*ég mundi hafa verið búinn að skrifa,* I should have just been writing

Each form of the indicative has been given here for the sake of completeness, and common sense will assist in selecting those forms that are of most use. To generalize, we may say that the first two forms of each construction are those most frequently met with.

Examples of Usage of these Constructions

Nú fer ég að fara. Now I am going (to go).
Hún fer að gera það. She is about to do that/going to do that.
Hún er að tala við mig. She is talking to me.
Hann var að lesa, þegar ég kom. He was reading when I arrived.
Þú ert búinn að vera mikið veik. You have (just) been very ill.
Nú er ég búinn að mála húsið. Now I have finished painting the house.
Ég er búinn að lesa bókina. I have just read the book.
Ég er búinn að eyða þeim öllum. I have just destroyed them all.
Það er búið að vera gott veður í vetur. There has been good weather this winter.

Note also: *Það er farið að dimma.* It is getting dark.
Það er farið að hvessa. It is blowing up.

The Subjunctive

You may possibly have wondered whether it has not been somewhat pedantic to mention the subjunctive forms as much as the ordinary indicative forms. The fact is, however, that the subjunctive is in constant use in Icelandic, in both the written and the spoken language.

Fundamentally, the subjunctive indicates something wished for, something existing in the imagination, something dependent on a condition, something possible but not certain, something doubtful. It is necessary to analyse this into different sections.

(1) *Wishes.*

Ég vil ekki, að hann segi eitt einasta orð. (I do not want him to say a single word.)
Hann vill að ég fari. (He wants me to go.)

Þú vildir, að ég tæki *mál hans að mér.* (You wanted me to take on his case.)

(2) *Verbs of Imagining, Thinking (Considering), etc.*

Ég held, að ég sé búinn að segja þér allar sögur, sem ég kann. (I believe that I have told you all the stories I know.)

Ég held, að það sé ef til vill hægt. (I think that is (may be) quite easy.)

Ég held, að það sé mögulegt. (I believe it is possible.)

Ég taldi víst, að einhver hefði *gleymt að gera það.* (I thought that someone had forgotten to do that.)

Hann hlýtur að vita, að ég sé að gera þetta fyrir þig. (He must realize that I am doing this for you.)

Ég er hræddur um, að þér verði *kalt á leiðinni.* (I am afraid that you will be cold on the way.)

Heldurðu, að þú munir *geta þetta*? (Do you believe that you will be able to do that?)

Ég hefði haldið, að þetta mundi *nægja.* (I thought that this would be enough.)

(3) *Conditions.* In English there are three main constructions:
if/present . . . future
if/past . . . conditional
if/past perfect . . . conditional perfect

These constructions vary somewhat from the Icelandic ones, which are as follows:
ef/present . . . future (or present)
ef/past subjunctive . . . past subjunctive
ef/past perfect subjunctive . . . past perfect subjunctive

Examples:

Ég skal vera kyrr, *ef þú segir* mér eina stutta sögu. (I will be quiet, if you tell me a short story.)

Ef þú ert að draga dár að mér, skal ég slá þig. (If you are pulling my leg, I shall hit you.)

Ég skyldi fara, ef ég gæti. (I would go if I were able.)

Ég kæmi, ef ég gæti. (I would come, if I could.)

Ég vildi vera blóm, *ef enginn* sliti *mig upp, og aldrei* kæmi *vetur með snjó og frost.* (I'd like to be a flower, if no-one pulled me up, and there never came winter with snow and frost.)

Ef hann hefði skrifað *þér þetta bréf,* hefði það verið undirritað *Pétur.* (If he had written you this letter, it would have been signed Peter.)

Ef ég hefði ekki séð *það með eigin augum,* hefði ég ekki trúað *því.* (If I hadn't seen that with my own eyes, I shouldn't have believed it.)

Ég hefði reynt *að hjálpa honum, ef hann* hefði leitað *til mín.* (I should have tried to help him if he had approached me.)

(4) *Indirect Speech.*

Fólkið segir, að hún sé *lík Dísu.* (People say that she is like D.)

Hann sagði, að þær væru *farnar.* (He said that they (fem.) had gone.)

Hann sagði þér, að hann væri *í Reykjavík.* (He told you that he was in Reykjavík.)

Þú sagðir honum, að þú hefðir ráðið *mig til þess að gera það.* (You told him that you had advised me to do that.)

(5) *Eins og.* The subjunctive is used after this expression in such sentences as the following:

Þetta var hrafnaspark, eins og það hefði verið *skrifað í myrkri.* (It was just scrawl, as if it had been written in the dark.)

Hún æpir eins og hún sé *óð.* (She screams as if she were mad.)

(6) In clauses introduced by "til þess að" or "svo að" (in order that), when the reason or purpose is given.

Vertu heima í kvöld, til þess að ég geti farið *út.* (Stay at home this evening, so that I can (may) go out.)

Note that in the sentence: *vindurinn hamaðist, svo að húsið skalf* (the wind raged so that the house shook), the subjunctive is not used, as there is no indication of reason or purpose, but only of effect or result.

(7) After *þótt* or *þó að* (although).

Þetta er lagleg gjöf, þótt lítil sé. (This is a handsome gift, although it is small.)

Han er í bláu fötunum, þó að það sé *ekki sunnudagur.* (He is in his blue suit (clothes), although it is not Sunday.)

Fullorðna fólkið skrökvar oft, þó að það segi*, að það* komi *svartur blettur á tunguna á mér, ef ég* skrökvi (Grown-up people often lie, although they say that I will get a black mark on my tongue if I lie.) Note in this sentence that we have the subjunctive in three instances; after *þó að,* after the verb "to say" (indirect speech), and in the conditional part of the sentence where *ef* is used. (Alternatively, the second instance of the subjunctive may be reckoned in the same category as the third.)

Miscellaneous

Ég skal sjá um, að hann gefi *sig fram klukkan fimm.* (I shall see to it that he gives himself up at five o'clock.)

Hann mun sjá, að ég hafi *tekið að mér mál hans.* (He will see that I have taken on his case.)

After *certain verbs* the subjunctive case is commonly used.

Guði sé *lof.* (God be praised.)

Guð sé *með þér.* (God be with you.)

The subjunctive is used in expressions of *desire cum imperative,* where it would be possible to use the word "may" in the English; "May God be praised", etc.

Komi *hvað koma vill.* (Come what may.)

The subjunctive is used in *certain fixed expressions.*

Vocabulary

although, *þótt*
before (time), *áður*
come, *koma (kem; kom; kominn)*
cry, *gráta*
(become) dawn, *daga*
foolish, *heimskulegur*
know, be aware of, *vita (veit; vissi; vitað)*
know, understand, *kunna (kann; kunni; kunnað)*
let, allow, *láta*
to make up (face), *mála sig*
never, *aldrei*

Norwegian (language), *norska*
say, *segja*
sing, *syngja*
somebody, *einhver*
stingy, *nízkur*
think, believe, *hyggja (hygg; hugði; hugað)*
think, consider, *halda (held; hélt; héldum; haldinn)*
true, *sannur, sönn*
ugly, hideous, nasty, *ljótur*
what?, *hvað?*
to wish, *óska*
younger, *yngri*

Exercise 7a

Translate into Icelandic:

(1) I think that I have seen him before.
(2) I thought that you knew that.
(3) The story is true, although it is horrible (ugly).
(4) Now she has read the book.
(5) He is writing a letter.
(6) I do not want Disa to see that I am beginning to cry.
(7) They did not want him to go (that he should go).
(8) The man has finished writing, but the girl has not finished reading.
(9) It is getting light (Dawn is breaking).
(10) She is speaking to me.
(11) I was not aware that you knew Norwegian.
(12) I have never said that I knew Norwegian.

Exercise 7b

Translate into English:

(1) Ég var að skrifa, þegar hún kom.
(2) Ef svo væri ekki, mundum við ekki vera hér.
(3) Hann var búinn að lesa bókina.
(4) Hvað ertu að gera?
(5) Hún vildi ekki láta Gerðu sjá, að hún færi að gráta.
(6) Einhver er að koma.
(7) Hann segir, að hún sé nízk.
(8) Ég vildi óska, að þú værir mörgum árum yngri.
(9) Stúlkan er búin að mála sig.
(10) Hvað hafi ég verið að segja?, sagði hann.
(11) Hún var að syngja, þegar ég kom.
(12) Ég held, að það sé heimskulegt.

LESSON 8

Strong Verbs

IN the past tense strong verbs do not add endings, but instead undergo a change of root vowel. Strong verbs are sometimes divided into the following six types, according to the change of vowel they undergo:

	infin.	*past sing.*	*past plural*	*supine*
(a)	bíta	beit	bitum	bitið
(b)	bjóða	bauð	buðum	boðið
(c)	bresta	brast	brustum	brostið
(d)	bera	bar	bárum	borið
(e)	taka	tók	tókum	tekið
(f)	heita	hét	hétum	heitið

Note also une *ri*-verbs and the verb *valda*. There are four verbs that take *-ri* in the past. These are:

> gróa—greri—gróið (grow)
> róa—reri—róið (row)
> núa—neri—núið (rub)
> snúa—sneri—snúið (turn)

Valda (cause) takes the following forms:

> pres. indic. *veld*; pres. subj. *valdi*; past indic. *olli*; past subj. *ylli*; supine *valdið*.

Group (a) therefore undergoes the changes: i—ei—i, e.g.,
> *bíta—beit—bitum* (bite)
> *rífa—reif—rifum* (tear)

Group (b) has these changes: jó, jú, ú—au—u—o, e.g.,
> *bjóða—bauð—buðum—boðið* (offer)
> *sjóða—sauð—suðum—soðið* (boil)
> *rjúka—rauk—rukum—rokið* (smoke)
> *strjúka—strauk—strukum—strokið* (stroke)

lúta—laut—lutum—lotið (bend)
súpa—saup—supum—sopið (sip)

Group (c) has these changes: e, i—a—u, o, e.g.,
bresta—brast—brustum—brostið (burst)
verpa—varp—urpum—orpið (throw)
binda—batt—bundum—bundið (tie)
finna—fann—fundum—fundið (find)

Group (d) has these changes: e, i—a—á—u, o, e.g.,
bera—bar—bárum—borið (carry)
nema—nam—námum—numið (learn)
svima—svam—svámum—sumið (swim)

Group (e) changes thus: a—ó, e.g.,
fara—fór (go)
taka—tók (take)

Note also these changes, not accounted for by gradation:

heita—hét—hétum—heitið (be called)
auka—jók—jukum—aukið (increase)
falla—féll—féllum—fallið (fall)
blása—blés—blésum—blásið (blow)
gráta—grét—grétum—grátið (cry)

The imperative of strong verbs is formed by dropping the final *-a* of the infinitive, but the *þ* in the following *þú* normally joins the verb (or else it changes as described in the pronunciation section). Sometimes, also, the final consonant of the verb is affected, so that, for example, the imperative of *binda* becomes *bittu*, that of *vinda* becomes *vittu*, and that of *ganga* becomes *gaktu*.

Conjugation of Strong Verbs

The following verbs are conjugated, to demonstrate the differences between the main groups: (a) *bíta*, (b) *bjóða*, (c) *bresta*, (d) *bera*, (e) *taka*, (f) *gráta*.

Bíta

	pres. indic.	*pres. subj.*	*past indic.*	*past subj.*
ég	bít	bíti	beit	biti
þú	bítur	bítir	beitst	bitir
hann	bítur	bíti	beit	biti
við	bítum	bítum	bitum	bitum
þið	bítið	bítið	bituð	bituð
þeir	bíta	bíti	bitu	bitu

imperative: s. *bít*, pl. *bítið* supine: *bitið*
past part.: *bitinn*

Bjóða

ég	býð	bjóði	bauð	byði
þú	býður	bjóðir	bauðst	byðir
hann	býður	bjóði	bauð	byði
við	bjóðum	bjóðum	buðum	byðum
þið	bjóðið	bjóðið	buðuð	byðuð
þeir	bjóða	bjóði	buðu	byðu

imperative: s. *býð*, pl. *bjóðið* supine: *boðið*
past part.: *boðinn*

Bresta

ég	brest	bresti	brast	brysti
þú	brestur	brestir	brast	brystir
hann	brestur	bresti	brast	brysti
við	brestum	brestum	brustum	brystum
þið	brestið	brestið	brustuð	brystuð
þeir	bresta	bresti	brustu	brystu

imperative: s. *brest*, pl. *brustuð* supine: *brostið*
past part.: *brostinn*

Bera

ég	ber	beri	bar	bæri
þú	berð	berir	barst	bærir
hann	ber	beri	bar	bæri
við	berum	berum	bárum	bærum

	pres. indic.	pres. subj.	past. indic.	past. subj.
þið	berið	berið	báruð	bæruð
þeir	bera	beri	báru	bæru

imperative: s. *ber*, pl. *berið* supine: *borið*
        past part.: *borinn*

Taka

ég	tek	taki	tók	tæki
þú	tekur	takir	tókst	tækir
hann	tekur	taki	tók	tæki
við	tökum	tökum	tókum	tækjum
þið	takið	takið	tókuð	tækjuð
þeir	taka	taki	tóku	tækju

imperative: s. *tek*, pl. *takið* supine: *tekið*
        past part.: *tekinn*

Gráta

ég	græt	gráti	grét	gréti
þú	grætur	grátir	grézt	grétir
hann	grætur	gráti	grét	gréti
við	grátum	grátum	grétum	grétum
þið	grátið	grátið	grétuð	grétuð
þeir	gráta	gráti	grétu	grétu

imperative: s. *græt*, pl. *grátið* supine: *grátið*
        past part.: *grátinn*

Verbs in Group A (The first person singular of the present indicative is given if there is any difference from the root vowel
of the infinitive.)

bíða, to wait

bíta, bite

drífa, drive

gína, gape

grípa, grasp

hníga, fall gently

hrífa, catch hold

hrína, squeal

hvína, whistle, whine

klífa, climb

klípa, pinch

kvíða (*kvíði*), dread

líða, elapse

líta, look

ríða, ride

rífa, tear

rísa, rise

síga, sink

skína, shine
skríða, creep
slíta, break
sníða, cut
stíga, step

svíða, singe/smart
svífa, soar
svíkja, deceive
víkja, yield, give way
þrífa, grasp, snatch

Verbs in Group B

bjóða (býð), offer
brjóta (brýt), break
drjúpa (drýp), drip
fjúka (fýk), blow
fljóta (flýt), float
fljúga (flýg), fly
frjósa (frýs), freeze
gjósa (gýs), gush
gjóta (gýt), have young (animals)
hljóta (hlýt), must
hnjóta (hnýt), stumble
hrjóta (hrýt), snore
kljúfa (klýf), split
kjósa (kýs), choose
krjúpa (krýp), creep
ljósta (lýst), strike
ljúga (lýg), lie
ljúka (lýk), end

lúta (lýt), bend
njóta (nýt), enjoy
rjóða (rýð), redden
rjúfa (rýf), break
rjúka (rýk), smoke
sjóða (sýð), boil
sjúga (sýg), suck
þrjóta (þrýt), end
skjóta (skýt), shoot
smjúga (smýg), creep through
strjúka (strýk), stroke
súpa (sýp), sip
þjóta (þýt), rush

Also:

hrökkva (hrekk), draw back
stökkva (stekk), spring
sökkva (sekk), sink
syngja (syng), sing

Verbs in Group C

binda (u), tie
brenna (u), burn
bresta, burst
detta, fall
drekka (u), drink
finna (u), find
gella, yell
gjalda geld, pay
gjalla (gell), scream
hrinda (u), push
hverfa, disappear
renna (u), run

skella, crash
skreppa, slip
sleppa, escape
snerta (snerti), touch
spinna (u), spin
spretta, grow
springa (u), burst
stinga (u), prick
svelgja, swallow
svelta, starve
sverfa, swear
vella, seethe

velta, overturn   *vinda* (*u*), wind
verða, become   *vinna* (*u*), work
verpa, throw

The bracketed (*u*) indicates that this is the vowel of the supine and past participle, the other verbs taking *o*.

Verbs in Group D

bera (*o*), carry   *lesa* (*lesinn*), read
biðja (*beðinn*), pray   *liggja* (*leginn*), lie
drepa (*drepinn*), kill   *meta* (*metinn*), value
fregna (*fregið*), ask   *nema* (*u*), learn
gefa (*gefinn*), give   *reka* (*rekinn*), drive
geta (*getinn*), be able   *sitja* (*setinn*), sit
kveða (*kveðinn*), say   *skera* (*o*), cut
leka (*lekinn*), play   *stela* (*o*), steal

Verbs in Group E

The first six take *e* in the past participle and supine, e.g. *dreginn*.

aka, drive   *grafa*, dig
draga, drag   *hefja*, lift/begin
flá (*flæ*, pres.), flay   *hlaða*, load
shaka, shake   *kala*, freeze
slá (*slæ*), strike   *mala*, grind
taka, take   *skafa*, scrape
ala, give birth to   *standa* (*stadinn*), stand
fara, go   *vaða*, wade
gala,* crow   *vega*, weigh

* But commonly *gala—galaði—galað*.

Verbs like *auka* are *ausa* (bale) and *hlaupa* (run). Like *heita* is *leika* (play). Like *blása* and *gráta* are *láta* (allow) and *ráða* (advise). With *falla* we may include *halda* (hold), *hanga* (hang) and *ganga* (walk). *Ganga* has the following parts: *geng* (pres.), *gekk*; *gengum* (past), *genginn* (past part.). Other strong verbs, difficult to classify, are the following:

búa	bý	bjó; bjuggum (y)	búinn,	live, etc.
deyja	dey	dó; dóum (æ)	dáinn,	die
éta	ét	át; átum (æ)	étinn,	eat
fá	fæ	fékk; fengum	fenginn,	get
hlæja	hlæ	hló; hlógum (æ)	hlegið,	laugh
höggva	hegg	hjó; hjuggum (y)	höggvinn,	hew, cut
koma	kem	kom; komum (æ)	kominn,	come
sjá	sé	sá; sáum (æ)	séður (sénn),	see
skjálfa	skelf	skalf; skulfum (y)	skolfið,	shake, tremble
sofa	sef	svaf; sváfum (æ)	sofinn,	sleep
spýja	spý	spjó; spjóum (y)	spúið,	vomit
sverja	sver	sór· sórum (æ)	svarinn,	swear
troða	treð	tróð; tróðum (æ)	troðinn,	tread
vefa	vef	óf; ófum (æ)	ofinn,	weave
þvo	þvæ	þó; þógum (æ)	þveginn,	wash

Note that the forms given are the infinitive, the present indicative, the singular and plural of the past (with the root vowel of the subjunctive in brackets) and the supine or past participle.

Vocabulary

alternately, á víxl
at home, heima
back of, á bak við
black, svartur
car, f. bifreið(-ar)
cup, m. bolli
in front of, framanvið
in order to, til þess að
keep on (doing), halda áfram
   að . . .
in (inside), inni
long into (time), langt fram á
notebook, f. minnisbók
opportunity, n. tækifæri

to take the opportunity, að
   grípa tækifærið
pocket, m. vasi
put on (coat), fara í . . .
put on (hat), setja á sig
   (colloq. setja upp)
river, f. á (r,- -r)
smile, að brosa
step (pace), n. skref
strong, sterkur
shop-window, m. búðargluggi
take up position, nema staðar
there (thither), þangað
while, meðan

Exercise 8a

Translate into Icelandic:

(1) I saw and heard a lot while I was living with you.
(2) You were not at home when I came.
(3) She laughed and cried alternately.
(4) I had taken up my position in front of the big shop-window.
(5) The dog bit me.
(6) I got a letter from him.
(7) He seized the opportunity and went in.
(8) The boy turned towards her.
(9) The girl took a step backwards.
(10) He pushed me into the river.
(11) She looked up and smiled.
(12) I went there and found him.

Exercise 8b

Translate into English:

(1) Ég stend upp till þess að gá.
(2) Han leit á klukkuna.
(3) Han hló að mér, þegar ég spurði hann, hvað ég ætti að gera.
(4) Hún braut kaffibollann.
(5) Ég hélt áfram að lesa langt fram á nótt.
(6) Hvað sáuð þér?
(7) Hún ók til bankans.
(8) Maðurinn tók minnisbók upp úr vasanum.
(9) Hann fór í frakkann, setti á sig (upp) hattinn og gekk síðan út.
(10) Hann sat inni í bifreiðinni sinni.
(11) Ég sá svartan hund.
(12) Drekktu ekki sterkt kaffi.

LESSON 9

The Passive Voice

As in the Active Voice, there are fourteen tenses, all formed by conjugating *vera* or *verða* with the past participle of the principal verb. Here are the tenses of the verb *kalla* (call) in the passive:

present indic.	ég er kallaður, þú ert kallaður, etc.
present subj.	ég sé kallaður
past indic.	ég var kallaður
past subj.	ég væri kallaður
perfect indic.	ég hefi verið kallaður
perfect subj.	ég hafi verið kallaður
past perf. indic.	ég hafði verið kallaður
past perf. subj.	ég hefði verið kallaður
future indic.	ég mun verða (vera) kallaður
future subj.	ég muni verða (vera) kallaður
future perf. indic.	ég mun hafa verið kallaður
future perf. subj.	ég muni hafa verið kallaður
conditional	ég mundi verða (vera) kallaður
conditional perf.	ég mundi hafa verið kallaður

Note that there are three common variations. These are as follows:

(*a*) In the Past Passive, the verb *verða* is sometimes used.

(*b*) In the Future Passive, the verb *verða* is used in the present tense without the verb *munu*. E.g., *hann verður flengdur*. (He will be flogged.)

(*c*) In the Conditional, the verb *verða* is used in the past subj. tense without the verb *munu*. E.g., *ég hélt, að hann yrði drepinn*. (I thought that he would be killed.)

The Middle Voice

This is a peculiarity of Icelandic of quite frequent occurrence. It is formed by adding -st to Active Verbs, being applicable to any tense. This -*st* is derived from the original reflexive *sik* (now *sig*), which became -*sk* and subsequently -*st*. If the verb ending is -*ur* or -*r*, e.g., *tekur*, these endings are dropped before the -*st*, e.g., *tekst*. Similarly, *sækir* becomes *sækist*.

When the letters *ds*, *ðs* or *ts* are together in the same syllable, and only the *s*-sound is pronounced, the *d*, *ð* or *t* is dropped and *z* substituted for *s*. For example, *stend/st* becomes *stenzt*, *bregð/st* becomes *bregzt*, and *læt/st* becomes *læzt*.

The Middle Voice is used in three senses:

(*a*) Passive. *Kallast* means, for instance, is called (*er kallaður*).

(*b*) Reciprocal. Here the Middle Voice ending indicates *hvor annan*, each other. For example, *þeir hittust* means *þeir hittu hvor annan*, they met (each other).

(*c*) Reflexive. This is the main use of the Middle Voice. For instance, *rödd hans lognaðist út af* means his voice died away (lit. quietened itself down).

A number of verbs, called Middle Voice Verbs, are used in the Middle Voice only. Such are: *nálgast* (approach), *annast* (take care of), *heppnast* (succeed), *óttast* (fear), *vingast við* (become friendly with), *öðlast* (obtain).

Here are the fourteen tenses of the Middle Voice:

present indic.	ég, þú, hann kallast; við köllumst, þið kallizt, þeir kallast
present subj.	ég kallist
past indic.	ég kallaðist; við kölluðumst, þið kölluðuzt, þeir kölluðust
past subj.	ég kallaðist
perfect indic.	ég hefi kallazt
perfect subj.	ég hafi kallazt
past perf. indic.	ég hafði kallazt
past perf. subj.	ég hefði kallazt
future indic.	ég mun kallast
future subj.	ég muni kallast
future perf. indic.	ég mun hafa kallazt
future perf. subj.	ég muni hafa kallazt
conditional	ég mundi kallast
conditional perf.	ég mundi hafa kallazt

Impersonal Verbs

Certain verbs are used only in the third person singular. These verbs indicate weather conditions, oncoming times of the day and year, and so on. Such verbs are:

það dagar, dawn	*það hitnar*, grow warm
„ *dimmir*, grow dark	„ *kólnar*, grow cold
„ *fennir*, snow	„ *kvöldar*, become evening
„ *geisar (ofviðri)*, (a violent gale) is raging	„ *rignir*, rain
	„ *snjóar*, snow
„ *haustar*, become autumn	„ *vorar*, become spring

Before certain impersonal verbs the accusative personal pronoun is placed; e.g.,

mig þyrstir, hungrar	I am thirsty, hungry
þig „ „	you are „ „
hann „ „	he is „ „
okkur „ „	we are „ „
ykkur „ „	you are „ „
þá „ „	they are „ „

There are a variety of other verbs which take this accusative pronoun; e.g.,

Það munar miklu. (It makes a great difference.)

Mig munar um hverja krónuna. (Every Krona makes a difference to me.)

Mig langar til að gera það. (I long to do that.)

Mig dreymdi vel (illa) í nótt. (I had a nice (bad) dream last night.)

See also Lesson 15 for such verbs.

Impersonal Use of Ordinary Verbs

This is strongly linked to the common Dative Construction in Icelandic. It should be emphasized that this impersonal construction is of common occurrence in Icelandic. Look at these sentences:

Mér hefur oft dottið í hug að læra dönsku. (To me it has often come to mind to learn Danish—I have often thought of learning Danish.)

Mér dettur ekki í hug að anza þér. (To me it does not come to mind to answer you.)

Mér blöskrar þessi eyðslusemi. (To me it shocks, this extrava
gance—this extravagance shocks me.)
Mér er heitt (kalt). (To me it is hot (cold).)
Mér þykir gaman. (I like.)
Honum hefði verið betra að fara eftir mínum ráðum. (To him
it would have been better to follow my advice.)
Mér líkar vel við þig. (To me it likes you well—I like you.)
Honum skeikar ekki. (To him it is not mistaken—he does not
make a mistake.)
Mér batnar (versnar). (I get better (worse).)
Honum batnaði seint. (He got well slowly.)
Mér finnst það undarlegt. (To me that finds itself strange—
I think that is strange.)

In the last example note the use of the Middle Voice in the
word *"finnst"*, here used in the reflexive sense.

Remember the dative forms of the personal pronouns, which
are:

mér, to me	*því*, to it
þér, to you	*okkur*, to us
honum, to him	*ykkur/yður*, to you
henni, to her	*þeim*, to them

As one last example, let us look at the verb *ljósta* (strong,
type b). This is an ordinary transitive verb meaning to strike,
hit. But it may also be used impersonally, as in this sentence:
miklu veðri laust á (much bad weather, blew up—a sudden
storm blew up). Further, we may use the dative construction
thus: *þeim laust saman* (to them it struck together—they came
to blows).

Vocabulary

athæfi, n. conduct, behaviour.
beinast á aðrar brautir, to change to another subject.
breytast, to change.
án afláts, incessantly, continuously.
gefast upp við að fá e-n til að gera e-ð, to give up trying to make
someone do something.

gægjast(i) út um, to peep out of.
hleypa brúnum, to frown.
hið sama, the same.
hægt, *adv*. slowly, gently, softly.
komast upp, to come to light, come out.
leggjast til svefns, to go to sleep.
leiðinlegur, *adj*. boring.
meðalhár, *adj*. of medium height.
mig langar í e-ð, I long for something.
rúða, *f*. window-pane.
röð (*raðar*, *raðir*), *f*. row, series; turn.
setjast, to sit down.
skömmu eftir, *adv*. shortly after.
snúa (*sný; sneri, snerum; snúinn*), to turn, go round.
takast á hendur, to undertake something.
varningur (*-s*), *m*. property; goods.

Exercise 9a

Translate into Icelandic:

(1) He sat down beside her.
(2) I long to ask some questions.
(3) They have gone to Akureyri.
(4) When she came into the room, the conversation changed to another subject.
(5) The letter was written by himself.
(6) They have changed a great deal.
(7) Now it was his turn to frown.
(8) We shall have to part here now.
(9) She did not dare to go to sleep.
(10) The door opened and in came a man of medium height.
(11) Many others have said the same thing.
(12) He gave up trying to make Dísa change her mind.

Exercise 9b

Translate into English:

(1) Hún hafði tekizt þessa ferð á hendur til þess að giftast honum.

(2) Þeir voru nú sendir til heimalands síns.

(3) Mig langar ekki í morgunverð.

(4) Skömmu eftir að dyrnar lokuðust á eftir Dísu, vaknaði ég.

(5) Drengurinn settist hægt niður.

(6) Með því að stolinn varningur fannst í fórum hans, komst allt athæfi hans upp.

(7) Hann berst með strauminum.

(8) Hestarnir voru sjúkir í morgun.

(9) Hún leit upp og gægðist út um rúðuna.

(10) Mér finnst hann leiðinlegur.

(11) Stúlkan snerist án afláts í kringum hana, meðan hún var að klæða sig.

(12) Hann stóð upp til hálfs, en settist svo aftur.

LESSON 10

Adjectives

ADJECTIVES are of two declensions, the strong and the weak. The strong declension is used when no article or pronoun is employed, and the weak is used with an article or pronoun. The weak declension always terminates in a vowel, the plural of all genders and cases ending in -u.

Note that adjectives agree in gender, number and case with their corresponding noun. Two main groups may be made, those ending in -r (-ur) and those ending in -inn, in the nominative singular masculine. More precisely we may specify five sub-divisions of the strong declension, for which see the Appendix. Here are examples of the main strong declensions:

	Singular		
	masculine	*feminine*	*neuter*
nom.	ríkur	rík	ríkt
acc.	ríkan	ríka	ríkt
dat.	ríkum	ríkri	ríku
gen.	ríks	ríkrar	ríks

Plural

nom.	ríkir	ríkar	rík
acc.	ríka	ríkar	rík
dat.	ríkum	ríkum	ríkum
gen.	ríkra	ríkra	ríkra

-*inn* type. *boginn* (bent, curved):

Singular

	masculine	*feminine*	*neuter*
nom	boginn	bogin	bogið
acc.	boginn	bogna	bogið
dat.	bognum	boginni	bognu
gen.	bogins	boginnar	bogins

Plural

nom.	bognir	bognar	bogin
acc.	bogna	bognar	bogin
dat.	bognum	bognum	bognum
gen.	boginna	boginna	boginna

Weak Declension of Adjectives

ríkur (rich).

Singular

	masculine	*feminine*	*neuter*
nom.	ríki	ríka	ríka
acc.	ríka	ríku	ríka
dat.	ríka	ríku	ríka
gen.	ríka	ríku	ríka

Plural

nom.	ríku	ríku	ríku
acc.	ríku	ríku	ríku
dat.	ríku	ríku	ríku
gen.	ríku	ríku	ríku

Examples of Usage

Presturinn átti unga og fríða dóttur. (The clergyman had a beautiful young daughter (literally: clergyman/the had young and beautiful daughter.) Here *dóttur* is the accusative case of *dóttir*, and *fríða* is therefore the accusative case strong declension femine of the adjective *fríður* (likewise with the adjective *ungur*). Remember that the strong declension is used when there is no article, as here.

Þetta er ungur drengur. (This is a young boy.) Here we have used the strong masculine nominative case, *ungur*.

Hann les í gamalli bók. (He reads (in) an old book.) Strong declension, feminine singular dative case. (Dative after *í*.)

Hann er í hreinni skyrtu. (He is wearing a clean shirt.) Strong declension, feminine singular dative case.

Kennarinn kom ríðandi á hvítum hesti. (The teacher came riding (up) on a white horse.) Strong declension, masculine singular dative case.

Þetta er reyndur maður. (This is an experienced man.) Strong declension, masculine singular nominative case.

Ég keypti þetta fallega hús af gömlum, ríkum manni. (I bought this beautiful house from an old rich man.) Here, *fallega* is the weak neuter accusative case of the adjective *fallegur* (beautiful, pretty)—the weak declension being used after the pronoun *þetta* (this)—while *gömlum* and *ríkum* are strong declension masculine singular dative of *gamall* (old) and *ríkur* (rich). Here the strong declension is used as there is neither article nor pronoun, and the dative case follows the preposition *af* (of, from).

Comparison of Adjectives

The regular comparison is thus:

ríkur—ríkari—ríkastur

The comparative is declinable only in the weak form, while the superlative can take both strong and weak forms.

Variations of the regular comparison are:

(a) *-ri*, *-stur*, together with root-vowel change; e.g., *stór—stærri—stærstur* (big, bigger, biggest), and *ungur—yngri—yngstur* (young, younger, youngest).

(b) *-ri*, *-astur*; e.g., *nýr—nýrri—nýjastur* (new, newer, newest), and *fallegur—fallegri—fallegastur* (pretty, prettier, prettiest).

Irregular Comparison

gamall—eldri—elztur (old)
góður—betri—beztur (good)
lítill—minni—minnstur (little)
margur—fleiri—flestur (many)
mikill—meiri—mestur (great, large)
vondur ⎫
illur ⎬—verri—verstur (bad)
slæmur ⎭

As stated, the comparative is declined only in the weak form: every case of the masculine and feminine singular and plural and all cases of the neuter plural have the same form: of the adjective *ríkur*, for example, this is *ríkari*. The neuter singular forms are all the same, namely *ríkara*.

Also as stated, the superlative can take both strong and weak forms, thus:

strong declension: *ríkastur* (masc.) *ríkust* (fem.) *ríkast* (neut.)

weak declension: *ríkasti* (masc.) *ríkasta* (fem.) *ríkasta* (neut.)

A certain number of adjectives exist only in the comparative and superlative. These are as follows (the form lacking is shown in brackets):

(austur)	eystri, farther east	austastur, most easterly.
(suður)	syðri, farther south	syðstur, most southerly
(vestur)	vestri, farther west	vestastur, most westerly
(norður)	nyrðri, farther north	nyrztur, most northerly
(aftur)	aftari, farther back	aftastur, hindmost
(fram)	fremri, more forward	fremstur, foremost
(fjarri)	firri, farther	firstur, farthest
(nær)	nærri, nearer	næstur, next
(for, fyrir)	fyrri, former	fyrstur, first, foremost
(síð)	síðari, latter	síðastur, latest
	síðri, inferior	síztur, worst
(handan)	handari, farther off	handastur, farthest off
(heim)	heimari, nearer home	heimastur, nearest home
(heldur)	heldri, better	helztur, best/main

(*hægur*)	*hægri*, right	—
(*inn*)	*innri*, inner	*innstur*, innermost
(*út*)	*ytri*, outer	*yztur*, outermost
(*niður*)	*neðri*, lower	*neðstur*, lowest
(*of*)	*efri*, upper	*efstur*, uppermost
(*sjaldan*)	*sjaldnari* rarer	*sjaldnastur*, rarest
	hindri, later	*hinztur*, last
	skárri, more bearable	*skástur*, most bearable
	vinstri, left	—
	æðri, superior	*æðstur*, supreme

Other Points about Adjectives

(1) A small number of adjectives are not declinable, and mostly end in -*a*.

Examples: *aflvana* (impotent); *dauðvona* (moribund); *einmana* (alone, lonely); *farlama* (decrepit); *rávita* (insane, crazy); *hugsi* (meditative).

(2) In the construction as . . . as, the correct literary constructions are:

eins . . . (*eins*) *og* . . .; *svo* . . . *sem* . . .

However, the first "as" is frequently not used, while the second one may be *eins og*, or *sem*.

Examples: *hvítur sem snjór*, as white as snow.
frjáls eins og fuglinn, free as a bird.

(3) Than, after the comparative, is either *en* or *heldur en*.

Ingibjörg er fallegri en Gerða, or
Ingibjörg er fallegri heldur en Gerða: Ingibjörg is prettier than Gerða.

(4) The genitive is used with the positive of adjectives in expressions of time or measure.

Examples: *átta vikna tími*, a space of eight weeks.
þriggja ára gamall, three years old.
tveggja feta hár, two feet tall (high).

(5) The comparative governs the dative case, in which case *heldur en* is omitted: *Bjarni er flestum mönnum fróðari*: B. is more learned than most men.

(6) The superlative governs the genitive case: *hún er fegurst allra kvenna*, she is the most beautiful of all women.

(7) Many adjectives have no ending in the masculine: e.g., *hvass*, sharp. After *l* or *n* preceded by a vowel, the final *-r* has changed into *l* or *n*: e.g., *mikill* for *mikilr*, *heiðinn* for *heiðinr*. Adjectives of this last group (*heiðinn*) take *ð* and not *t* in the neuter: e.g., *heiðinn*, *heiðið*.

(8) When the stem of the adjective ends in *æ* or *ý* (and also in the word *miður*) there is a *-j* placed before *a* and *u*: e.g., *gagnsær* (transparent) has the accusative case *gagnsæjan* and the dative case *gagnsæjum*. *Miður* (amid) becomes *miðjan* in the accusative and *miðjum* in the dative. Note also that in some words there is a *-v* before *a* and *u* in all endings: e.g., *fölur*, pale, becomes *fölvan* in the accusative singular and *fölvir* in the nominative plural.

Vocabulary

búast við, to expect
fölleitur, adj. pale
glaðlyndur, adj. cheerful, jovial
harla, adv. very
hnugginn, adj. sad, downcast
nótt (nætur, nætur), f. night

opinn, adj. open
sann (satt), adj. true
skemmtilegur, adj. pleasant
svalur (svöl), adj. cool
svipur (-s, -ir), m. look, countenance
venjulegur, adj. usual, general

Exercise 10a

Translate into English:

(1) Kjöt er venjulega dýrara en fiskur.
(2) Landið er fagurt.
(3) Skipið er harla sterkt og fallegt.
(4) Andlitið var fölleitt, en svipurinn hreinn og drengilegur.
(5) Hér eru fleiri drengir en stúlkur.
(6) Stúlkunum er kalt.
(7) Hann ók grænum Ford.

(8) Ég er hærri en Siggi.

(9) Hann er glaðlyndur og skemmtilegur.

(10) Maðurinn er blindfullur.

(11) Dagurinn var heitur en nóttin var svöl.

(12) Það er ekki satt.

Exercise 10b

Translate into Icelandic (make use of the Vocabulary and Idiomatic sections):

(1) The mountain is high.

(2) The valley is beautiful.

(3) This is the broadest street in the town.

(4) She is as poor as a churchmouse.

(5) The windows in the room are not open.

(6) She is smaller than he is.

(7) I am not sad, but she is very sad.

(8) Winter is the coldest time of the year.

(9) He is more clever than I expected.

(10) The house is green.

(11) She is younger than he is.

(12) We are very tired.

LESSON 11

Numerals

Cardinal Numbers

1 einn	11 ellefu
2 tveir	12 tólf
3 þrír	13 þrettán
4 fjórir	14 fjórtán
5 fimm	15 fimtán
6 sex	16 sextán
7 sjö	17 sautján, seytján
8 átta	18 átján
9 níu	19 nítján
10 tíu	20 tuttugu

21 tuttugu og einn	90 níutíu
22 tuttugu og tveir	100 (eitt) hundrað
23 tuttugu og þrír, etc.	101 (eitt) hundrað og einn
30 þrjátíu	121 (eitt) hundrað tuttugu og einn
31 þrjátíu og einn, etc.	200 tvö hundruð
40 fjörutíu	300 þrjú hundruð
50 fimmtíu	1000 (eitt) þúsund
60 sextíu	1959 nítján hundruð fimmtíu og níu
70 sjötíu	2000 tvö þúsund (tvær þúsundir)
80 áttatíu	1,000,000 (ein) milljón

The cardinal numbers that it is possible to decline are the first four and *hundrað*, *þúsund* and *milljón*.

Declension of *einn*

Singular

	masculine	feminine	neuter
nom.	einn	ein	eitt
acc.	einn	einna	eitt
dat.	einum	einni	einu
gen.	eins	einnar	eins

Plural

nom.	einir	einar	ein
acc.	eina	einar	ein
dat.	einum	einum	einum
gen.	einna	einna	einna

Einn may also be declined weak: *hinn eini, hin eina, hið eina*, etc.

Declension of *tveir*

nom.	tveir	tvær	tvö
acc.	tvo	tvær	tvö
dat.	tveim/ur	tveim/ur	tveim/ur
gen.	tveggja	tveggja	tveggja

Declension of *þrır*

	masculine	feminine	neuter
nom.	þrír	þrjár	þrjú
acc.	þrjá	þrjár	þrjú
dat.	þrem/ur	þrem/ur	þrem/ur
gen.	þriggja	þriggja	þriggja

Declension of *fjórir*

	nom.	feminine	neuter
nom.	fjórir	fjórar	fjögur
acc.	fjóra	fjórar	fjögur
dat.	fjórum	fjórum	fjórum
gen.	fjögurra,	fjögurra,	fjögurra,
	fjögra	fjögra	fjögra

When used as adjectives, *hundrað* and *þúsund* are not declined, except that the plural of *hundrað* is *hundruð*. However, when used as nouns, *hundrað* is declined in the same way as other neuter nouns, while *þúsund* may be declined like the feminine noun *tíð* or like the neuter noun *skip*. *Milljón* is feminine.

Ordinal Numbers

1st	fyrsti	20th	tuttugasti
2nd	annar	21st	tuttugasti og fyrsti
3rd	þriðji	22nd	tuttugasti og annar
4th	fjórði	23rd	tuttugasti og þriðji
5th	fimmti	30th	þrítugasti
6th	sjötti	40th	fertugasti
7th	sjöundi	50th	fimmtugasti
8th	áttundi	60th	sextugasti
9th	níundi	70th	sjötugasti
10th	tíundi	80th	áttugasti
11th	ellefti	90th	nítugasti
12th	tólfti	100th	hundraðasti
13th	þrettándi	101st	hundraðasti og fyrsti
14th	fjórtándi	200th	tvö hundraðasti
15th	fimmtándi	300th	þrjú hundraðasti
16th	sextándi	1000th	þúsundasti
17th	sautjándi	2000th	tvö þúsandasti
18th	átjándi	1,000,000th	milljónasti
19th	nítjándi		

All ordinal numbers, with the exception of *annar*, are de-clined as weak adjectives (*fyrsti* may also be declined as *fyrstur* in the strong declension).

Declension of *annar*

Singular

	masculine	feminine	neuter
nom.	annar	önnur	annað
acc.	annan	aðra	annað
dat.	öðrum	annarri	öðru
gen.	annars	annarrar	annars

Plural

nom.	aðrir	aðrar	önnur
acc.	aðra	aðrar	önnur
dat.	öðrum	öðrum	öðrum
gen.	annarra	annarra	annarra

Group Numerals

These refer to things associated in twos, threes, and so on. Such words are: *einir* (pair); *tvennir* (2 pairs); *þrennir* (3 pairs); *fernir* (4 pairs).

These are declined like adjectives.

Examples: *einir sokkar* (a pair of stockings);
tvennir skór (2 pairs of shoes);
skipta í fernt, í tvennu lagi (divided into four sides, into two teams).

Numeral Nouns

In English we have *dozen* corresponding to *twelve* and *score* corresponding to *twenty*. In Icelandic there exist a large number of such nouns:

eining	corresponding to		einn
eind	,,	,,	einn
tvenning	,,	,,	tveir
tvend	,,	,,	tveir
þrenning	,,	,,	þrír
fimt	,,	,,	fimm

sjöund corresponding to sjö
áttund   ,,   ,,   átta
níund   ,,   ,,   níu
tíund   ,,   ,,   tíu
tugur   ,,   ,,   tíu
tylft   ,,   ,,   tólf

Nouns Denoting Fractions

helmingur (-s, -ar) *m.*	half	fjórðungur	fourth
þriðjungur	third	fimtungur	fifth

and so on.

Adjectives may be formed from cardinal numbers by adding
-*faldur* (fold), in the following manner: *einfaldur* (single);
tvöfaldur (double), and so on.

> Examples of fractions: half, *hálfur*; one-third, *einn þriðji*;
> one-tenth, *einn tíundi*; two and a half, *hálfur þriðji* or
> *tveir og hálfur*; two-sevenths, *tveir sjöundu*; three
> quarters, *þrír fjórðu*; seven and a quarter, *sjö heilir og
> einn fjórði*.

Adjectives Relating to Age, Depth, Length and Height

Numbers from 20 to 70 add -*tugur* to the stem, and numbers
from 80 to 120 add -*ræður*: e.g., *tvítugur*, twenty years old,
twenty standards of length, etc. *þrítugur*, *fertugur*, and so on.

> Examples: *tvítugur maður*, a twenty-year old man (20 *ára
> gamall maður*);
> *þrítugur hamar*, a thirty-fathom high precipice
> (30 *faðma hár hamar*);
> *sextugt dýpi*, a depth of sixty fathoms (60 *faðma
> dýpi*);
> *tvítugur hvalur*, a twenty-aln long whale (20
> *álna langur hvalur*).

To multiply, the word *sinn* is used. (Also there are the words
tvisvar, twice, and *þrisvar*, thrice.) *Eitt sinn, tveim sinnum*, and
so on.

Vocabulary

algengast, adj. most common,
most usual
dýpka (a), v.i. become deeper,
deepen
flest, most
hæð, f. height

um hríð, adv. for a while
undarlegur, adj. strange
vakna (a). v.i. wake up
þumlungur, m. inch
þyngd, f. weight
ör, n. scar

Exercise 11a

Translate into English:

Hann er fimm fet og ellefu þumlungar á hæð, fjörutíu og fimm ára gamall, hundrað og áttatíu pund á þyngd, með ljósan hatt, í bláum fötum, og ·með undarlegt ör á andlitinu. Hann ók grænum Austin.

Exercise 11b

Translate into English:

Flest sofum við fast fyrstu tvo klukkutímana, svo verður svefninn ekki eins djúpur um hríð, uns hann dýpkar aftur í svo sem tvo tíma, áður en við byrjum að búa okkur undir að vakna. Þetta er algengast.

Exercise 11c

Translate into Icelandic:

One day in November, 1905, a little Danish boy was carried off (*var borinn úr*) the ship *"Heimdal"*, on to the quay (*hafnargarður*) in Oslo. His father held him (*hélt á honum*) in his arms (*á handleggnum*). On the quay, the then (*þáverandi*) Prime Minister (*forsætisráðherra*) of Norway, Chr. Michelsen, bade father and son (*þá feðga*) welcome. This was the first journey of the little prince to Norway, his new fatherland (*föðurland*). A short time ago King Olaf V came to Copenhagen, and that was the first time that he had come to Denmark as the King of Norway.

LESSON 12

Adverbs

In the first place, many adverbs are formed by adding *-a* to the stem of adjectives: e.g.,

prýðileg/ur—prýðilega, beautiful/ly
falleg/ur—fallega, pretty—prettily

Adverbs derived from adjectives have degrees of comparison, e.g.,

prýðilega—prýðilegar—prýðilegast.

Some have somewhat different endings, e.g.,

lengi—lengur—lengst
fram—fremur—fremst (*fremur* means preferably, and *fremst* means most of all).
nærri—nær—næst, near, nearly, almost, next.

Irregular Comparison of Adverbs

gjarna/n, willingly	*heldur*, rather	*helzt*, most of all
illa, badly	*verr*, worse	*verst*, worst
lítt, little	*midur*, less	*minnst*, least
litið, little	*minna*, less	*minst*, least
mjög, very	*meir*, more	*mest*, most
snemma, early	*fyrr*, before, sooner	*fyrst*, first
vel, well	*betur*, better	*bezt*, best

Some neuter adjectives are used as adverbs, and are compared as follows:

bágt, difficult	*bágar/a*	*bágast*
hart, hard	*harðar/a*	*harðast*
seint, late	*seinna*	*seinast*
hátt, high, highly	*hærra*	*hæst*
langt, long, far	*lengra*	*lengst*

Adverbs of Time

nú, now	*stundum*, sometimes
þá, then	*ávalt*, always
lengi, for a long time	*alltaf*, always
aldrei, never	*sjaldan*, seldom
oft, often	

Adverbs of Place

heima, at home	*héðan*, from here
hér, *hérna*, here	*hingað*, here, hither
þar, *þarna*, there	*þangað*, there, thither
úti, out/side	*hvaðan*, where from
inni, in	*hvert*, whither
ofan, down	*fyrir*, in front of
hvar, where	*undan*, before

Adverbs of Manner and Degree

vel, well	*svona*, thus
illa, badly	*svo*, so
þannig, thus, in this way	*mjög*, very
hvernig, how	*alveg*, quite

Adverbs of Cause

þessvegna, therefore	*hversvegna*, why

Adverbs of Adversity

þó, however	*þar á móti*, on the other hand
samt, yet	*annars*, or else, otherwise

Affirmative Adverbs

já, *jú*, yes (*jú* is used to deny a negative statement or question)

sannlega, *sannarlega*, indeed, really

vissulega, *vist*, certainly

reyndar, *raunar*, really

Negative Adverbs

nei, no	*eigi*, *ekki*, not

Examples of Usage

Maðurinn hérna er bróðir minn.   The man here is my brother.
Hún er stundum úti allan daginn.   She is sometimes out all day.
Er ekki báturinn farinn? Jú, fyrir löngu.   Hasn't the boat left? Yes, long ago.
Hann gerði svo.   He did so (thus).
Ég fer oft í leikhús.   I often go to the theatre.
Hann er alltaf að lesa.   He is always reading.

Prepositions

eftir, after, behind, by, along, according to, for.
This preposition governs the dative in expressions denoting space.

> *eftir hundunum*, after the dogs
> *senda eftir*, to send for
> *spyrja eftir*, to ask for, inquire for
> *taka eftir*, to notice, take notice of
> *telja eftir*, to grudge someone something
> *niður eftir hæðinni*, down the hill
> *eftir endilöngu*, from end to end
> *eftir málavöxtum*, as the case may be
> *eftir því sem*, according as

eftir governs the accusative when it refers to time and also when it denotes something done or left by someone.

vor kemur eftir vetur, spring comes after winter
eftir jól, after Christmas
árið 1959 *eftir Krists burð*, the year 1959 A.D.
dag eftir dag, day after day
taka arf eftir . . ., to inherit from someone
koma til ríkis eftir . . ., to succeed . . . to the throne
vera eftir sig, to be exhausted, fagged out
þessi bók er eftir . . ., this book is by . . .

Note the following adverbial expressions using *eftir*:

daginn eftir, the following day
árið eftir, the following year
tveim dögum eftir, two days later

é hefi skilið peninga mína eftir, I have left my money behind
eftir á, later on
eftir á að hyggja, on second thoughts, after thinking about it

frá

This means *from*, and takes the dative case.

> *segja frá . . .*, to speak about . . .
> *dag frá degi*, day after day
> *heyra frá . . .*, to hear from . .
> *hindra mann frá að koma*, to hinder someone from coming

Note the adverbial expressions:

> *til og frá*, to and fro
> *þaðan í frá*, from then on, thenceforwards
> *héðan í frá*, from now on, henceforth

fyrir

This means: before, in front of; for, because of.
Governing the dative case we have:

flýja fyrir, to flee from
vera fyrir (fremri) . . ., to be before (superior to) . .
biðja fyrir, to pray for; ask (someone) to look after
gera fyrir . . ., to make allowances for
vægja fyrir . . ., to yield to . . .
hún þoldi ekki við fyrir verkjum, she could not rest for the pain
frammi fyrir . . ., before, in the presence of . . .
verkur fyrir brjóstinu, pains in the chest
fyrir skömmu, a short time ago, recently
fyrir löngu, a long time ago
fyrir fimm dögum, five days ago
fyrir því, therefore

Fyrir with the accusative means: for, on behalf of; (*sökum*) for, on account of (*í staðinn fyrir*) instead of.

> *stefna . . . fyrir dómstól*, to summon . . . to court
> *hlaupa fyrir borð*, to jump overboard
> *taka fyrir kverkar . . .*, to take . . . by the throat

koma fyrir ekki, to come to nought
fyrir sólarlag, before sunset
fyrir Krists burð, B.C.
fyrir mitt minni, before I can remember
fyrir hvern mun, by all means
fyrir engan mun, by no means
fyrir framan dyrnar, in front of the door
fyrir austan ána, east of the river
fyrir neðan brúna, below the bridge

Vocabulary

afgreiðslumaður, m. shop-assistant
bréfpoki, m. paper-bag
deig, n. dough
ennþá, adv. still
flýta sér, v. reflex. hurry (up)
gjósa (past—*gaus*), v.i. gush up
grunlaus, adj. unsuspecting
hengibrú, f. suspension bridge
húsfreyja, f. lady of the house
leyndardómsfullur, adj. mysterious
málverk, n. portrait, picture
ópefur, m. bad smell
sement, n. cement
skammur, adj. short
skápur (-s, -ar), m. cupboard
stál, n. steel
stöpull (-s, *stöplar*) m. upright, pillar
slá í tvennt, divide, break in two
viðburðaríkur, adj. eventful, exciting
þreytulegur, adj. tired-looking
æfi, f. life-time; *æfisaga*, f. life-story, biography

Exercise 12a

Translate into English:

"Eitt síðasta málverk sem málað var af Lill málaði Haukur Berg fyrir tveim árum." Hið þreytulega andlit hennar var ennþá frítt og leyndardómsfullt. Málverk þetta er meistarverk, og segir æfisögu Lill. Æfi hennar var skömm, en viðburðarík.

Exercise 12b

Translate into English:

Húsfreyja var að búa til kökudeig og tók út úr skápnum bréfpoka með eggjum, sem fimm ára sonur hennar hafði keypt fyrir hana um morguninn. Grunlaus sló hún eggið í tvennt, en þá gaus upp míkill ópefur.

—"Heyrðu, Óli minn," sagði hún við son sínn. "Sagði afgreiðslumaðurinn að þessi egg væru ný?"

—"Nei, hann sagði bara að ég skyldi flýta mér heim með þau."

Exercise 12c

Translate into Icelandic:

The Golden Gate Bridge is the longest suspension bridge in the world. It is over the harbour in San Francisco, in California. The floor of the bridge is of (*úr*) cement and steel. The length of the road between the uprights is 1250 metres, and the largest ocean liners are able to sail under the bridge.

LESSON 13

Conjunctions
Co-ordinating Conjunctions

og, and

en, but

eða, or

bæði . . . og, both . . . and

hvorki . . . né, neither . . . nor

hvort . . . eða, whether . . . or

annaðhvort . . . eða, either . . . or

Subordinating Conjunctions
Cause

af því að, because

því að, for, because

fyrir því að, as, because

sökum þess að, since

úr því að, seeing that, since

vegna þess að, as, owing to the fact that

þar sem, since, as

fyrst, as, since

Condition

> *ef*, if
> *svo framarlega sem*, provided that, so long as
> *nema*, unless

Result

> *svo að*, so that　　　　*að*, that

Concession

> *þó að*, though, although
> *þótt*, although; notwithstanding
> *enda þótt*, although, even if
> *þrátt fyrir það að*, in spite of the fact that

Purpose

> *til þess að*, in order that
> *til að*, (so) that
> *svo að*, (so) that
> *til þess að ekki*, lest, for fear that

Comparison

> *eins og*, as
> *og*, as
> *heldur en*, than
> *sem, svo sem*, as
> *því . . . því*, the . . . the . . .

(e.g., *því fyrr, því betra*, the sooner the better).

Time

> *þegar*, when
> *áður en*, before
> (*á*) *meðan*, while
> *eftir að*, after
> *er*, when
> *þegar er*, as soon as
> *fyrr en*, before
> *jafnskjótt sem*, as soon as, the moment
> *óðar en*, so sooner . . . than
> *síðan*, since
> *undireins og*, as soon as
> *strax og*, as soon as
> *um leið og*, as, at the same time as
> *þangað til að*, till, until
> *þar til er*, till, until
> *þá er*, when
> *unz*, till, until

Place

> *þar sem*, where
> *hvert sem*, wherever
> *hvert er*, wherever
> *þangað sem*, where, whither
> *hvar sem*, wherever

Prepositions

í

This preposition generally means *in*.

As stated previously, this is one of the words that can take both the accusative and dative cases. Remember that generally the accusative is used when there is an idea of motion or change, and the dative when there is an idea of rest: look at these two expressions:

> *vera í fötum*, to have one's clothes on
> *fara í föt*, to put one's clothes on

In these examples the first case used is the dative, as there is the indication of rest, of being, while the second one is the accusative, as here there is definitely a question of change.

Here are some examples of the dative case:

í fyrstu, at first
í kafi, under water
í vikunni, sem kemur, next week
í sumum greinum, in some ways
í öllum greinum, in every respect, in every way
vera í kröggum, to be hard up
vera í góðu skapi, to be in high spirits
að hitna í hamsi, to become excited
í þessu efni, in this respect
allt í einu, suddenly
rjóður í andliti, red in the face
veri í góðum holdum, to be fat, in good condition, be fit
hóf er bezt í hverjum hlut, moderation is best in everything
það rofar til í lofti, it is clearing up
tala í óráði, to rave
róa í spiki, to be very fat
innst í hjarta sínu, in his innermost heart

Here are examples of the accusative case:

í bráð/ina, at present
í bráð og lengd, for ever
ganga í garð, to enter, set in
sofa í ró, to sleep in peace

lenda í ónáð hjá . . ., fall into disgrace with . . .
taka í höndina á . . ., to shake someone by the hand
taka í hönd . . ., to shake someone's hand
í nokkra daga, for some days
í margar vikur, for many weeks
gefa . . . í afmælisgjöf, to give something as a birthday present

Notice the following expressions:

í dag, today
í gær, yesterday
í nótt (sem var), last night
í nótt (sem fer í hönd), tonight
í kvöld, this evening
í fyrramálið, tomorrow morning
í myrkri, in the dark

með

This preposition means *with*, normally. When the meaning is to bring or to keep someone or something, *með* governs the accusative case. For example: *að koma með bókina* (to bring the book); *að vera með bókina* (to have the book). In other cases, *með* governs the dative case, as in the following:

margfalda með þremur, multiply by three
deila með þremur, divide by three
það var siður með sjómönnum, it was the custom among sailors
vera með hinnum fyrstu, to be among the first
með öllu, quite, altogether
með réttu, rightly
með röngu, wrongly
vakna með sólu, to get up with the sun

Examples with the accusative case:

hann kom með hesta, he came with (some) horses
hann kom með hestinn, he came with the horse
hann kom með hestana, he came with the horses
vera ánægður með . . ., to be satisfied with
verzla með . . ., to deal in . . .

Vocabulary

að meðaltali, on an average
ferðast (a), v. reflex. travel, go
   along
flytja, v.t. carry
færa (i), v.t. bring, shift, transport
grunnflötur, m. base
hábúar, colloq. "air-dwellings"
hádegi, n. midday
hella (i), v.t. with dat. pour
   (out)

hraðlyfta, f. express-lift
hylja, v.t. hide, cover
ský, n. cloud
sólarsýn, f. sight of the sun
stórfenglegur, adj. magnificent
útsýnispallur (-s, -ar), m. view-
   platform
vera til, v.i. exist, be
yfirsýn, f. view
þaðan sem, from which
þoka, f. fog, mist

Exercise 13a

Translate into English:

Á hverju ári flytur hraðlyftan í Empire State Building,
hæstu byggingu heimsins, að meðaltali 500.000 ferðamenn frá
öllum löndum heims upp á útsýnispallinn, en þaðan má fá
stórfenglega yfirsýn yfir heimsborgina. Það eru til aðrar
byggingar, sem hafa stærri grunnflöt, en í engri annarri eru svo
margar skrifstofur svo hátt yfir jörðu. Stundum, þegar lág ský
eða þoka hylja sólarsýn neðan af götunni, er glaðasólskin í
skrifstofunum á efstu hæðunum, og stundum horfa þessir
"hábúar" niður á sólböðuð ský, sem hella úr regnskálum sínum
yfir þá, sem ferðast um göturnar.

Exercise 13b

Translate into Icelandic:

Grandfather sat by the window and looked down at the
street. The nurse, Vera, had moved his chair there. Usually it
stood over by the door, but today grandfather wanted to sit
by the window. He had his 79th birthday today. He looked at
his watch. Half an hour to midday. Then the nurse would
bring him his food. And half an hour later he could expect the
post. Today he ought to get a lot (*heilmörg*) of letters.

Notes: hjúkrunarkona, nurse; *eiga 79 ára afmæli,* celebrate one's
seventy-ninth birthday; *eiga von á e-u,* expect.

LESSON 14

Pronouns

PERSONAL pronouns, relatives, reflexives and possessives, were dealt with in Lesson 4. Here we must look at demonstrative pronouns, interrogative pronouns and indefinite pronouns.

Demonstrative Pronouns

There are three of these in Icelandic: *sá* (that), *þessi* (this) and *hinn* (the other). *Hinn* is declined in the same way as the article, except that the nominative singular neuter is *hitt* (instead of *hið*). *Sá* and *þessi* are declined thus:

	Singular		
	masculine	*feminine*	*neuter*
nom.	sá	sú	það
acc.	þann	þá	það
dat.	þeim	þeirri	því
gen.	þess	þeirrar	þess

	Plural		
nom.	þeir	þær	þau
acc.	þá	þær	þau
dat.	þeim	þeim	þeim
gen.	þeirra	þeirra	þeirra

	Singular		
nom.	þessi	þessi	þetta
acc.	þenna/n	þessa	þetta
dat.	þessum	þessari	þessu
gen.	þessa	þessarar	þessa

	Plural		
nom.	þessir	þessar	þessi
acc.	þessa	þessar	þessi
dat.	þessum	þessum	þessum
gen.	þessara	þessara	þessara

It is as well to note the use, in familiar style as in conversation, of the pronouns *hann* and *hún*. These are used to anticipate a following noun, especially a personal name. *Það er hún Imba gamla*, it is Old Imba (literally: it is she Imba old). This is of very frequent occurrence in speaking and in everyday writing.

Interrogative Pronouns

There are four interrogative pronouns: *hver* (who, which (of many)); *hvor* (who, which (of two)); *hvaða* (what); and *hvílíkur* (what, what sort).

Declension of *Hver*.

Singular

	masculine	feminine	neuter
nom.	hver	hver	hvert (hvað)
acc.	hvern	hverja	hvert (hvað)
dat.	hverjum	hverri	hverju
gen.	hvers	hverrar	hvers

Plural

	masculine	feminine	neuter
nom.	hverjir	hverjar	hver
acc.	hverja	hverjar	hver
dat.	hverjum	hverjum	hverjum
gen.	hverra	hverra	hverra

Hvað was originally an independent pronoun, but it has now run together with *hver*. *Hvað* is now used only as a noun.

The word *Hvaða* cannot be declined.

Hvor is declined like the possessive *Vor* (see Lesson 4).

Hvílíkur is declined like *Ríkur* in the strong form. It is seldom used nowadays except in exclamations such as, for instance, *Hvílík heimska!* (What nonsense!), or in poetry

Remember the difference between *Hver* and *Hvor*. *Hver* is used when there are more than two to choose from; for example: *hver drengjanna braut það?* (which of the boys—which boy—broke that?). *Hvor* is used to choose between two, as in this sentence: *hvor drengjanna braut það?* (which of the two boys broke that?).

Indefinite Pronouns

The main indefinite pronouns are the following: *einn* (one); *neinn* (some, any); *annar* (another); *nokkur* (any, one); *enginn* (no, none); *hver* (each, every); *einhver* (someone, somebody); *sérhver* (everyone, everybody); *hvor* (each); *annarhvor* (one of the two, either); *hvortveggja* (both); *ýmis* (various); *allur* (all); *hvorugur* (neither); *sumur* (some, some part of); *sumir* (some); *báðir* (both); *fáeinir* (few).

These words are declined as follows:

(1) *Einn and Neinn* like the numeral *Einn* (see Lesson 11).

(2) *Annar* like the numeral *Annar* (see Lesson 11).

(3) *Nokkur* thus:

| | *Singular* | | |
	masculine	*feminine*	*neuter*
nom.	nokkur	nokkur	nokkurt (nokkuð)
acc.	nokkurn	nokkra	nokkurt (nokkuð)
dat.	nokkrum	nokkurri	nokkru
gen.	nokkurs	nokkurrar	nokkurs

	Plural		
nom.	nokkrir	nokkrar	nokkur
acc.	nokkra	nokkrar	nokkur
dat.	nokkrum	nokkrum	nokkrum
gen.	nokkurra	nokkurra	nokkurra

The form *nokkuð* is used only as a noun.

(4) *Enginn* thus:

	Singular		
nom.	enginn (engi)	engin (engi)	ekkert (ekki)
acc.	engan (öngvan)	enga (öngva)	ekkert (ekki)
dat.	engum (öngvum)	engri (öngri)	engu (einigu)
gen.	einskis (einkis)	engrar (öngrar)	einskis (einkis)

Plural

	masculine	feminine	neuter
nom.	engir (öngvir)	engar (öngvar)	engin (engi)
acc.	enga (öngva)	engar (öngvar)	engin (engi)
dat.	engum (öngvum)	engum (öngvum)	engum (öngvum)
gen.	engra (öngra)	engra (öngra)	engra (öngra)

The forms using *ö* are found only in colloquial language and familiar style.

(5) *Hver* like the interrogative pronoun. This also applies to *einhver* and to *sérhver*. The neuter nominative and accusative of *einhver* and *sérhver* are *eitthvert, eitthvað* (corresponding to *Hvað*), and *sérhvert, sérhvað*.

(6) *Hvor* like the interrogative pronoun *Hvor*.

(7) *Annarhvor* has a double declension, *annar* and *hvor* being declined separately.

(8) *Hvortveggja* is declined in the first part like *Hvor*, while the ending, *tveggja*, is unchanged.

(9) *Ýmis* thus:

Singular

	masculine	feminine	neuter
nom.	ýmis	ýmis	ýmist
acc.	ýmsan	ýmsa	ýmist
dat.	ýmsum	ýmissi	ýmsu
gen.	ýmiss	ýmissar	ýmiss

Plural

nom.	ýmsir	ýmsar	ýmis
acc.	ýmsa	ýmsar	ýmis
dat.	ýmsum	ýmsum	ýmsum
gen.	ýmissa	ýmissa	ýmissa

(10) *Allur, hvorugur* and *sumur* (plural *sumir*) are declined like strong adjectives (see Lesson 10).

(11) *Báðir* thus:

	masculine	feminine	neuter
nom.	báðir	báðar	bæði
acc.	báða	báðar	bæði
dat.	báðum	báðum	báðum
gen.	beggja	beggja	beggja

(12) *Fáeinir* is declined like a strong adjective in the plural (Lesson 10).

Vocabulary

ás (-s, -ar), m. ace
eiga, ekki, not
fátækt, f. poverty
forstjóri, m. manager
gjörla, adv. quite, fully, clearly
hann þótti, he was regarded as, looked upon as
mikill á lofti, adj. "stuck-up"
reistur, adj. straight, erect; aloof, superior
sagt er, it is said
samtíðarmaður, m. contemporary (same-time man)
starfsmaður, m. employee, clerk
uppnefna (i), v.t. dub, give a nickname
vinna, f. work
ýkja (i), v.t. exaggerate
því, conj. as, for

Exercise 14a

Translate into English:

Guðmundur hét maður nokkur, sem samtíðarmenn hans uppnefndu og kölluðu "Spaða". Eigi vita menn gjörla hvernig spaða-nafnið var í fyrstunni tilkomið. Sumir halda að hann hafi verið svartur sem spaðaás, en aðrir hyggja, að það sé til orðið vegna þess, að hann þótti nokkuð "reistur" og mikill á lofti, því sagt er að sjálfsálit (self-esteem) hans hafi verið ýkjið. Guðmundur var fæddur að Bakkaseli í Fnjóskadal 21. janúar árið 1815, og þar ólst hann upp hjá foreldrum sínum við mikla fátækt.

Exercise 14b

Translate into Icelandic:

"How is (*líða*) your wife, Palli?"

"Oh, sometimes she is better and sometimes she is worse. But when she is better, it sometimes seems to me that she is better when she is worse."

Exercise 14c

Translate into Icelandic:

Manager (to employee who comes to work too late): "You always come too late. Don't you know when we begin to work here?" Employee: "No, everybody has always started (they are always all begun to work) when I arrive."

LESSON 15

Cases

WE have seen that there are four cases in Icelandic: the nominative, the accusative, the dative and the genitive. Further, we have seen that Icelandic prepositions govern cases, some always the same case, others one or another of two cases, according to circumstances. For this, see the notes on the various prepositic. s. Note also that the case is necessary only when the preposition comes before the noun. E.g.,

Þarna er stóllinn, sem ég sat í.
Ég sat í stólnum. (Dative case, rest or position after *í*).

This last point is also valid in the question of verbs that require different cases. This is quite a complicated matter in Icelandic. Perhaps we might compare it with the difficulty that learners of English have with the gerund and the infinitive, with or without "to". It is a question of learning just what type of verb it is as you come across a new one. Some Icelandic verbs govern the accusative (the majority), some govern the dative, while others govern the genitive.

Ég sá manninn í gær. (Accusative case.)
Ég mætti manninum í gær. (Dative case.)
Ég vitjaði sjúklingsins í gær. (Genitive case.)

In these examples we note the following:

sjá (to see) takes the accusative case.
mæta (to meet) takes the dative case.
vitja (to visit) takes the genitive case.

Further examples:

Hann tók bókina (*taka* (to take) plus accusative).
Hann stal hestinum (*stela* (to steal) plus dative).
Hann neytti matar { (*neyta* (to use) plus genitive).
{ (*neyta matar* means to eat).

Naturally, some verbs govern two cases: when, for instance, there are direct and indirect objects.

There are various combinations of cases that single verbs may govern. For example:

Hann spurði mig frétta. (He asked me (about) the news.)
Hann gaf mér bókina. (He gave (to) me the book.)
Han hét honum liðveizlu. (He promised him support.)
Hann synjaði honum peninganna. (He refused him the money.)

In these sentences we note the following patterns:

(1) *spyrja* (to ask) plus accusative plus genitive.
(2) *gefa* (to give) plus dative plus accusative (direct object).
(3) *heita* plus dative (to promise) plus dative.
(4) *synja* (to refuse) plus dative plus genitive.

The verb *heita* means to call, name; but in this case it is followed by the accusative. With the dative case, the meaning is to promise.

Nouns occasionally govern the genitive case, or even perhaps the dative.

Examples:

Hérna er hús sjómannsins. (This is the sailor's house.)
Bókin segir frá ferðalagi konungsins. (The book tells of the journey of the king.)
Hann steig á bak hestinum. (He mounted the horse.)

In the first and second examples there is the idea of "of": "the house of the sailor", "the journey of the king". In the third example the dative follows rather unnaturally where you would perhaps expect the genitive (the back of the horse).

Pronouns also occasionally govern the genitive case.

Nokkrir hestanna hafa týnzt. (Some of the horses have perished.)

Hvor bræðranna kom í dag? (Which brother came today?)

Here again there is a natural idea of genitive case (some *of* the horses, which *of* the brothers).

Adjectives may take the accusative case or the genitive case.

Hann er vinveittur mér. (He is friendly (towards) me.)

Nú er ég laus allra mála. (Now I am free of all ties.)

Numerals may govern the genitive case, as in this example:

Aðeins tveir þeirra komu aftur. (Only two of them came back.)

Adverbs may take the dative or the genitive.

Hann stendur nær mér en þú. (He is standing nearer (to) me than you.)

Hann skrifar bezt allra drengjanna. (He writes the best *of* all the boys.)

Notes on the Cases

Accusative

This is used with measure, time, place or direction, and with some impersonal verbs.

(a) *Hann stóð* **tvo faðma** *frá mér.* (He stood two fathoms from me.)

(b) **Næsta dag** *var veður gott.* (The next day the weather was good.)

(c) *Hann fór* **bæ** *frá bæ.* (He went from village to village.)

(d) **Mig** *þyrstir.* (I am thirsty).

On this point, here are the verbs of this category, which require the accusative form before them.

Impersonal Verbs Introduced by mig, *etc.*

mig dreymir, I dream	*órar (fyrir),* have a presentiment of
fýsir, desire	
grunar, suspect	*skortir,* lack
hryllir, shudder at	*svimar,* am dizzy
hungrar, am hungry	*syfjar,* get sleepy
kelur (keli), freeze	*uggir,* am afraid that . . .
langar, long	*undrar,* I am amazed at
daginn lengir, the day draws out	*vantar,* want, need, lack
	þrýtur, want, lack
lystir, desire	*þyrstir,* am thirsty
minnir, seems to me	
munar (i), makes a difference	

Dative Case

(*a*) This is sometimes used to give the idea of "with" when there is a deed or action performed or done.

Hann var gyrður sverði. (He was girded with a sword.)

(*b*) The dative is also used occasionally to indicate the manner in which an action is done.

Hann lét **illum látum.** (He behaved badly.)
Þeir gengu **þurrum fótum** *yfir hafið.* (They crossed the sea with dry feet.)

(*c*) The dative can be used with time expressions, sometimes together with the word *saman.*

Hann situr hér **öllum stundum.** (He sits here the whole time.)
Ég hefi unnið að þessu **árum saman.** (I have worked at this for years.)

(*d*) The dative is used with the words *fyrir, eftir, fyrir sunnan, fyrir neðan, of* and *til.*

Hann kom heim **mánuði** *fyrir jól.* (He came home a month, before Christmas.)

*Hann kom heim **viku** eftir jól.* (He came home a week after Christmas.)
*Þetta er **þrem metrum** of stutt.* (This is three metres too short.)

(e) Note the following:

*Hann er **mikill vexti**.* (He is tall (large in growth).)
*Hann er friður **sýnum**.* (He is good-looking (good of looks).)

(f) The dative is used together with many impersonal verbs:

***Mér** finnst leiðinlegt hér.* (I consider it boring here.)
***Honum** þykir sopinn góður.* (He is fond of drink.)

Genitive Case

The most typical use of this case is to denote "of the" (or the possessive construction with 's or s'). Example: **Allir gluggar húsanna voru opnir** (all the windows of the houses were open—genitive plural).

It must be emphasized that the main points to remember are that prepositions require case forms in the nouns they govern, and that different verbs take different cases. On this subject, note the various possibilities with such a verb as *hlaða*, to load. In the dictionary you will find:

Hlaða (hleð; hlóð; hlaðinn): transitive verb: to load, lade (*hlaða skip*); load, charge (*hlaða byssu*); pile up; build (*hleður vegg*); with the dative case, to fell, lay low, prostrate; *hlaða seglum*, furl or stow the sails; impersonal verb: *snjónum hleður niður*, there is a heavy fall of snow.

Therefore *hlaða* may take the accusative or the dative case, and it may also be used impersonally. Some verbs also may be used with a special meaning for the middle voice. Here is *Skifta*, for example:

Skifta (i): trans. verb with dative: to divide, distribute, exchange, change (*skifta litum*, change colour; *skifta bankaseðli*, change a banknote). Impersonal verb: *það skiftir engu*, it makes no odds; *mig skiftir engu*, it makes no difference to me. *Skifta um föt, hesta, nafn*; to change clothes, horses, name.

Reflexive verb, *skiftast*: change, branch. *Skiftast á að gera það*, to take turns at doing that.

In the following piece see how the case endings are very important with the prepositions.

Vestur *frá Vogsvogum*, en norður *frá bænum* Vogi *í Akranessókn*, er hátt klettabelti í sjó fram, sem kallað er Helgrindur. Það er *gamalla manna* sögn, að þar hafi rekið útlent skip *með dauðum mönnum*. Var fyrst tjaldað *yfir þeim með viðum og seglum*, en *að lokum* voru þeir dysjaðir *í gjá einni*.

West of Vogsvogur but north of the village of Voga in the parish of Akranes, there is a high chain of rocks along by the coast, called Helgrindur. The old story is that a foreign ship with dead men (on board) ran aground there. At first they erected a tent over them with wood and sails, but eventually they were buried in a rocky cleft. (Note the subjunctive (hafi) after the verb "say", and also note the genitive case endings of *"gamalla manna"*: of old men (*það er gamalla manna sögn* = it is a tale of old men = the old story is). *Það er sögn manna, að*: people say that . . . Another point to note is the somewhat emphatic word-order in this style of writing, smacking rather of Old Icelandic.)

Vocabulary

aflangur, adj. oblong
alls, adv. altogether
blátt áfram, adv. quite simply
eiga því láni að fagna, enjoy (have) the good fortune (luck)
erindi, m. verse
frétta (i), v.i. hear, learn, get news
(i) gipsi, (in) plaster
hávaði, m. din, noise
hugmynd, f. idea
iðandi, adj. busy
lestur, m. reading
lýsa, v.t. describe
meðan það stóð, while that lasted
ógurlegur, adj. awful, terrible
óþolandi, adj. unbearable

síður en svo, quite the contrary
truflaður, adj. disturbed
það er mikils vert, it is well worth
þó, adv. however
þrátt fyrir það, in spite of that

Exercise 15a

Translate into English:

Fyrir nokkru ætlaði ég að hlusta á kvæðalestur í útvarpinu mínu. Var það skáld frá Ísafirði er las ný kvæði. Er hann var nýbyrjaður að lesa, flaug flugvél með ógurlegum hávaða yfir húsið, og var ómögulegt að heyra neitt í útvarpinu meðan á því stóð. Alls var kvæðalestur þessi truflaður fimm sinnum af flugvélum. Til þess að njóta upplesturs eða erinda, þó einkum kvæða, má ekkert orð missast. Það er nú síður en svo, að við hlustendur hér í Reykjavík eigum slíku láni að fagna. Flugvöllur inni í miðri borg er blátt áfram óþolandi.

Exercise 15b

Translate into Icelandic:

Now I will describe this room for you, as it is well worth your getting (that you get) a clear picture of it. This is an oblong room with pale yellow panelling (*með ljósbleikum þiljum*). On the inner side of the room there is a window, which it is easy to open. At first I thought only the wall of the next house could be seen out of it, but I quickly heard otherwise, however. The man in the inside bed could only look straight ahead, like us (others), as he was also in plaster from head to foot (*frá hvirfli til ilja*). In spite of that he was able to see between two houses. This space (*millibil*) gave him a view of a limited part (*sýn á takmarkað svæði*) of the busy street-life (*lífi götunnar*).

LESSON 16

Further Prepositions

Til

The basic meaning of this word is *to, towards,* but, as with other prepositions, there are a variety of possibilities. *Til* takes the genitive case.

að fara til Reykjavíkur, to go to Reykjavík
til dæmis, for example
til gamans, for amusement, for pleasure
til hægri handar, on the right hand
til lítils gagns, of little use
til merkis um, as a token of
til minningar um, in memory of
til reynslu, by way of experiment
til skiftis, in turns, alternately
til sölu, for sale
frá morgni til kvölds, from morning to night
til skamms tíma, until a short time ago
hestur til reiðar, horse for riding
búast til ófriðar, prepare for war
ljúga til e-s, tell a lie in order to
muna til e-s, remember something
vita til e-s, know of or about something
koma til vits og ára, reach the age of discretion
koma til ríkis, come to the throne

um

This takes the accusative case, and has a great variety of meanings, including the following: of, about, around, across, over, approximately, during, by, for, at (time).

hugsa, tala, vita um, think, speak, know of or about
um nóttina, in the night
um mitt sumar, by midsummer
um sumarið, during the summer
um daga, nætur, kvöld, in the daytime, at night, in the evening
um allan aldur, forever
um alla hluti fram, above all
um leið, at the same time
um morguninn, kvöldið, in the morning, evening
að ganga um staðinn, to walk about the place
um háls sér, about one's neck
detta um stein, fall over a stone
um allt landið, throughout the country
spila um peninga, gamble

£50 *um mánuðinn,* £50 a month
mér er um og ó, I'm between two minds
mér er ekki mikið um hann. I'm not very taken by him.

við

This preposition takes the accusative case, and its meanings include: against, at, near, by, from, to, with. With the dative case, see below.

> *við dyrnar, gluggann,* at the door, window
> *við hvert orð,* at every word
> *við morgunverð,* at breakfast
> *við sólaruppkomu,* at sunrise
> *við veginn,* by the roadside
> *við þetta tækifæri,* on this occasion
> *sitja við stýri,* sit at the rudder
> *vera við e-ð,* be present at
> *sverja við e-ð,* swear by
> *hræddur við,* afraid of
> *bærinn liggur við ána,* the town is on the river
> *orustan við Hastings,* the Battle of Hastings
> *í sýn við húsið,* within sight of the house
> *í samanburði við,* in comparison with
> *góður við e-n,* be kind to
> *vanur við e-ð,* be used to [but also *vanur e-u*]
> *bæta við e-ð,* add to
> *fara í mál við e-n,* bring an action against someone

Use of *við* with the Dative Case

Here the meaning is against, from, or at. *Við lágu verði,* at a low price, of little worth. *Selja við litlu verði,* sell cheaply. *Snúa baki við e-m,* turn one's back on.

Við is also used as an adverb. *Komast við,* for instance, means to be touched. *Snúa sér við,* turn round. *Talast við,* speak together.

The Infinitive and the -ing Form

One of the complications of English is the treatment of verbs that follow other verbs. Some verbs, such as to enjoy, take the -ing form; others require the infinitive with "to" (e.g. to want);

some require prepositions, as, for instance, to be interested in, followed of course by the -ing form; others again take "to" together with the -ing form, as does the verb "to look forward to", for example. Now, in Icelandic the system is much more straightforward; verbs regularly take the infinitive introduced by "*að*", even if there is a preposition (or adverb) following the verb. For instance, look at the following sentences:

Ég hefi gaman af að lesa. (I am fond of reading.)
Það er þess vert að sjá það. (It is worth seeing that.)
Það kom honum til að hlæja. (That made him laugh.)
Maðurinn var fljótur til að hjálpa. (The man was quick in helping.)

The only modification of this is the use of the present participle with certain verbs to describe for example that someone *comes running*, or *looks laughingly*. The Icelandic here is:

Hann kom hlaupandi. (He came running up.)
Hún leit hlæjandi á hann. (She looked laughingly at him.)

When in English the -ing (gerund) is used as a noun, as in the expression "betting is forbidden", or in "seeing is believing", Icelandic cannot use this form. It is natural in Icelandic to re-phrase such expressions as "betting is forbidden": they prefer to say: It is forbidden to bet. Here the infinitive is used, which is the rule unless there is a completely different form of expression to give the same idea. "Seeing is believing", for example, is rendered as "*sjón er sögu ríkari*" or "sight is stronger than story".

Icelandic Names

In Iceland there is not the same method of using surnames as in most countries. Mr. Magnússon's son does not himself receive automatically the surname of his father. Instead, he will append -son to the father's Christian name. Thus, Björn Magnússon's son will be called, for instance, Valdimar Björnsson. His sister Þóra, on the other hand, would be called Þóra Björnsdóttir. Brother and sister thus have somewhat different surnames.

Days of the Week

Sunday, *sunnudagur.*	Thursday, *fimmtudagur.*
Monday, *mánudagur.*	Friday, *föstudagur;* Good Friday,
Tuesday, *þriðjudagur.*	*föstudagurinn langi.*
Wednesday, *miðvikudagur.*	Saturday, *laugardagur.*

Months of the Year (All masculine.)

January, *janúar* (*-rs*).	July, *júlí.*
February, *febrúar.*	August, *ágúst.*
March, *marz.*	September, *september* (*-rs*).
April, *apríl* (*-s*).	October, *október* (*-rs*).
May, *maí.*	November, *nóvember* (*-rs*).
June, *júní.*	December, *desember* (*-rs*).

Seasons of the Year. (*Árstíð, f.*)

Spring, n. *vor;* m. *vortími*	Autumn, n. *haust.*
Summer, n. *sumar.*	Winter, m. *vetur* (*-rar, vetur*).

Vocabulary

afgreiðslumaður, m. clerk	*líta út,* to look, seem
birtast, to appear	*ná í samband,* to get a con-
brýnt erindi, n. urgent mess-	nexion
age (matter)	*óttast* (*a*), to fear, be afraid
endurtaka, to repeat	*rétt strax,* straight away
gjarnan, adv. willingly (would	*skila* (*a*), *v.t.* with dat. bring
like to)	back; deliver a message
koma á fætur, to be up (and	*skrá* (*yfir*), *f.* catalogue, list
about)	(of)
hinum megin, on the other	*teygja* (*i*), to stretch
side	*veita viðtal,* to see (receive)
líða, v.i. to elapse	someone

Exercise 16a

Translate into English:

Í fyrstu leit út fyrir, að enginn í gistihúsinu væri kominn á fætur. Er hún hafði beðið nokkra stund, birtist afgreiðslumað-urinn hinum megin við afgreiðsluborðið.

"Býr hér ekki maður, Hansen að nafni?"

"Hansen?" Hann endurtók nafnið, tók síðan skrána yfir gesti hótelsins og leitaði í henni. Góð stund leið, án þess að hann fyndi nafnið, og Gerður var farinn að óttast, að hún hefði komið of seint—Siggi væri farinn. Loks leit maðurinn upp. "Hann býr hérna," sagði hann. "Herbergi nr. 47."

"Viljið þér gjöra svo vel að skila til hans, að hér sé stúlka, sem vilji tala við hann—hún eigi mjög brýnt erindi."

Translate into Icelandic (continuation of foregoing piece):

He stretched for (after) the telephone, got a connexion and spoke to Siggi. "Mr. Hansen would like to know (will willingly get to know) what your name is," (what you are called), he said. "He says also, that if it is someone from the papers (that be it someone from the papers), he does not want to see him."

"Tell him that my name is Andrésdóttir," said Gerd.

"Please wait (do so well to wait), he is coming straight away," said the man, when he had delivered the message to Siggi.

"You can wait in the small saloon (*salur*, m.) here—I'll go with you (*fylgja*) there." The man accompanied her up to the next floor and showed her into a small saloon. "Thank you very much," said Gerd.

LESSON 17

In this chapter it is intended to give some indication of the changes that have taken place to differentiate Modern Icelandic from Old Icelandic. It should be realized that the great wealth of literature in the Sagas and the Eddas lies within easy reach of all speakers of the modern language. It is owing to the fact that Icelanders are able easily to reach such ancient literary works written in the twelfth and thirteenth centuries, that these works continue to exert a preserving influence on the language. Therefore, the changes are worth studying, as they are not so extensive as to constitute a formidable barrier, either in the realm of grammatical endings or in that of word-order.

Nor has there been any great modification in vocabulary, with perhaps one important exception. In poetry, especially, and to some extent in the sagas, they made use of synonyms, *heiti* and *kennings*. *Heiti* are specific poetic words, that is, used only in poetry. *Kennings* (from the Icelandic noun *kenning*, plural *kenningar*) are rather complicated metaphors, in large part based on mythology; we may call them poetic circumlocutions or descriptive compounds. As mentioned, in poetry great use was made of these devices, since poets (skalds) went to considerable lengths to avoid conventional designations for things. Saga writers, on the other hand, more frequently restricted themselves to plain, unadorned words. They were objective and intent above all on portraying characters, and are outstanding for their lack of effusion and their use of understatement. But even saga writers had recourse to synonyms in order to counter any monotonous effect there might otherwise have been.

Since the sea enters so much into Icelandic writing, there are many different ways of referring to ships and the sea. Battles, men, women, the sky . . . these and other things have their fair share of synonyms and *kennings*. Here by way of example are the *kennings* used in a single work for men, battles and the sky.

Men	*Battles*		*The Sky*
brandareynir	eldþruma	orraveður	herjanssalur
darrabendir	darrafundur	skjómagnýr	herjasalur
fleinabrjótur	hildardanz	sverðakviða	himinsteigur
geirarunnur	hildarleikur	sverðaraun	ragnabraut
hjörvagrjer	hjörvaleikur	vigrafundur	ragnastóll
randaskelfir	hjörvasláttur	vigrasenna	ragnatjald
stálarunnur	hjörþryma		sjafnarsalir
vargfæðandi	hræeldahríð		sólarborð
	járnaþrá		sólarhvel
			stjörnusalur

To exemplify the construction of these *kennings*, we may take the compound word *vargfæðandi* in the list of metaphors for man above. *Vargr* means "wolf", and the accusative form is *varg*; *fæða* means "to feed", and *fæðandi* is the present participle.

Apart from these long-winded ways of avoiding the use of the object itself, there are, as mentioned, direct synonyms in this older literature. Taken from the same book, here are the manners in which the author refers to the sea and to men, for instance.

The Sea		Men	
alda	hrönn	bragnar	rekkur
bára	lá	drengur	sjöt
boði	löður	drótt	sjót
breki	lögur	firðar	skatnar
djúp	mar	garpur	sveinn
dröfn	rán	greppur	virðar
flóð	röst	gumi	ýtar
gráður	unnur	halur	þegn
græðir	ægir	höldur	þjóð
hlér		lýðir	öld
		mæringur	

It is really not a question of learning large numbers of special words, but rather of being on your guard and often expecting a word to refer to something rather different from what the dictionary will ordinarily tell you. Take the word "*djúp*", for example. The dictionary tells you that the word means deep, while you may see in the above list of synonyms for "sea" that "*djúp*" means "sea". This is, admittedly, a rather obvious example, and, what is more, an example that can be translated exactly into English, as the same treatment of this word, "deep", is used in English. Remember, however, that there are far more instances of this in Icelandic than in English or other languages.

Other Differences
Vowel Addition

Between a consonant and a final -*r* we now find a -*u*- added. For instance, *gestr* has become *gestur*, and *fagr* has become *fagur*. This is a quite extensive modification, although it is not found in every case. *Akr* became *akur*, but other cases of this word are: *akri*, *akra*, etc.

Vowel Loss

Unaccented vowels have often disappeared after stressed ones, e.g., *féit* has become *féð*, and *skóar* changed to *skór*.

Unstressed vowels have also often disappeared in endings: *sumari—sumri, gamalir—gamlir*, and so on.

Lengthening of Vowels

(*a*) When there was originally a following -*l* and another consonant: *halfr—hálfur, folk—fólk, holmr—hólmur, hjalpa—hjálpa*.

(*b*) When there was an original -*ht* following(this -*ht*- becoming -*tt*-): *ahta—átta, dohtir—dóttir*.

(*c*) At the end of certain words: *sa—sá, þu—þú*.

(*d*) Where a consonant has disappeared at the end of a word: *lag—lá, an—á, ansts—ást, fram—frá, in—í*.

Consonant Changes

The foremost consonant changes are in words where the initial letter has been dropped, as:

v before -*r* (*vreka—reka*).

g plus a (*galandi—landi*).

v before -*o*, -*ó* and -*u* in strong verbs . (*vorðinn—orðinn, vunnum—unnum*).

Consonants also often disappeared in word-endings. For example, *fuglr—fugl, annart—annat—annað*.

There are several instances of double consonants becoming single ones, but this change is so obvious that no examples are necessary.

In many cases the former of two consonants excludes the latter, itself being doubled in the process: *steinr—steinn, fanþ—fann, stólr—stóll* (thus, -*lr* became -*ll*, -*nr*— -*nn*, -*lþ*— -*ll* and -*nþ*— *nn*).

The reverse process is also extensively noted: *glaðt—glatt, kamp—kapp* (thus, -*dt* became -*tt*, -*ðl*— -*ll*, -*ðt*— -*tt*, -*ht*— -*tt*, -*mp*— -*pp*, -*nk*— -*kk*, -*nt*— -*tt*, -*rs*— -*ss*, -*tk*— -*kk*).

Most words formerly beginning with *kn*- changed to *hn*-, although a few of them retained the *kn*-form, sometimes as an alternative to the newer *hn*-form. So, *knífr* became *hnífur*, *knje* became *hné*, etc.

Unstressed -*k* has often changed into -*g*, and -*t* into -*ð*. For example, *ek*—*eg*, *mik*—*mig*, *sik*—*sig*, *mjök*—*mjög*, *at*—*að*, *þat* —*það*.

Old -*r* sometimes became -*ð*: *frerinn*—*freðinn*.

Before -*r*, -*nn* became -*ð*: *mannr*—*maðr*—*maður*, *minnr*— *miðr*—*miður*.

Lastly, notice the change in position of consonants in a number of words: *harðr* became *hraðr*, *argr* became *ragr*, and so on.

Another point to notice while on the subject of change is the modern writing of the combination *je* as accented *é*. Therefore you will find in modern books *tré* where formerly there was *trje*, and *ég* where the word formerly appeared as *jeg* (note also here that the form *eg* belongs to poetic writing).

Dual Form

Remember that what is today used as the ordinary plural form of verbs is in reality the old Dual Form (I and you). Therefore in Old Icelandic you find the three distinct forms, Singular, Dual and Plural, this last having no use in current Icelandic, being used solely in very solemn high style, or in polite addressing of strangers among older people.

Word Order

Ancient writers attached great importance to *stress*, and allowed themselves much more freedom in arranging their sentence patterns than is common today, in order to bring out this stress. The outstanding difference of this type is the custom of placing the verb, especially when in the past tense, *before* the noun or pronoun. Examples of this are:

Kallaði Njáll þetta lögvörn. (Called Njáll this lawful defence.)
Ríða þeir nú heim. (Ride they now home.)

Another point is that prepositions are frequently placed *behind* the verb in relative sentences, principally where the demonstrative pronoun is not declined. For example: *Sverrir konúngr hafði viðsét þessi snöru er þeir ætluðu hann í veiða.* King Sverrir had observed the trap which they intended to catch him in (literally, him in to catch).

In conclusion, here is a short extract from Egils Saga.

Upphaf ríkis Haralds hárfagra

Haraldr, son Hálfdánar svarta, hafði tekit arf eptir föður sinn; hann hafði þess heit streingt, at láta eigi skera hár sitt né kemba, fyrr en hann væri einvaldskonúngr yfir Noregi; hann var kallaðr Haraldr lúfa.

The Origin of the Kingdom of Harald the Finehair

Harald, son of Halfdan the Black, had succeeded his father; he had made a solemn vow (this solemn vow made) neither to cut nor to comb his hair (to have neither cut hair his nor comb) until he was king of all Norway; he was called Harald the Scruffy-Haired.

LESSON 18

Translation with Notes

THERE are, as we have seen, a number of characteristics in Icelandic which take some getting used to. Such things as the article suffixed to the noun, and the possessive placed after the noun, are points that tend to confuse at first, but once you are accustomed to them the confusion disappears. The extract given here for translation is chosen in large part because the simple ideas in it are an aid to understanding the language. It is taken from a detective story, in which a burglar is about to break into a private house.

Hljóðlaust opnaði hann gluggann utan frá, og vatt sér yfir karminn og inn í stofuna. Fætur hans sukku í mjúk teppin, sem gleyptu sérhvert hljóð og hjálpuðu honum næstum því líknsamlega til þess að komast fram á ganginn og upp á aðra hæð. "En hvað þetta er skrautlegt heimili," hugsaði hann með sér. "Dýrindis húsgögn, ekta málverk og indversk teppi á öllum gólfum—jæja, þegar maður var okrari og lánaði gegn meira en 100% vöxtum, þá gat maður vel leyft sér að kaupa það, sem mann langaði til."

Literally, this piece reads thus in translation:

Soundlessly opened he window/the outside from and jumped (himself) over window-sill/the and in-to room/the. Feet his sank into soft carpets/the, which swallowed every sound and helped him almost mercifully (in order) to reach corridor/the and up to second floor. "But what this is splendid house," thought he with himself. "Expensive furniture, genuine paintings and Indian carpets on all floors—yes, when one was money-lender and lent against more than 100 % interest, then could one certainly allow oneself to buy that which one longed for."

In reasonable English, and keeping to the ideas expressed in the piece, we have the following:

Soundlessly he opened the window from the outside and vaulted over the window-sill into the room. His feet sank into the soft carpets, which absorbed every sound and almost merci-fully helped him to reach the corridor and up to the second floor. "But what a splendid house this is," he thought to him-self. "Expensive furniture, genuine paintings and Indian carpets on every floor—well, if you were a money-lender and lent money for more than 100 % interest, then you could certainly permit yourself to buy whatever you desired."

Having given the literal and free translations of the piece, we shall now make a number of notes on certain things:

(1) Soundless: *hljóðlaus*. The adverb is formed by adding *-t* to this (that is, by using the neuter form of the adjective).

(2) Inverted word order, as the sentence is introduced by an adverb, and the verb must be the second idea.

(3) Window—*gluggi* (weak masc.). *Gluggann* is the accusa-tive case with the article affixed.

(4) *Vatt* is the past tense, third person singular, of the strong verb *vinda*, which means normally to wind, twist, wring. With the dative case the meaning is to wriggle or to jump. Here the dative is used in *sér*, which is the dative case of *sig*, the reflexive pronoun.

(5) The preposition *yfir* takes the accusative case when there is motion, as here. *Karminn* is the definite form of the accusa-tive case.

(6) *í* also takes the accusative case here, as there is motion. The noun *stofa* is weak feminine, and the accusative case with article is *stofu/na*.

(7) *Fætur hans:* here is an example of the use of the possessive placed after the noun.

(8) *Sukku* is the third person plural of the past tense of the strong verb *sökkva* (to sink): *sökkva; sekk; sökk, sukkum; sykk; sokkinn.*

(9) *Sérhvert* is the neuter form of the indefinite pronoun *sérhver* (every one, each). The case here is the accusative.

(10) The verb *hjálpa*, to help, takes the dative case (hence *honum*, dative case of the pronoun *hann*, he). It is a weak verb of the *elska* type, and *hjálpuðu* is the third person plural of the past tense, referring to the subject *teppin*, the carpets.

(11) *Næstum því* means next to or almost. *Næstum því ekkert*, next to nothing.

(12) *Líknsamur* means merciful. Here the adverbial form is used, the adverb being formed from the adjective by dropping *-ur* and adding *-lega.*

(13) *Til þess að*, means in order to.

(14) *Koma, kem, kom, kominn.* This verb means to come. The reflexive form of this verb is *komast*, which means to get, reach, come to the end. *Ég komst ekki* means I was not able to come, I could not reach. There are a variety of meanings using different prepositions.

(15) *Gangur (-s, -ar)* masculine: walk, gait; walking—(in house) corridor, passage. The preposition *á* here governs the accusative case, with the article affixed: *á ganginn.*

(16) The feminine noun *hæð* means height, hill, storey, floor. Note that there is no indefinite article. The preposition *á* here governs the accusative case, as there is motion, and therefore we have the form *aðra* of the numeral *annar* (second), this being the feminine singular accusative.

(17) *Hvað* (what) introduces an exclamation.

(18) *Heimili* is a neuter noun meaning home, house. As it is neuter, we have the neuter nominative of *þessi*—viz. *þetta.* Also we have the neuter form of the adjective *skrautlegur*, splendid, magnificent, viz. *skrautlegt.*

(19) *Með* here takes the dative case. *Sér* is the dative of *sig.*

(20) *Dýrindis*, precious, valuable, is one of the comparatively few adjectives that cannot be declined.

(21) *Húsgögn* is neuter plural, meaning furniture.

(22) The preposition *á* here governs the dative case, as there

is no motion. *Öllum* is the dative plural of the adjective *allur* (all), while *gólfum* is the dative plural of the neuter noun *gólf* (floor).

(23) *Maður*, man, is here used with the general meaning of one, you.

(24) Notice the construction: *meira en* . . ., more than . . .

(25) *Vöxtur* (*vaxtar, vextir*), m. means growth, increase. In the plural the meaning is, as here, interest on money.

(26) *Gat* is the past tense of the verb *geta*, to be able. Remember that this verb has the peculiarity of taking the supine instead of the infinitive, as if one should say in English, for instance, "I could not *bought* that". Therefore we have here the form *leyft*, this being the supine of the verb *leyfa* (i), to permit, allow. *Sér* is the dative of *sig*, himself.

(27) The construction *mig langar til* means I long to. Note the use of *mig* (Lesson 9, impersonal verbs). Hence *mann*, impersonal accusative.

Exercise 18a

Notes

smábarnagæzluleikvellir—divide this compound word up thus:

smá/barna/gæzlu/leik/vellir. *Smá* means small, referring to the following word, *barna* (gen. pl. of *barn*, child). *Gæzlu* means guarded, minded, controlled, watched, supervised, *leik* means play/ing, and the termination (which is the part of all compound words which determines the gender, here masculine) is the nom. plural of *völlur*, field, ground. Therefore the whole word gives the idea of: infants' supervised playgrounds, supervised playgrounds for infants.

Fræðslumálastjóri. *Stjóri* means head, chief, and so on. The whole word means Director of Educational Affairs.

Hverfum: neuter dative singular (after the preposition *í*): quarter, district.

Kvað: this is the past tense of the verb *kveða*, to say, recite, etc.

Skýra (i), *v.i.* and *v.t.*, to state, explain; *skýra frá e-u*, report, inform about.

Stefna að e-u, to aim at something.

Translate into English:

Í gær voru opnaðir tveir nýir smábarnagæzluleikvellir hér í Reykjavík. Vellir þessir eru fyrir börn á aldrinum tveggja til fimm ára og er annar þeirra við Faxaskjól og hinn við Stakkahlíð. Fréttamönnum var boðið að líta á gæzluvellina í gær. Jónas Jónsson fræðslumálastjóri skýrði svo frá, að í september hefðu verið opnaðir þrír gæzluvellir, við Dúnhaga, Rauðalæk og Hlíðargerði. Kvað hann hafa verið stefnt að því að koma upp smábarnagæzluleikvöllum í hinum ýmsu hverfum bæjarins.

Exercise 18b

Notes

aðstandendur, m. pl. relatives; friends
að tölu, in number
dveljast, to stay, wait. Supine of *dvelja* is *dvalið,* thus here we have *dvalizt*
fjölga (a), v.t. with dat. increase; *v.i.* increase
gjald, n. payment
hádegi, n. noon
í öruggri gaezlu, under careful supervision
skilja eftir, to hand over, leave
tilskilja, to stipulate

Translate into Icelandic:

The grounds are intended for children of two to five years, and mothers and other relatives of the children can leave them at these grounds; there they are under careful supervision, and are not let out (*komast út*) of the grounds (by) themselves. The children can stay there 2–3 hours a day before and after midday. It is stipulated that the children (shall) not be sent unless they are healthy, and they are collected if the weather is very bad.

These grounds are open from 9 a.m. to 12 and 2 to 5 p.m. On Saturdays they are open only to noon (say; is only open till noon). No payment is taken for the supervision (*gæzla,* f.). In the last (few) years the playgrounds have increased greatly in number. In the year 1952 the playgrounds were five in number, and now they are fifteen in number.

LESSON 19
Translation

ANNA Þórborg var fædd 28. maí 1895, að Vestdalseyri við Seyðisfjörð. Foreldrar hennar voru þau Gunnar Gunnarsson og seinni kona hans Guðrún Stefánsdóttir. Anna var yngst sex barna foreldra sinna. Þegar hún fæddist, var Gunnar faðir hennar orðinn blindur fyrir nokkru. Systkinahópurinn dreifðist og var komið fyrir í fóstur til vina og vandamanna. Anna fór þannig aðeins vikugömul í fóstur til sæmdarhjónanna Elísabetar Aradóttur og Jóns Wilhelmssonar, kennara á Seyðisfirði, og ólst hún þar upp við mikið ástríki. Minntist Anna ávallt fósturforeldra sinna sem eigin foreldra. Þar naut hún þess einnig að alast upp með tveimur öðrum stúlkum, Maríu dóttur þeirra hjóna, er dó ung, og bróðurdóttur Elísabetar Aradóttur, Ingibjörgu. Var hún Önnu alla tíð sem systir.

Here is a fairly literal translation of this piece.

Anna Thorborg was born on the 28th May 1895, on Vestdal Neck by Seydisfjörd. Her parents were Gunnar Gunnarsson and his second wife Gudrún Stefánsdóttir. Anna was the youngest of her parents' six children. When she was born, Gunnar her father had been blind for some little time. The brothers and sisters were scattered, and sent out as foster children to friends and relatives. Thus Anna was only a week old when she was adopted by the worthy couple Elizabeth Aradóttir and Jón Wilhelmsson, schoolmaster in Seydisfjörd, and there she was brought up with great love. Anna always remembered her foster-parents as her own parents. There she had the good fortune, moreover, to be brought up with two other girls: the couple's own daughter Mary, who died young, and Ingiborg, a niece of Elizabeth's. She was just like a sister to Anna.

Notes

(1) The past participle *fæddur* means born. Here the feminine form is used, without the ending -*ur*.

(2) *Foreldrar hennar*. The possessive pronoun follows the noun. *Hennar* is the genitive case of *hún*.

(3) *Þau.* This is the very common introductory pronoun (here neuter plural), preceeding the names of persons. This cannot, of course, be translated.

(4) *Seinni.* This word means second or later. Note the word order here—later wife his, i.e. second wife.

(5) *Yngst sex barna foreldra sinna.* There are three examples of the genitive plural case here: *barna, foreldra* and *sinna. Yngst* is the superlative of *ungur*, young. The youngest of six children of parents her.

(6) Word order. The verb takes the second position, after the time expression "when". When she was born, *was* Gunnar. . . . Note also the form *fæddist*, was born.

(7) Literally, *var orðinn blindur fyrir nokkru* means was become blind shortly before. *Orðinn* is the past participle of *verða. Nokkru* is in the dative case after *fyrir* (expression of time).

(8) *Systkin* means brother/s and sister/s, collectively. *Hópur* (-*s*, -*ar*) m., means a crowd, flock, and so on. The flock of brothers and sisters.

(9) *Dreifa* (i), is a transitive verb taking the dative case, and means to scatter, disperse. The form *dreifðist* is the past of the reflexive form *dreifast*, meaning to be scattered, be spread out or about.

(10) *Til vandamanna. Vandamenn* is a masculine plural noun meaning relatives. The genitive case is used after *til.*

(11) *Fara í fóstur til* . . . To go as foster-child to . . . (to be adopted by . . .).

(12) *Þannig* means therefore, thus.

(13) *Hjón* is a neuter plural noun meaning man and wife. *Sæmdar-* used as a prefix is a honorific, worthy.

(14) *Seyðisfirði.* The nominative singular is *Seyðisfjörður.* The form here is the dative singular, after the preposition *á* (dative when no change or movement is involved).

(15) The form *ólst* is the past of the reflexive *alast*, which is formed from the verb *ala* (present *el*; past *ól*; past part. -*alinn*). *Alast upp* means to be brought up.

(16) The neuter noun *ástríki* means love, affection. The accusative case is used after the preposition *við.*

(17) *Naut* is the past of the verb *njóta* (*nýt; naut, nutum; notið*). This verb means to enjoy, get advantage from, etc.,

and governs the genitive case. *Þess* is the genitive case of the word *það*.

(18) The preposition *með* governs the dative case: *með tveimur öðrum stúlkum*. Note that *tveimur* is the dative form (masc., fem. and neuter) of the numeral *tveir*, two. *Maríu* also is dative, of *María*.

(19) *Þeirra* is another example of the use of the introductory pronoun. *Þeirra* is the genitive plural case (masc., fem. and neuter). Remember that *hjón* is neuter plural.

(20) *Er dó ung*. *Er* is an alternative to *sem*, who, that, which. *Dó* is the past of *deyja*, to die. *Ung* is the feminine form of *ungur*, young.

(21) *Bróðurdóttur*. The Icelandic method of denoting nieces, nephews, aunts, uncles, and so on, is to say "brother–daughter", "sister–son", etc. The word is here in the dative case, as is *Ingibjörgu*, being governed by the preposition *með*.

(22) The stressed word order is employed in this last sentence, putting the verb *var* in first position.

(23) *Önnu* is the dative case of the name Anna. The sentence means literally: Was she (to) Anna all time as sister.

Exercise 19a

Notes

aðstoða, to be present at, attend
bil, *n*. moment; interval—*um hádegisbilið*, at midday
botnlangakast, *n*. appendicitis attack
fela e-m e-ð, to leave something in someone's charge
kauptún, *n*. (market-)town
kvaðst, *hann kvaðst*, he said he would
lagðist, lay
sjóliði, *m*. marine
tundurspillir, *m*. destroyer
veikur, *adj*. sick, ill.

Translate into English:

Um hádegisbilið í gær kom brezki tundurspillirinn *Diana* til Patreksfjarðar með veikan sjóliða. Lagðist herskipið utan við kauptúnið og skipslæknirinn fylgdi sjúklingnum í land í litlum bát. Þar tók Björn Sigvaldason læknir við piltinum, sem heitir Smith og er átján ára gamall. Hafði hann fengið botnlangakast um nóttina. Spurði Björn skipslækninn hvort hann vildi aðstoða við uppskurðinn (operation), en hann kvaðst fela íslenzka lækninum sjúklinginn.

Exercise 19b

Notes

á hæð, in height
að heiman, from home
bíða bana, to be killed
dráttarvél, f. tractor
fara hjá, to pass by
eyðibýli, n. deserted farmhouse
koma í ljós, to appear, come to light
lenda, to fall
slys, n. accident
spyrjast fyrir um e-ð, to make inquiries about
upp ur hádeginu, round about midday
vegarbrún (ir), f. edge of the road
velta (supine, *oltið*), to tumble over, overturn

Translate into Icelandic:

Yesterday there was an accident near Seyðisfjörður. Magnús Óskarsson left home round about midday yesterday (going) towards Seyðisfjörður. One or two hours later people began to wonder (*var farið að undrast*) about him, and then inquiries were made at Selstað, the next village before Brimnes. It then appeared that Magnús had not passed by there. He was found by a deserted farmhouse, Borgarhóli, between the villages. The tractor had tumbled off the edge of the road, which is one to two metres in height there, and Magnús fell under it and was killed.

LESSON 20

Translation

Í vor og sumar hefur Kristleifur Jóhannesson frá Sturlu-reykjum unnið að brúarsmíði eins og undanfarin ár. Hann hefur haft tíu til tuttugu menn í þjónustu sinni, eftir þörfum á hverjum stað. Smíðaðar hafa verið sex brýr í fjórum sýslum.

Fyrsta brúin var byggð yfir Geirsá í Reykholtsdal, fjórtán metra löng, önnur, fjórtán metra, yfir Kaldá hjá Húsafelli í Hálsaveit, sú þriðja yfir Þverá í Norðurádal, hjá Hermundarstöðum, þrettán metra löng, og sú fjórða og lengsta þessara brúa yfir Kaldá hjá Snorrastöðum í Kolbeinsstaðahreppi í Snæfellsnessýslu, og er hún þrjátíu metra að lengd. Fimmta brúin var byggð yfir á Fellsströnd, nálægt Litlutungu, fimmtán metra löng, og sú sjötta yfir ána Skraumu í Hörðudal, báðar í Dölum. Hún er átján metra löng og byggð yfir djúp gljúfur, svo að fimmtán metrar eru frá brúnni niður að vatnsborði Skraumu. Búizt er við, að brúarsmíðinni yfir Skraumu ljúki í þessari viku.

In translation, this piece reads as follows:

This spring and summer Kristleifur Jóhannesson, from Sturlureykur, as in previous years, has been engaged in building bridges. He has had ten to twenty men in his employment, according to requirements in each place. Six bridges have been constructed in four counties. The first bridge was built over the river Geir in Reykholt Valley, and is fourteen metres long, the second over the river Kald at Húsafell in the Hálsa district, fourteen metres, the third over the river Thver in the Northur Valley, near Hermundarstadur, thirteen metres long, and the fourth and longest of these bridges over the river Kald near Snorrastadir in Kolbeinsstad parish in Snæfellsnes county; this one is thirty metres in length. The fifth bridge was built across to Fellsstrand, near Litlatunga, fifteen metres long, and the sixth over the river Skrauma in Hördu valley, both in the Dales. It is eighteen metres long and built over a deep ravine, so that it is fifteen metres from the bridge down to the surface of the river Skrauma. It is expected that construction work on the bridge over the Skrauma will end this week.

Notes

(1) Order of words. The verb *hefur* comes before the name as the sentence opens with a time expression, and the verb must be the second idea in Icelandic sentences.

(2) *ár* is a neuter noun, and the singular is the same as the plural. The word here must be plural as the adjective *undanfarin* is in the plural form. *Farinn* is an adjective of the *boginn* type.

(3) *Unnið* is the supine of the verb *vinna*, to work, etc. Followed by *að*, the verb has the meaning to be engaged on something, in doing something.

(4) *Brúarsmiði* means bridge-building. The form of the first part of the word, *brúar-*, is the genitive of the feminine noun *brú*.

(5) *Þjónusta* is a feminine noun meaning service, employment. The form of the word used here is the dative after the preposition *í*, just as *sinni* is the dative case of *sinn*, his.

(6) *Þörf* (*þarfar*, *þarfir*) is a feminine noun meaning requirement/s, need, etc. *Eftir þörfum* means as required, according to requirements. Note the expression *ef þörf gerist*, meaning if need be.

(7) *Sýsla* is a feminine noun which means both job, work, business and, as here, county. *Sýslu* is the dative case after *í*.

(8) *Brúin* means the bridge. Note the feminine suffixed article, *-in*. In the case of masculine nouns and neuter nouns, this suffix is respectively *-inn* and *-ið*, remember.

(9) Note 4 points out that the first part of the word *brúar-smiði* is the genitive of the word *brú*. Likewise *Geirsá* consists of two parts: *Geirs*, which is the genitive case of *Geir* (a name) and *á*, river.

(10) *Langur* means long, and the feminine form of the word is *löng*. Compare with *svalur* (cool), for instance, which becomes *svöl* in the feminine. The neuter forms are *langt* and *svalt*.

(11) The preposition *hjá* controls the dative case, and the dative of *fell*, mountain or fell, is *felli*. Hence the form *Húsa-felli* of the name *Húsafell*. Likewise *Hermundarstaður* becomes *Hermundarstöðum* (dat. plural).

(12) *Staður* (*-ar*, *-ir*) can mean place, spot, town, etc., but it can also mean church, as it does in several names.

(13) *Hreppur* (*-s*, *-ar*) is a masculine noun meaning parish or district. The parish does not mean necessarily church-parish, as these divisions are of very ancient formation, before church districts were made.

(14) *Yfir á* means across, over to the other side.

(15) *Gljúfur* is a neuter noun, and therefore the nominative and accusative cases both singular and plural are the same. In this case the word could logically be either singular or plural (accusative case, after *yfir*). The key is given by the adjective

djúp, which is the feminine nominative singular or else the neuter nominative and accusative plural of *djúpur*. Here it must obviously be the last-named case.

(16) *Svo að fimmtán metrar eru frá.* . . . Literally, so that fifteen metres are from.

(17) *Frá brúnni.* Dative singular case, after the preposition *frá.*

(18) *Vatnsborði.* The neuter noun is *vatnsborð.* The case is dative singular, after *niður að*, down to. Literally, down to the water's-surface. Note that the first part of the word is the genitive singular of *vatn.*

(19) *Skraumu.* This is the genitive case of the name *Skrauma,* of the (river) Skrauma.

(20) *Búizt er við.* *Búast við* means to expect. Literally: Expected is that. . . . Note that the verb is separated by the verb *er.*

(21) To end, finish, conclude, can be translated *ljúka* (*lýk; lauk, lukum; lokinn*). The form *ljúki* is the present subjunctive, third person singular. The subjunctive is required after the verb to expect, *búast við.*

Vocabulary

buxur, f. pl. trousers
dálítið, adv. somewhat, a little
eldhús, n. kitchen
félagi, m. companion, pal
fyrirskipa (a), v.t. order, prescribe
gegnum (with *acc.*) *prep.,* through
liðka (a), v.t. smooth, make supple
lögregluskipun (-anir), f. police-order
mál, n. case, matter
mega, v.aux. may, might, be allowed
næturvörður, m. night-watchman
ringlaður, p.p. muddled, confused, mixed up
skýring (-ar), f. interpretation, explanation
skyrta, f. shirt
staddur, p.p. situated
stirður, adj. stiff
strjúka, v.t. brush back, smooth down
teygja (i), *v.t.* stretch

torg, *n.* market-place

úti, *adv.* out, outside (N.B. *út* is the prep. out; *að vera úti*, to be out/side)

veggur, *m.* wall

velta (i), *v.t.* with dat. roll; *velta e-u fyrir sér*, turn s.t. over in one's mind

þekkja (i), *v.t.* know (*um*, about)

þurrka (*a*), *v.t.* dry; *þurrka sér um* . . ., wipe one's . . .

Exercise 20a

Translate into English:

Eitt sinn var það fyrirskipað í Höfn (Copenhagen), að menn mættu ekki syngja eða gjöra annan hávaða, á götum, þegar þeir færu heim um nætur. Fáum nóttum síðar var Haukur með nokkrum félögum sínum úti á götu, og sungu þeir mikinn (or mikið). Næturvörður kom þegar og spurði þá, hvort þeir þekktu ekki hina nýju lögregluskipun um að menn mættu ekki syngja um nætur, er þeir færu heim. "Jú," sagði Haukur, "en það er ennþá langt þangað til við förum heim." Næturverðinum brá við, og meðan hann var að velta fyrir sér þessari skýringu málsins, héldu hinir leiðar sinnar.

Notes

Mættu is the third person plural past subjunctive of the verb *mega*. The subjunctive is used after "ordered". Likewise, *færu*, from *fara*.

Jú means yes, *jú* being used after a negative question.

Bregða, to move quickly, takes the dative case. The construction, *e-m bregður* (past, *brá*) *við*, means to be taken aback.

Héldu (*halda*, keep on) *hinir leiðar sinnar*, they continued on their way.

Exercise 20b

Translate into Icelandic:

He was somewhat confused when he woke up, and did not remember where he was (situated). He stretched out his hand for (after) his trousers and shirt, and then he found that he had them on (that he was in them). Through the wall he heard the morning noise from (*úr*) the kitchen and outside from (*utan af*) the market square. He wiped his mouth, smoothed his hair back and stood up, a little stiff at first, but became more supple (*liðkaðist*) as he went up to the door. The night-watchman had (was) gone, and the sun was shining. The town was awake.

IDIOMS, IDIOMATIC EXPRESSIONS AND PROVERBS IN ICELANDIC

Proverbs

Hamra skal járn meðan heitt er. Strike while the iron is hot.

Eins dauði er annars brauð. One man's meat is another man's poison.

Mistök eru mistök, hversu nærri sem þau eru markinu. A miss is as good as a mile.

Sjaldan er ein báran stök. Misfortunes never come singly.

Gleymt er þá gleypt er. Out of sight, out of mind.

Engin rós utan þyrna. No rose without a thorn.

Viljinn dregur hálft hlass. Willingness is half the battle (where there's a will there's a way).

Oft veltir lítil þúfa þungu hlassi. A small leak will sink a great ship.

Vaninn gefur listina. Practice makes perfect.

Líkur sækir líkan heim. Birds of a feather flock together.

Sjaldan grær um oft hrærðan stein. A rolling stone gathers no moss.

Verkin tala. Actions speak louder than words.

Flas er ekki til fagnaðar. More haste, less speed.

Fátt er svo með öllu illt, að ekki boði nokkuð gott. It's an ill wind that blows nobody any good.

Betur sjá augu en auga. Two heads are better than one.

Sá er vinur, sem í raun reynist. A friend in need is a friend indeed.

Öllu böli fylgir jafnan einhver bót. Every cloud has a silver lining.

Ekki er sopið kálið þótt í ausuna sé komið. There's many a slip 'twixt cup and lip.

Eins og maðurinn sáir, svo skal hann og uppskera. As you sow, so shall you reap.

Enginn verður óbarinn biskup. Spare the rod and spoil the child.

Oft er í lygnu vatni langt til botns. Still waters run deep.

Allt er gott sem endar vel. All's well that ends well.

Náttúran er náminu ríkari. What's bred in the bone will
    come out in the flesh.
Margt smátt gerir eitt stórt. Many a mickle makes a muckle.
Verkið lofar meistarann. The workman is known by his work.
Ekki er allt gull, sem glóir. All that glistens is not gold.
Neyðin kennir naktri konu að spinna. Necessity is the mother
    of invention.
Dramb er falli næst. Pride goes before a fall.
Sultur gerir sætan mat. Hunger is the best sauce.
Grípa gæsina meðan hún gefst. Make hay while the sun shines.
Hóf er bezt í hverjum hlut. Moderation is best in all things.
    (Enough is as good as a feast.)
Skamt er öfganna á milli. Extremes meet.
Öl er innri maður. In vino veritas.
Það sem einum er gott er öðrum gott. What's good for the
    goose is good for the gander.

Pointers for Use in Conversation

Góðan dag. ⎫
Góðan daginn. ⎬ Good day; good morning.

Gott kvöld. Good evening.

Komdu sæll. ⎫
Komið þér sælir. ⎬ Good day; how do you do?

Vertu sæll. ⎫
Verið þér sælir. ⎬ Goodbye.

Þakk' (yður) fyrir. Thank you.
Þökk. Thanks.
Nei, þökk fyrir. No, thanks.
Ég vildi gjarna . . . I'd like to . . .
Viljið þér gera svo vel og (bíða). Would you please (wait).
Getið þér gert svo vel og sagt mér . . . Could you please tell
    me . . .
Gerið svo vel og (látið mig fá) . . . Please (let me have) . . .
Því miður ekki. I'm sorry.
Það var leiðinlegt. What a pity.
Ég verð að fara að fara. I must be going.
Ég verð að flýta mér. I must hurry.
Hve langt er héðan til . . . ? How far is it (from here) to . . .?
Við skulum (líta á . . .). Let's (look at . . .).
Fyrir mitt leyti. For my part.

Ef ég man rétt. If I remember aright.

Í stuttu máli. In a nutshell.

Í fáum orðum sagt. To cut a long story short.

Gerið þér svo vel. Certainly; please do; help yourself.

Ég er að hugsa um að (fara í langferð upp í sveit). I'm thinking of (going on a journey into the country).

Viljið þér ekki gera svo vel að . . . Would you mind . . .

Hugsaðu um það, sem þér kemur við. Mind your own business.

Biddu augnablik. Just a moment.

. . . (eða) þar um bil. . . . or thereabouts. (More or less.)

Mér datt það líka í hug. I thought as much.

Hamingjan góða. My goodness.

Guð minn góður. My God.

Það gerir ekkert til. It makes no odds.

Hvað gengur að? What's the matter?

Það er ekkert. Oh, it's nothing.

Minnstu ekki á það. Don't mention it.

Mig hálflangar að fara. I've half a mind to go.

Í mínum augum. To my mind.

Að mínu áliti. In my opinion.

Það er auðskilið. It stands to reason.

Vera í kröggum. To be hard up.

Eftir á að hyggja. On second thoughts.

Það getur ekki komið til greina. That is out of the question.

Þegar til lengdar lætur. In the long run.

Fyrirvaralaust. On the spur of the moment.

Í veði. Í húfi. At stake.

Frá upphafi til enda. From beginning to end.

Allt í lagi. All right. O.K.

Með réttu. By rights.

Ef nauðsyn krefur. If need be.

Að undanteknu. Apart from this.

Fyrsta flokks. First rate.

Ef svo er. Ef svo færi. In that case.

Að minnsta kosti. Anyway.

Hvað sem öðru líður. In any case.

Og svo framvegis. And so on.

Eins og sagt er. As the saying goes.

Það er augljóst, að . . . It stands to reason that . . .

Í raun og veru. In reality.

Af ásettu ráði. On purpose.
Að öllum líkindum. In all probability.
Út í bláinn. At random.
Hvað sem tautar. Come what may.
Mér stendur alveg á sama. I don't care a rap.
Þetta er augljóst. It speaks for itself.
Ef satt skal segja. To speak the truth.
Ekkert, sem tali tekur. Nothing to speak of.
Í fyrsta lagi. In the first place.
Hugsaðu þér bara. Just fancy that.
Hverju skiptir það? What does that matter?
Það skiptir engu. It makes no difference.
Á hinn bóginn. On the other hand.
Satt að segja. In fact. (Truth to tell.)
Sannleikurinn er sá . . . As a matter of fact ..
Þykja vænt um . . .⎫
Hafa mætur á . . . ⎬ To be fond of . . .
Þykja gott . . . ⎭
Steinsnar. A stone's throw.
Mig svimar. My head is reeling.
Allt hringsnýst fyrir mér. My head is going round.
Skipta um skoðun. To change one's opinion.
Breyta áformi sínu. To change one's mind.
Að ég ekki minnist á, að . . . Not to mention . . .
Í mesta lagi. At most.
Mestann tímann. Most of the time.
Ég var ekki fæddur í gær. ⎫
Ég er eldri en tvævetur. ⎬ I was not born yesterday.
Það lítur út fyrir rigningu. It looks like rain.
Hann er alltaf að núa mér því um nasir, að ég . . . He's always
   rubbing it in that I . . .
Eins og ekkert væri um að vera. As if nothing had happened.
Það er skrambi kalt. It's jolly cold.
Ég er því ekki mótfallinn að . . . I have no objection to . . .
Mér dettur í hug, að . . . It occurs to me that . . .
Ég átti ekki annars úrkosta en að . . . I had no option but
   to . . .
Skál! Cheers!
Auðvitað. Vitanlega. Of course.
Í klípu. Í vandræðum. In the soup. In hot water.

Lof mér að sjá. Let me see.

Sjáum nú til, hvað var ég að segja? Let me see, what was I saying?

Sjáðu það þá sjálfur. See for yourself.

Ég hefi ekki séð þig í óratíma. I haven't seen you for ages.

Ég skil. I see. I understand.

Ég hefi ekki efni á því. I can't afford it.

Nú á dögum. Nowadays.

Ekki á morgun heldur hinn. The day after tomorrow.

Viltu ekki koma með? Won't you come too?

Á leiðinni. On the way.

Eftir því sem ég lít á. To my way of looking at it.

Fara til fjandans. ⎫
Fara í hundana. ⎬ To go to the devil.

Leggja saman tvo og tvo. To put two and two together.

Í eitt skipti fyrir öll. Once and for all.

Hver fjandinn. Damn it.

Skrattinn hafi þig. The devil take you.

Useful Idioms and Expressions

Fylgjast með tímanum. To keep abreast of the times.

Hafa margt í takinu. To have many irons in the fire.

Kaupa köttinn í sekknum. To buy a pig in a poke.

Löturhægt. At a snail's pace.

Halda loforð sitt. To keep one's word.

Hlaupa af sér hornin. To sow one's wild oats.

Vera farinn að stirðna. To be out of practice.

Fá mætur á . . . To take a fancy to . . .

Hafa gát á . . . Keep one's eye on . . .

Þola bæði súrt og sætt. To go through thick and thin.

Gera úlfalda úr mýflugu. To make a mountain out of a molehill.

Kunna til fullnustu. To have at one's fingertips.

Hafa ekki nema til hnífs og skeiðar. To lead a hand-to-mouth existence.

Læra (kunna) utanbókar. To learn (know) by heart.

Herða upp hugann. To pluck up courage.

Verða hnugginn. To lose heart.

Hafa hjartað á réttum stað. To have the heart in the right place.

Sneiða hjá . . . To steer clear of . . .
Gera gys að e-m. To pull someone's leg.
Jafna sig. To pull oneself together.
Vera ástfanginn af . . . To be in love with . . .
Verða ástfanginn af . . . To fall in love with . . .
Ást við fyrstu sýn. Love at first sight.
Drekka eins og svampur. To drink like a fish.
Hafa öðrum og mikilsverðari störfum að sinna. To have other and better fish to fry.
Sleppa nauðulega. To have a close shave.
Segja eins og manni býr í brjósti. To speak one's own mind.
Líta fljótlega á . . . To give . . . a quick glance.
Kyrkja (kæfa) í fæðingunni. To nip something in the bud.
Koma auga á . . . To catch sight of . . .
Missa sjónar á . . . To lose sight of . . .
Gefa ró reiði sinni. To blow off steam.
Vera með hártoganir. To split hairs.
Nefna hlutinn sínu rétta nafni. To call a spade a spade.
Fara á túr. To go on the spree.
Vera á einu máli. To be of one mind.
Vera á báðum áttum um . . . To be in two minds about . . .
Hafa bein í nefinu. To have a mind of one's own.
Vera kominn á grafarbakkann. To have one foot in the grave.
Hitta naglann á höfuðið. To hit the nail on the head.
Nauðuleg undankoma. To have a narrow escape.
Ráða með sér. To make up one's mind.
Taka afleiðingunum af gjörðum sínum. To take the consequences for one's actions.
Fara á fætur fyrir allar aldir. To get up with the lark.
Vera komið að óvörum. To be caught napping.
Vinna eins og þræll. To work like a Trojan.
Greiða okurverð. To pay through the nose.
Grípa tækifærið. To seize the-opportunity.
Halda sér við efnið. To keep to the subject.
Víkja frá efninu. To digress.
Taka í sig kjark. To screw up courage.
Setja í sig kjark. To pluck up courage.
Brjóta heilann (um . . .). To rack one's brains (about . . .).
Vera mjög í tízku. To be all the rage.
Versna stöðugt. To go from bad to worse.

Vera milli steins og sleggju. To be between the devil and the deep blue sea.

Sigla milli skers og báru. To steer between Scylla and Charybdis.

Sofa eins og steinn. To sleep like a log.

Neita að taka sönsum. To refuse to listen to reason.

Tala af sér. To let the cat out of the bag.

Vera ekki með öllum mjalla. To be round the bend. To be mad.

Með réttu máli. In one's right mind.

Steindauður. Dead as a doornail.

Blindfullur. As drunk as a lord.

Fátækur eins og kirkjurotta. As poor as a churchmouse.

Háll eins og áll. As slippery as an eel.

Úlfur í sauðargæru. A wolf in sheep's clothing.

Með (móti) straumnum. With (against) the current.

Í húð og hár. To the core.

Hann er klaufi í höndunum. His fingers are all thumbs.

Hann er alveg eins og hann faðir hans. He is just like his father.

Alveg heyrnarlaus. As deaf as a post.

Augliti til auglitis. Face to face.

Framtakslaus. Faint-hearted.

Með fullum (sæmilegum) hraða. At full (a good) speed.

Í beina línu. As the crow flies.

Allur í uppnámi. All in a dither.

Frá hvirfli til ilja. From head to foot.

Yfir holt og hæðir. Up hill and down dale.

Í góðu skapi. In high spirits.

Í þungu (döpru) skapi. In low spirits. Down in the dumps.

Pennaglöp. A slip of the pen.

Mismæli. A slip of the tongue.

Allt var á tjá og tundri. Everything was upside down.

Hann er sinn eigin herra. He is his own master.

Frá morgni til kvölds. From morning to night.

Aldrei fyrr og aldrei síðan. Never before or since.

Af alefli. With all one's might and main.

Ef út í það er farið. For that matter.

Frá ómunatíð. From time immemorial.

Því meir, því betra. The more the merrier.

Langt í burtu. Far away.
Einu sinni enn. Once more.
Við og við. Öðru hverju. Now and again.
Hvað eftir annað. Again and again.
Strax á morgun. First thing tomorrow.
Fyrir skömmu. A short time ago.
Fyrir skemstu. A very short time ago.
Innan skamms. Shortly.
Hvað sem það kostar. At any price.
Snarræði. Presence of mind.
Hvaða höfn sem er í roki. Any port in a storm.
Spara eyrinn og eyða krónunni. Penny wise, pound foolish.
Gjalda líku líkt. To pay back in the same coin.
Um allan heim. All over the world.
Leynileg bending. A veiled hint.
Ur öskunni í eldinn. Out of the frying-pan into the fire.
Fegurðarsvefn. Beauty sleep.
Dapur í bragði. Down in the mouth.
Hann er ekki mikill fyrir mann að sjá. He's not much to
  look at.
Engan veginn. By no means.
Hins vegar. On the other hand.

Expressions for Use in Letters

Kæri vinur. Heiðraði herra. Dear friend. Dear Sir.
Kærar kveðjur. My best regards.
Yðar einlægur. Yours sincerely.
Virðingarfyllst. Yours faithfully.
. . . biður að heilsa þér. . . . wishes to be remembered to you.
Berðu . . . kveðju mína. Give . . . my best regards.
Með alúðarkveðju. Kindest regards.

Here is a short selection of idiomatic expressions in sentences
to illustrate their use.

(1) *Ég er nú búinn að byggja hús; það var dýrt að koma því
upp, og nú skulda ég mikið og er í kröggum.* I have now finished
building my house; it was expensive to build, and now I owe
a great deal and am in financial straits.

(2) *Þú skrifaðir mér bréf í janúar, ef ég man rétt.* You wrote
me a letter in January, if I remember aright.

(3) *Þykir þér ekki leiðinlegt að leiðrétta stíla, þegar til lengdar*

lætur? Don't you think it's boring to correct exercises, in the long run?

(4) *Hann sló manninn fyrirvaralaust. Maðurinn fór frá konunni fyrirvaralaust.* He struck the man without warning. The man left his wife without any warning.

(5) *Þú átt að minnsta kosti tvö bréf hjá mér, svo að ég verð að fara að skrifa þér.* I owe you at least two letters, so I must write to you.

(6) *Það er hægt að vera í margs konar klípu. Til dæmis, ég týndi lyklunum að íbúðinni og kemst ekki inn; ég er í mikilli klípu. Kakan brann í ofninum og gestirnir eru komnir; konan er í voðalegri klípu.* It is possible to be in many kinds of trouble. For example, I lost the key of the flat and cannot get in; I am in a fix. The cake burnt in the oven and the guests have arrived; the woman is in a terrible fix.

(7) *Hann lét eins og ekkert væri um að vera, þegar vinur hans kom í heimsókn, þó að þau hjónin væru mjög ósátt.* He pretended that nothing was the matter when his friend paid them a visit, although they (the couple) were having a quarrel.

(8) *Bíllinn fór löturhægt. Hesturinn gekk löturhægt.* The car was going at a snail's pace. The horse was walking dead slow.

(9) *Ég hef miklar mætur á enskri tungu.* I am very fond of the English language.

(10) *Ég vinn frá morgni til kvölds, og þú líka. Sumir vinna enn lengri tíma.* I work from morning to night, and so do you. Some people work even longer hours.

APPENDIX 1

Strong Nouns

Masculine, type 1*a* (-s, -ar)

	Singular		Plural
nom.	heimur	*nom.*	heimar
acc.	heim	*acc.*	heima
dat.	heimi	*dat.*	heimum
gen.	heims	*gen.*	heima

Masculine, type 1*b* (-s, -ar)

nom.	drottinn	*nom.*	drottnar
acc.	drottin	*acc.*	drottna
dat.	drottni	*dat.*	drottnum
gen.	drottins	*gen.*	drottna

Masculine, type 1*c* (-s, -ar)

nom.	hamar	*nom.*	hamrar
acc.	hamar	*acc.*	hamra
dat.	hamri	*dat.*	hömrum
gen.	hamars	*gen.*	hamra

Masculine, type 1*d* (-s, -ar)

nom.	læknir	*nom.*	læknar
acc.	lækni	*acc.*	lækna
dat.	lækni	*dat.*	læknum
gen.	læknis	*gen.*	lækna

Masculine, type 2*a* (-s, -ir)

nom.	gestur	*nom.*	gestir
acc.	gest	*acc.*	gesti
dat.	gesti	*dat.*	gestum
gen.	gests	*gen.*	gesta

Masculine, type 2*b* (-s, -ir)

nom.	dalur	*nom.*	dalir
acc.	dal	*acc.*	dali
dat.	dal	*dat.*	dölum
gen.	dals	*gen.*	dala

Masculine, type 2c (-s, -ir)

	Singular		Plural
nom.	bekkur	*nom.*	bekkir
acc.	bekk	*acc.*	bekki
dat.	bekk	*dat.*	bekkjum
gen.	bekks (bekkjar)	*gen.*	bekkja

Masculine, type 3a (-ar, -ir)

nom.	fundur	*nom.*	fundir
acc.	fund	*acc.*	fundi
dat.	fundi	*dat.*	fundum
gen.	fundar	*gen.*	funda

Masculine, type 3b (-ar, -ir)

nom.	köttur	*nom.*	kettir
acc.	kött	*acc.*	ketti
dat.	ketti	*dat.*	köttum
gen.	kattar	*gen.*	katta

Masculine, type 3c (-ar, -ir)

nom.	fjörður	*nom.*	firðir
acc.	fjörð	*acc.*	firði
dat.	firði	*dat.*	fjörðum
gen.	fjarðar	*gen.*	fjarða

Notes on Masculine Nouns

(1) Like *drottinn*, we have two-syllable words ending in -*inn*, -*all*, -*ill*, -*ull*, -*ann*, -*unn*. Examples include: *arinn* (hearth); *aðall* (nobility), *gaffall* (fork); *ferill* (way, track), *lykill* (key), *pistill* (thistle); *djöfull* (devil), *ígull* (sea-urchin), *jökull* (glacier), *öxull* (axle); *aftann* (evening); *jötunn* (giant).

(2) Like *hamar* are declined the following: *akur* (field), *aldur* (age), *árangur* (yield, result), *Baldur*, *faraldur* (epidemic), *farangur* (luggage), *galdur* (witchcraft), *hlátur* (laughter), *humar* (lobster), *leiðangur* (levy), *mokstur* (great quantity), *otur* (otter), *staðaldur* (continuance).

(3) In Group SM 1d are found two-syllable words ending in -*ir*. These include: *deilir* (divisor), *einir* (juniper), *flýtir* (haste), *geymir* (reservoir), *Geysir*, *greinir* (grammatical article), *hirðir* (shepherd), *léttir* (relief; grampus), *mælir* (measure), *reynir* (rowan), *víðir* (willow), *vísir* pointer, indicator, hand (of clock).

(4) Like *köttur* are: *börkur* (bark), *göltur* (hog), *köstur* (pile), *lögur* (liquid), *mögur* (son), *svörður* (sward, skin (of head)), *völlur* (field), *vörður* (guard, watch), *vöxtur* (growth), *þröstur* (thrush), *örn* (eagle).

(5) Like *fjörður* are: *björn* (bear), *hjörtur* (stag), *kjölur* (keel), *mjöður* (mead).

Feminine Nouns

Type 1a (-ar, -ir)

	Singular		*Plural*
nom.	borg	*nom.*	borgir
acc.	borg	*acc.*	borgir
dat.	borg	*dat.*	borgum
gen.	borgar	*gen.*	borga

Type 1b (-ar, -ir)

nom.	sög	*nom.*	sagir
acc.	sög	*acc.*	sagir
dat.	sög	*dat.*	sögum
gen.	sagar	*gen.*	saga

Type 1c (-ar, -ir)

nom.	verzlun	*nom.*	verzlanir
acc.	verzlun	*acc.*	verzlanir
dat.	verzlun	*dat.*	verzlunum
gen.	verzlunar	*gen.*	verzlana

Type 2a (-ar, -ar)

nom.	skál	*nom.*	skálar
acc.	skál	*acc.*	skálar
dat.	skál	*dat.*	skálum
gen.	skálar	*gen.*	skála

Type 2b (-ar, -ar)

nom.	elfur	*nom.*	elfar
acc.	elfi	*acc.*	elfar
dat.	elfi	*dat.*	elfum
gen.	elfar	*gen.*	elfa

In this group are found: *flæður* (high water), *gunnur* (poet. battle), *hildur* (poet. battle), *reyður* (rorqual), *æður* (eider). Also, names of females ending in -*dís*, -*unn*, -*ur*: *Valdís*, *Þórunn*, *Ástríður*.

Type 2c (-r, -r)

	Singular			Plural
nom.	á		nom.	ár
acc.	á		acc.	ár
dat.	á		dat.	ám
gen.	ár		gen.	áa

In this group are: *flá* (net-float), *forsjá* (foresight), *spá* (prediction), *þrá* (longing).

Type 3a (-ar, -ur)

nom.	bók		nom.	bækur
acc.	bók		acc.	bækur
dat.	bók		dat.	bókum
gen.	bókar		gen.	bóka

Type 3b (-ar, -r)

nom.	brú		nom.	brýr
acc.	brú		acc.	brýr
dat.	brú		dat.	brúm
gen.	brúar		gen.	brúa

Type 3c (-ur, -ur)

nom.	mörk		nom.	merkur
acc.	mörk		acc.	merkur
dat.	mörk		dat.	mörkum
gen.	merkur		gen.	marka

Irregular Nouns

	Kýr *f.* (cow)			Ær *f.* (ewe)	
	Singular	Plural		Singular	Plural
nom.	kýr	kýr	nom.	ær	ær
acc.	kú	kýr	acc.	á	ær
dat.	kú	kúm	dat.	á	ám
gen.	kýr	kúa	gen.	ær	áa

Brúður *f.* (bride)

	Singular	*Plural*
nom.	brúður	brúðir
acc.	brúði	brúðir
dat.	brúði	brúðum
gen.	brúðar	brúða

Vættur *f.* (supernatural being)

	Singular	*Plural*
nom.	vættur	vættir
acc.	vætt	vætti
dat.	vætti	vættum
gen.	vættar	vætta

Neuter Nouns

Type 1a (-s, --)

	Singular	*Plural*
nom.	blóm	blóm
acc.	blóm	blóm
dat.	blómi	blómum
gen.	blóms	blóma

Type 1b

	Singular	*Plural*
nom.	ber	ber
acc.	ber	ber
dat.	beri	berjum
gen.	bers	berja

Type 2

nom.	tré	tré
acc.	tré	tré
dat.	tré	trjám
gen.	trés	trjáa

Type 3

nom.	snæri	snæri
acc.	snæri	snæri
dat.	snæri	snærum
gen.	snæris	snæra

Type 4

nom.	hreiður	hreiður
acc.	hreiður	hreiður
dat.	hreiðri	hreiðrum
gen.	hreiðurs	hreiðra

Type 5

nom.	folald	folöld
acc.	folald	folöld
dat.	folaldi	folöldum
gen.	folalds	folalda

APPENDIX 2

Weak Masculine Nouns

Type 1

	Singular	*Plural*
nom.	tími	tímar
acc.	tíma	tíma
dat.	tíma	tímum
gen.	tíma	tíma

Type 2

	Singular	*Plural*
nom.	einyrki	einyrkjar
acc.	einyrkja	einyrkja
dat.	einyrkja	einyrkjum
gen.	einyrkja	einyrkja

Type 3

	Singular	Plural
nom.	nemandi	nemendur
acc.	nemanda	nemendur
dat.	nemanda	nemendum (nemöndum)
gen.	nemanda	nemenda (nemanda)

Weak Feminine Nouns

Type 1

	Singular	Plural
nom.	tunga	tungur
acc.	tungu	tungur
dat.	tungu	tungum
gen.	tungu	tungna

Type 2

	Singular	Plural
nom.	lilja	liljur
acc.	lilju	liljur
dat.	lilju	liljum
gen.	lilju	lilja

Type 3

	Singular	Plural
nom.	lygi	lygar
acc.	lygi	lygar
dat.	lygi	lygum
gen.	lygi	lyga

APPENDIX 3

Weak Verbs, Group 4

Infinitive	Present	Past	Supine
berja (*beat*)	ber	barði	barið
bylja (*roar, resound*)	byl	buldi	bulið
dvelja (*live*)	dvel	dvaldi	dvalið
dylja (*hide*)	dyl	duldi	duldinn (*past part.*)
flýja (*flee*)	flý	flýði	flúinn (*past part.*)
fremja (*commit*)	frem	framdi	framinn (*past part.*)
gleðja (*gladden*)	gleð	gladdi	gladdur (*past part.*)
hemja (*restrain*)	hem	hamdi	haminn (*past part.*)
hlymja (*roar*)	hlym	hlumdi	hlumið
hrekja (*refute*)	hrek	hrakti	hrakinn (*past part.*)
hvetja (*sharpen*)	hvet	hvatti	hvattur (*past part.*)
hyggja (*think*)	hygg	hugði	hugað

kremja (*crush*)	krem	kramdi	kraminn (*past part.*)
kveðja (*say goodbye*)	kveð	kvaddi	kvaddur (*past part.*)
leggja (*lay*)	legg	lagði	lagður (*past part.*)
lykja (*close*)	lyk	lukti	luktur (*past part.*)
ná (*reach*)	næ	náði	náð
selja (*sell*)	sel	seldi	seldur (*past part.*)
setja (*set*)	set	setti	settur (*past part.*)
skilja (*understand*)	skil	skildi	skilinn (*past part.*)
smyrja (*grease*)	smyr	smurði	smurður (*past part.*)
spyrja (*ask*)	spyr	spurði	spurður (*past part.*)
spýja (*be sick*)	spý	spjó	spúinn (*past part.*)
telja (*count*)	tel	taldi	talinn (*past part.*)
temja (*tame*)	tem	tamdi	taminn (*past part.*)
tyggja (*chew*)	tygg	tugði	tugginn (*past part.*)
valda (*bring about*)	veld	olli	valdið
vekja (*awaken*)	vek	vakti	vakinn (*past part.*)
velja (*choose*)	vel	valdi	valinn (*past part.*)
venja (*accustom*)	ven	vandi	vaninn (*past part.*)
verja (*defend*)	ver	varði	varinn (*past part.*)
ymja (*groan*)	ym	umdi	umið
þekja (*cover*)	þek	þakti	þakinn (*past part.*)
þrymja (*thunder*)	þrym	þrumdi	þrumið

APPENDIX 4

Adjectives of the Strong Declension
A. *Ríkur*

Singular

	masculine	*feminine*	*neuter*
nom.	ríkur	rík	ríkt
acc.	ríkan	ríka	ríkt
dat.	ríkum	ríkri	ríku
gen.	ríks	ríkrar	ríks

Plural

nom.	ríkir	ríkar	rík
acc.	ríka	ríkar	rík
dat.	ríkum	ríkum	ríkum
gen.	ríkra	ríkra	ríkra

B. *Hlýr*

Singular

	masculine	feminine	neuter
nom.	hlýr	hlý	hlýtt
acc.	hlýjan	hlýja	hlýtt
dat.	hlýjum	hlýrri	hlýju
gen.	hlýs	hlýrrar	hlýs

Plural

nom.	hlýir	hlýjar	hlý
acc.	hlýja	hlýjar	hlý
dat.	hlýjum	hlýjum	hlýjum
gen.	hlýrra	hlýrra	hlýrra

C. *-inn* type

Singular

	masculine	feminine	neuter
nom.	boginn	bogin	bogið
acc.	boginn	bogna	bogið
dat.	bognum	boginni	bognu
gen.	bogins	boginnar	bogins

Plural

nom.	bognir	bognar	bogin
acc.	bogna	bognar	bogin
dat.	bognum	bognum	bognum
gen.	boginna	boginna	boginna

Likewise, adjectives ending in *-inn* (e.g., *fyndinn*), and past participles of strong verbs (e.g., *roðinn*). Also the past participles of *some* weak verbs which end in *-ja* in the infinitive, e.g., *flúinn* (*flýja*, to flee), *kafinn* (*kefja*, to subdue); and also the past participles of *ri*-verbs—*róinn*, *gróinn*.

D. *Lítill*

Singular

	masculine	feminine	neuter
nom.	lítill	lítil	lítið
acc.	lítinn	litla	lítið
dat.	litlum	lítilli	litlu
gen.	lítils	lítillar	lítils

Plural

	masculine	feminine	neuter
nom.	litlir	litlar	lítil
acc.	litla	litlar	lítil
dat.	litlum	litlum	litlum
gen.	lítilla	lítilla	lítilla

Likewise—*mikill.*

E. *Framinn*

Singular

	masculine	feminine	neuter
nom.	framinn	framin	framið
acc.	framinn	framda	framið
dat.	frömdum	framinni	frömdu
gen.	framins	framinnar	framins

Plural

nom.	framdir	framdar	framin
acc.	framda	framdar	framin
dat.	frömdum	frömdum	frömdum
gen.	framinna	framinna	framinna

Likewise, the past participles of *most* weak verbs ending in *-ja* in the infinitive, e.g., *hulinn* (*hylja*, to cover), *talinn* (*telja*, to count).

APPENDIX 5

Gradation (*hljóðskipti*) and Fracture (*klofning*)

Gradation is the substitution of one vowel for another, and occurs in the conjugation of strong verbs. See the section on strong verbs for these changes in full. Examples: *nema—nam —námum—numið, bera—bar—bárum—borið.*

Fracture is the name given to the sound-change when *e* becomes *ja*, which by reason of *u*-mutation becomes *jö*. It sometimes appears as though the *ja* has developed from *i* and not *e*, but in these cases the *i* itself is developed from an original *e*. Example: *firði—fjarðar—fjörður.* In this case the original root-word was *ferð.* Note that fracture takes place only in the case of unaccented syllables, although not even here in every case; fracture does not occur, for example, after *v*, *l*, or *r* (see *velta*, *lesa* and *reka*).

Note also the following points regarding mutations: the *u* in the masculine nominative ending -*ur* does not lead to any mutation, owing to the fact that the ending in Old Icelandic was -*r*, e.g., *garður* was originally *garðr*. In this connexion it is as well to note that in some cases mutation appears to take place when it should not; see *barn* (child), plural *börn*. Here there is no following *u* to give rise to the mutation, but there was a *u* in the original form of the word, and it was this which caused mutation before the *u* itself was lost. Likewise, *hús* (house) changes to *hýsa* (to house), there having originally been an *i*-sound in the ending, since lost.

KEY

Exercise 1

Strong masculine, group 1a (-s, -ar)

hestur	foss	karl
garður	háls	leikur
bátur	haukur	lax
fiskur	hrafn	munnur

Strong masculine, group 1b (-s, -ar)

bíll	gaffall	jökull
djöfull	hæll	öxull

Strong masculine, group 2a (-s, -ir)

gestur	skrækur	stafur
selur	staður	drengur

Strong feminine, group 1a (-ar, -ir)

ást	hurð	lest
borg	lengd	

Strong neuter, group 1a (-s, -)

blóm	hús	sjónvarp
fjall	ljós	skáld
haf	regn	skip
hross	rúm	tungl

Exercise 2a

(1) Hundurinn og drengurinn.
(2) Ég tek bókina.
(3) Ég læt bókina á borðið.
(4) Ég keypti hestinn.
(5) Hún keypti kött.
(6) Hvar er bókin?
(7) Drengurinn er hér.
(8) Báturinn er nýr.
(9) Konan og maðurinn eru frá Reykjavík.
(10) Drengurinn er frá togaranum.
(11) Í garðinum.
(12) Maðurinn sækir hestana.

Exercise 2b

(1) She has a pen and (some) paper.
(2) The ship is not here.
(3) The dictionary is on the table.
(4) He bought the ships in Reykjavík.
(5) The book is (lying) on the table.
(6) The house is new.

(7) I read the book in the garden.
(8) The man is not here.
(9) Here are a boy and a girl.
(10) I have a knife and a spoon.
(11) The girl has a dog.
(12) He bought the books.

Exercise 3a

(1) He came to the town yesterday.
(2) The horses are in the field.
(3) The watch is (of) gold.
(4) Can you wade over the stream?
(5) From there I travel to England.
(6) For example.
(7) He knelt down (went down on his knees).
(8) He got to his feet.
(9) There are trees along the road (way).
(10) The boy is from Reykjavík.

Exercise 3b

(1) Hann talaði um bókina.
(2) Hefur þú komið til Reykjavíkur?
(3) Hún keypti bókina fyrir stúlkuna.
(4) Láttu mig í friði.
(5) Á sunnudaginn.
(6) Hann sat gegnt mér.
(7) Hann fór í kirkju.
(8) Hún býr í Reykjavík.
(9) Ég fer oft í leikhús.
(10) Drengurinn gekk kringum húsið.

Exercise 4a

(1) Sigurður, bróðir þinn, er heima.
(2) Hann gekk út með konunni sinni.
(3) Hún klæddi sig.
(4) Það er faðir þinn.
(5) Hann fór með mér til systur minnar.
(6) Hann hefur beðið hennar.
(7) Þú situr og ég stend.
(8) Hundurinn beit mig.
(9) Hún elskar hann.
(10) Þú tefur mig.
(11) Hún jafnar sig fljótt.
(12) Hann hneigði sig og gekk út.

Exercise 4b

(1) He greets me.
(2) I burnt myself.
(3) She drowned herself in the well.

(4) I understand him.
(5) You offend me.
(6) I (shall) never forget you.
(7) That really pleased me.
(8) I keep my word (promise).
(9) I know you.
(10) Did you meet my brother?
(11) I answer you.
(12) The girl is washing her hair.

Exercise 5a

(1) Ég skal sýna þér nokkuð merkilegt.
(2) Ég hefi aldrei séð það. (Það hefi ég aldrei séð.)
(3) Hefurðu talað um það við pabba?
(4) Hann ætlar að búa hérna.
(5) Ég skal vaka í kvöld og rifja upp allar óreglulegu sagnirnar
í ensku.
(6) Hefurðu aldrei séð sjóinn?
(7) Hvar hefur þú verið allan þennan tíma?
(8) Hún vill hjálpa systur sinni.
(9) Þú þarft að kaupa það.
(10) Við vildum fá að tala við hana.
(11) Ég fæ aldrei að sofa neitt.
(12) Ég get sagt yður nákvæmlega, hvað hann mun segja.

Exercise 5b

(1) Now I should like to know where John is.
(2) I have told you everything I know about him.
(3) I have to catch a train.
(4) We would far sooner play bridge than sleep.
(5) He is the man who wants to speak to you.
(6) She came yesterday.
(7) I intend to answer the first (former) question first.
(8) Have you read this book?
(9) He did not want to leave without seeing you.
(10) They have had news of John.
(11) I intend to be (become) a surgeon.
(12) We will go to the pictures together.

Exercise 6a

(1) Nú er presturinn kominn að finna pabba.
(2) Hún klappaði saman höndunum.
(3) Hann kinkaði kolli.
(4) Ég skrifaði bréf í gær.
(5) Hún varð reið, þegar hún sá, hvað í skálinni var.
(6) Skipið er komið að landi.
(7) Hann er orðinn duglegur að skrifa.
(8) Hún hringdi til hans, og heyrði rödd hans í símanum.
(9) Nú verð ég að fara.

(10) Ég talaði við hana í gær.
(11) Telpan blandaði sér nú inn í samtalið.
(12) Það er út af bréfi, sem þú skrifaðir.

Exercise 6b

(1) She intends to stay only a few days.
(2) I don't know (that).
(3) The boy travelled to Norway six years ago.
(4) Inga has turned twelve.
(5) We are going to Iceland this winter.
(6) The girl will be gone when he comes.
(7) He could not speak.
(8) Spring began cold, but the weather gradually became warmer.
(9) She had not understood.
(10) They spoke about doing that.
(11) The boy painted the trawler today.
(12) The people have come home to eat.

Exercise 7a

(1) Ég held, að ég hafi séð hann áður.
(2) Ég hélt, að þú vissir þetta.
(3) Sagan er sönn, þótt ljót sé (þótt hún sé ljót).
(4) Nú er hún búin að lesa bókina.
(5) Hann er að skrifa bréf.
(6) Ég vil ekki láta Dísu sjá, að ég fari að gráta.
(7) Þeir vildu ekki, að hann færi.
(8) Maðurinn er búinn að skrifa, en stúlkan er ekki búin að lesa.
(9) Það er farið að daga.
(10) Hún er að tala við mig.
(11) Ég vissi ekki til, að þú kynnir norsku.
(12) Ég hefi aldrei sagt, að ég kynni norsku.

Exercise 7b

(1) I was writing when she came.
(2) If it were not so, we should not be here.
(3) He had just finished reading the book.
(4) What are you doing?
(5) She did not want to let Gerda see that she was going to cry.
(6) Someone is coming.
(7) He says that she is stingy.
(8) I wish that you were many years younger.
(9) The girl has just put her make-up on.
(10) "What have I been saying?" he said.
(11) She was singing when I came.
(12) I think that is foolish.

Exercise 8a

(1) Ég sá og heyrði margt, meðan ég bjó hjá þér.
(2) Þú varst ekki heima, þegar ég kom.
(3) Hún hló og grét á víxl.

(4) Ég hafði numið staðar fyrir framan stóran búðarglugga.
(5) Hundurinn beit mig.
(6) Ég fekk bréf frá honum.
(7) Hann greip tækifærið og fór inn.
(8) Drengurinn sneri sér að henni.
(9) Stúlkan steig eitt skref aftur á bak.
(10) Hann hratt mér í ána.
(11) Hún leit upp og brosti.
(12) Ég fór þangað og fann hann.

Exercise 8b

(1) I stand up (in order) to go.
(2) He looked at the clock.
(3) He laughed at me when I asked him what I ought to do.
(4) She broke the coffee-cup.
(5) I went on reading long into the night.
(6) What did you see?
(7) She went (drove) to the bank.
(8) The man took a note-book out of his pocket.
(9) He put his coat on, put his hat on, and then went out.
(10) He sat in his car.
(11) I saw a black dog.
(12) Don't you drink strong coffee?

Exercise 9a

(1) Hann settist við hlið hennar.
(2) Mig langar til að spyrja nokkurra spurninga.
(3) Þeir eru farnir til Akureyrar.
(4) Þegar hún kom inn í stofuna, beindist samtalið á aðrar brautir.
(5) Bréfið var ritað af honum sjálfum.
(6) Þau hafa breytzt mjög.
(7) Nú var röðin komin að honum að hleypa brúnum.
(8) Hér munum við nú skiljast.
(9) Hún þorði ekki að leggjast til svefns.
(10) Dyrnar opnuðust og inn kom maður meðalhár.
(11) Margir aðrir hafa sagt hið sama.
(12) Hann gafst upp við að fá Dísu til að skipta um skoðun.

Exercise 9b

(1) She had undertaken this journey in order to marry him.
(2) They were now sent to their homeland.
(3) I don't feel like any breakfast.
(4) Shortly after the door was closed behind Disa I woke up.
(5) The boy sat down slowly.
(6) As stolen goods were found in his possession, all his past behaviour came up.
(7) He was carried (along) with the current.
(8) The horses were sick this morning.
(9) She looked up and peeped through the window (pane)
(10) I find him boring.

(11) The girl bustled around her without a pause while she was dressing.
(12) He half stood up, but then sat down again.

Exercise 10a

(1) Meat is generally dearer than fish.
(2) The country is beautiful.
(3) The ship is very strong and beautiful.
(4) (His) face was pale, but (he) had a frank and bold look.
(5) There are more boys than girls here.
(6) The girls are cold. (To the girls it is cold.)
(7) He was driving a green Ford.
(8) I am taller than Siggi.
(9) He is cheerful and pleasant.
(10) The man is blind drunk.
(11) The day was hot but the night was cool.
(12) That is not true.

Exercise 10b

(1) Fjallið er hátt.
(2) Dalurinn er fallegur.
(3) Þetta er breiðasta gatan í bænum.
(4) Hún er fátæk eins og kirkjurotta.
(5) Gluggarnir í stofunni eru ekki oþnir.
(6) Hún er minni en hann.
(7) Ég er ekki hnugginn, en hún er mjög hnuggin.
(8) Veturinn er kaldasti tími ársins.
(9) Hann er duglegri en ég bjóst við.
(10) Húsið er grænt.
(11) Hún er yngri en hann.
(12) Við erum mjög þreyttir.

Exercise 11a

He is five feet eleven inches in height, forty-five years old, one hundred and eighty pounds in weight, with a light hat, a blue suit (clothes), and has a strange scar on his face. He was driving a green Austin.

Exercise 11b

Most of us sleep soundly for the first two hours, then the sleep is not at all deep for a while, until it becomes deep again for about two hours before we begin to get ready to wake up. This is the most usual.

Exercise 11c

Dag nokkurn í nóvember árið 1905 var lítill danskur drengur borinn úr skipinu Heimdal upp á hafnargarðinn í Ósló. Faðir hans hélt á honum á handleggnum. Á hafnargarðinum bauð þáverandi forsætis-ráðherra Norðmanna, Chr. Michelsen, þá feðga, velkomna. Þetta

var fyrst ferð litla prinsins til Noregs, nýja föðurlandsins. Fyrir
skömmu kom Ólafur V konungur til Kaupmannahafnar, og var það
í fyrsta sinn, sem hann kom til Danmerkur sem konungur Noregs.

Exercise 12a

One of the last portraits (that were) painted of Lill was painted by
Haukur Berg two years ago. Her tired-looking face was still beautiful
and mysterious. This portrait is a masterpiece, and tells (us) Lill's
life-story. Her life was short, but eventful (exciting).

Exercise 12b

A lady was getting a cake-mixture ready and took out from the
cupboard a paper-bag with (containing) eggs which her five-year-old
son had bought for her that morning. Quite unsuspecting, she broke
the egg in two, and then a very bad smell gushed up.
"Listen, Óli," she said to her son. "Did the shop-assistant say that
these eggs were fresh?"
"No, he just said that I should hurry home with them."

Exercise 12c

Golden Gate-brúin er lengsta hengibrú í heimi. Hún er yfir höfnina
í San Francisco í Kaliforníu. Brúargólfið er úr sementi og stáli.
Vegalengdin milli stöplanna er 1250 metrar og stærstu hafskip geta
siglt undir brúna.

Exercise 13a

Every year the express lift in the Empire State Building, the
tallest building in the world, takes an average of 500,000 tourists
from every country in the world up to the view-platform, from which
a magnificent view can be had of the (world-) city. There exist other
buildings which have a larger base (which cover a greater area), but
in no others are there so many offices so high above the ground (above
ground level). At times, when low clouds or fog hide the sun from
down in the streets, there is bright sunshine on the topmost floors,
and occasionally these "air-dwellings" look down on sun-drenched
clouds, which are pouring out their bowls of water on the people
going along the streets.

Exercise 13b

Afi sat við gluggann og horfði niður á götuna. Vera hjúkrunarkona hafði fært stólinn hans þangað. Venjulega stóð hann frammi
við dyrnar, en í dag vildi afi sitja við gluggann. Hann átti 79 ára
afmæli í dag. Hann leit á úrið sitt. Hálftími til hádegis. Þá mundi
hjúkrunarkonan færa honum matinn. Og hálftíma seinna gæti hann
átt von á póstinum. Í dag hlaut hann að fá heilmörg bréf.

Exercise 14a

Guðmundur was the name of a certain man, whom his contempor-
aries nicknamed (and called) "Spade". Men do not know clearly how
the name Spade (the Spade-name) first came into existence. Some

hold that he was as black as the ace of spades, but others think that it came about in this way—that he was regarded as somewhat superior and "stuck-up", for it is said that his self-esteem was exaggerated. Gudmundur was born at Bakkaseli in Fnjóskadal on the 21st January, 1815, and there he was brought up by his parents in great poverty.

Exercise 14b

"Hvernig líður konunni þinni, Palli?"
"O, stundum er hún betri og stundum er hún verri. En þegar hún er betri, finnst mér stundum, að hún sé betri þegar hún er verri."

Exercise 14c

Forstjórinn (við starfsmann, sem kemur of seint til vinnunnar): "Þér komið alltaf of seint. Vitið þér ekki hvenær við byrjum að vinna hérna?"
Starfsmaðurinn: "Nei, það eru alltaf allir byrjaðir að vinna þegar ég kem."

Exercise 15a

A short time ago I was going to listen to some poetry reading on the radio. It was a poet from Ísafjörður who was reading some new poems. When he had just begun to read (when he was new-begun to read), an aeroplane flew over the house with an awful noise, and it was impossible to hear anything on the radio while this lasted. Altogether this poetry reading was interrupted five times by planes. In order to enjoy readings or verses, though especially poems, not a word should be missed. We listeners here in Reykjavík, on the contrary, have no such good luck now. An airfield in the middle of the town is, quite simply, intolerable.

Exercise 15b

Nú skal ég lýsa þessu herbergi fyrir þér, því að það er mikils vert að þú fáir ljósa hugmynd um það. Þetta er aflangt herbergi með ljósbleikum þiljum. Á innri hlið herbergisins er gluggi, sem hægt er að opna. Fyrst hélt ég, að út um hann sæist aðeins í vegginn á næsta húsi, en ég frétti þó fljótlega annað. Maðurinn í innsta rúminu gat aðeins horft beint fram, eins og við hinir, því að hann var líka í gipsi frá hvirfli til ilja. Þrátt fyrir það gat hann séð á milli tveggja húsa. Þetta millibil gaf honum sýn á takmarkað svæði af iðandi lífi götunnar.

Exercise 16a

At first it seemed that no-one in the hotel was up and about. When she had waited for a while, the clerk appeared on the other side of the desk.
"Isn't there a man here by the name of Hansen?"
"Hansen?" He repeated the name, then picked up the list of hotel visitors and looked in it. A fair while elapsed without his finding the

name, and Gerd was beginning to be afraid that she had come too late—Siggi was gone. Suddenly the man looked up. "He is staying here," he said. "Room nr. 47."
"Would you please tell him that there is a girl here who wants to speak to him—she has a very urgent message."

Exercise 16b

Hann teygði sig eftir símanum, náði í samband og talaði við Sigga. "Hr. Hansen vill gjarnan fá að vita, hvað þér heitið," sagði hann. "Hann segir líka, að sé það einhver frá blöðunum, vilji hann ekki veita viðtal."
"Segið honum, að nafn mitt sé Andrésdóttir," sagði Gerður.
"Gjörið svo vel að bíða, hann kemur rétt strax," sagði maðurinn, er hann hafði skilað þessu til Sigga. "Þér getið beðið í litla salnum hérna—ég skal fylgja yður þangað." Maðurinn fylgdi henni upp á næstu hæð og vísaði henni inn í lítinn sal. "Þakka yður fyrir," sagði Gerður.

Exercise 18a

Yesterday two new infants' playgrounds were opened here in Reykjavík. These grounds are for children of two to five years of age, and one of them is at Faxaskjól and the other at Stakkahlíð. Reporters were invited to look at the playgrounds yesterday. Jónas Jónsson, Director of Education, informed (them) that three playgrounds had been opened in September, at Dúnhaga, Rauðalæk and Hlíðargerði. He said that the aim was to set up supervised infants' playgrounds in (all) the various districts of the town.

Exercise 18b

Vellirnir eru ætlaðir börnum tveggja til fimm ára og geta mæður og aðrir aðstandendur barnanna skilið þau eftir á þessum völlum; þar eru þau í öruggri gæslu og komast ekki út af vellinum sjálf. Börnin geta dvalizt þarna 2–3 stundir á dag fyrir og eftir hádegi. Það er tilskilið, að börnin séu ekki send nema þau séu frísk, og þau verði sótt, ef veður er mjög slæmt. Vellir þessir eru opnir kl. 9–12 f.h. og 2–5 e.h. Á laugardögum er aðeins opið til hádegis. Ekkert gjald er tekið fyrir gæsluna. Á síðustu árum hefur gæsluvöllum fjölgað mjög. Árið 1952 voru gæsluvellir fimm að tölu, en nú eru þeir fimtán að tölu.

Exercise 19a

At midday yesterday the British destroyer "Diana" came into Patreksfjörður with a sick marine. The warship lay off the town, and the ship's doctor accompanied the sick man ashore in a small boat. There Dr. Björn Sigvaldason received the youth, who is called Smith and is eighteen years old. He had had an appendicitis attack during the night. Björn asked the ship's doctor whether he wished to be present during the operation, but he said he would leave the patient in the charge of the Icelandic doctor.

Exercise 19b

Í gær varð slys við Seyðisfjörð. Magnús Óskarsson fór að heiman frá sér (frá heimili sínu) áleiðis til Seyðisfjarðar upp úr hádegi í gær. Einum til tveimur klukkustundum síðar var farið að undrast um hann og var þá spurzt fyrir á Selstað, næsta bæ fyrir innan Brimnes. Kom þá í ljós að Magnús hafði ekki farið þar hjá. Hann fannst hjá eyðibýlinu Borgarhóli, milli bæjanna. Hafði dráttarvélin oltið út af vegarbrúninni, sem er þarna 1 til 2 metrar á hæð, og Magnús lent undir henni og beið bana.

Exercise 20a

It was once prescribed in Copenhagen that people were not allowed to sing or make other noise in the streets when they were going home at night. A few nights later, Haukur and (with) some of his companions were out in a street, and they were singing lustily. The night-watchman then came (up) and asked them whether they did not know (about) the new police-order (law), about men not being allowed to sing at night when they were going home. "Yes," said Haukur, "but there is still a long time to go till we go home." The night-watchman was taken aback, and while he was turning this explanation over in his mind, they continued on their way.

Exercise 20b

Hann var dálítið ringlaður, þegar hann vaknaði, og mundi ekki, hvar hann var staddur. Hann teygði út hendina eftir buxunum og skyrtunni, og þá fann hann, að hann var í þeim. Gegnum vegginn heyrði hann morgunhávaðann úr eldhúsinu og utan af torginu. Hann þurrkaði sér um munninn, strauk aftur hár sitt og stóð upp, dálítið stirður fyrst, en liðkaðist um leið og hann gekk fram að dyrunum. Næturvörðurinn var farinn, og sólin skein. Bærinn var vaknaður.

VOCABULARY SECTION: ENGLISH–ICELANDIC, ICELANDIC–ENGLISH

Introduction

THE following abbreviations are used:

acc.	accusative case.
adj.	adjective.
adv.	adverb.
conj.	conjunction.
dat.	dative case.
e-ð	*eitthvað* (something).
e-m	*einhverjum* (someone), masculine singular dative.
e-n	*einhvern* (someone), masculine singular accusative.
e-s	*einhvers* (someone, something), masculine and neuter singular genitive.
e-u	*einhverju* (something), neuter singular dative.
f.	feminine noun.
gen.	genitive case.
m.	masculine noun.
n.	neuter noun.
p.p.	past participle.
pl.	plural.
prep.	preposition.
pron. dem.	demonstrative pronoun.
pron. pers.	personal pronoun.
pron. poss.	possessive pronoun.
s.o.	someone.
s.t.	something.
v. aux.	auxiliary verb.
v.i.	intransitive verb.
v. impers.	impersonal verb.
v. reflex.	reflexive verb.
v.t.	transitive verb.

Note that strong masculine nouns are given in the Icelandic–English part with the genitive singular and nominative plural forms in brackets. These forms are not given in the English–Icelandic section unless the noun appears only in that section: otherwise, look the noun up in the Icelandic–English part to ascertain its main forms.

Strong feminine nouns ending in *-ar* in the nominative plural have this noted in brackets. If the nominative plural is *-ir*, however, no note of this is made. Further, the genitive ending *-ar* is generally not given, unless the root vowel undergoes a change.

138

Strong neuter nouns are given only in the nominative singular. Note that the last component of compound nouns indicates the gender, e.g., *klukkustund* is a feminine word because *stund* is feminine. Adjectives are given in the masculine form only. Verbs are indicated as follows:

kalla (*a*); *læra* (*i*); *halda* (*held*; *hélt*, *héldum*; *haldinn*). In the first instance, the bracketed (*a*) indicates that the verb belongs to the weak conjugation, first (regular) group, and the parts are thus: present, *kalla*; past indic., *kallaði*; past. participle, *kallaður*. In the second case the (*i*) shows that this verb belongs to weak conjugation but not in the first group. Thus: *læri*, present indic.; past, *lærði*; past participle, *lærður*. In the third case, the verb belongs to the strong variety, and the parts given are the first person singular, present indic. (held); the first person singular, past indicative, and the first person plural, past indicative (*ég hélt*, *við héldum*); and the past participle (or supine), (*haldinn*).

Lastly, note that a number of prefixes have been included, some of which are not normally listed as actual prefixes. This has been done when many words begin thus, to avoid having to repeat large numbers of words modified by the prefix.

ENGLISH–ICELANDIC VOCABULARY

A

abandon *v.t.* yfirgefa; hætta við; leggja niður (*habit, etc.*).
ability *m.* hæfileiki; *m.* dugnaður (-ar); *f.pl.* gáfur; *to the best of his ability*, eins vel og hann get.
able *adj.* fær (um); duglegur; *be able*, geta.
aboard *adv.* úti á skipi, um borð; út á skip.
about *prep.* um, umhverfis; við, hjá; hér um bil (*approx.*); *be about to*, ætla að fara að; *think about*, hugsa um; *adv.* um, kringum; hér um bil; hringinn í kring; *bring about*, orsaka; *come about*, verða.
above *prep. & adv.* yfir; (*adv.*) uppi; fyrir ofan; (*more than*) fram yfir, meir en; *above all*, umfram allt.

abroad *adv.* erlendis; út, úti; *go abroad*, fara utan.
abruptly *adv.* snögglega.
absence *f.* fjarvera; *m.* skortur; *f.* vöntun (vantanir).
absent *adj.* fjarverandi.
absolute *adj.* fullkominn, algjör.
absolutely *adv.* fullkomlega, algjörlega; alveg.
abuse *v.t.* skamma (swear); nota ranglega, misbeita (*misuse*); *f.pl.* skammir (bad words); *f.* misbeiting (-ar).
accent *m.* framburður (-ar, -ir) (*good, bad, foreign*); *f.* áherzla; *n.* áherzlumerki.
accept *v.t.* taka við; þiggja.
accident *n.* slys; *n.* óhapp.
accidentally *adv.* af tilviljun.
accommodation *n.* húsrúm.
accompany *v.t.* fylgja.
according to *adv.* samkvæmt, eftir.

accordingly *adv.* þess vegna; eftir því.

account *m.* reikningur (-s, -ar); *f.* skýrsla (*report*); *turn to account*, færa sér í nyt; *on account of*, sökum, sakir, vegna; *on no account*, fyrir engan mun; *take into account*, taka til greina; *not to take into account*, reikna ekki með; *v.t.* account *for*, skýra.

accountant *m.* reikningsmaður; reikningshaldari; bókari.

accustom *v.t.* venja (við).

accustomed *adj.* vanur (*used*); venjulegur (*customary*); *be accustomed to*, vera vanur að gera e-ð; *become accustomed to*, venja sig á.

ace *m.* ás (-s, -ar) (*cards*).

ache *m.* verkur (-jar, -ir); *v.i.* verkja.

across *adv. & prep.* yfir, þvert yfir.

act *v.i.* framkvæma; leika (*on stage, etc.*); vera (*as*); breyta eftir (*upon*). *n.* verk *f.* athöfn; *n.pl.* (*law*); *m.* þáttur (-ar, þættir) (*theatre*).

active *adj.* starfsamur, framtakssamur, snarpur; (*gram.*) germynd.

address *n.* heimilisfang; *f.* utanáskrift (*on letter*); *n.* ávarp (*speech*). *v.t.* skrifa utan á (*letter*); ávarpa (*speech*).

adrift *adv.* á reki, út í bláinn.

advertise *v.t. & i.* auglýsa (eftir).

aerodrome *m.* flugvöllur.

aeroplane *f.* flugvél.

afraid *adj.* hræddur (við); *I'm afraid* (*deprec.*), því miður.

after *adv.* síðar; *prep.* eftir, vegna; *after all*, þegar allt kemur til alls.

again *adv.* aftur, að nýju, á hinn bóginn; *again and again*, hvað eftir annað; *now and again*, við og við.

age *f.* öld; *m.* aldur; *of age*, full-

veðja; 5 *years of age* (*aged*), fimm ára gamall.

agent *m.* umboðsmaður (*representative*).

ago *adv.* fyrir; *twenty years ago*, fyrir tuttugu árum; *long ago*, fyrir löngu; *a short time ago*, fyrir skömmu.

agree *v.i.* samþykkja; koma sér saman (um).

air *n.* loft; *m.* svipur; *n.* útlit (*look*).

alive *adv.* lifandi, á lífi.

all *adj.* allur; *all of them*, þeir allir; *all my life*, alla ævi mína. *adv. all at once*, allt í einu; *all over the place*, alls staðar; *not at all*, alls eigi; *all but*, næstum.

allow *v.t.* játa, leyfa, kannast við.

almost *adv.* næstum, hér um bil.

alone *adj.* aleinn, einn.

along *prep.* langs með, fram með. *adv.* áfram; *along with*, ásamt; *all along*, alltaf.

already *adv.* nú þegar.

also *adv.* einnig, líka.

although *conj.* þó að, þótt.

altogether *adv.* alveg.

always *adv.* ávallt, alltaf.

among *prep.* á milli, á meðal, meðal.

anchor *n.* akkeri.

and *conj.* og.

anger *f.* reiði.

annoy *v.t.* ónáða, angra (a).

another *pron.* annar.

answer *n.* svar. *v.t. & i.* svara.

any *pron.* nokkur, neinn.

anybody *pron.* hver sem vera skal; nokkur, neinn; sérhver.

anything *pron.* nokkuð. neitt; hvað sem er.

anywhere *adv.* nokkurstaðar, nokkurs staðar; neinstaðar.

appear *v.i.* koma í ljós; koma út (*book*); virðast: *it appears to me*, mér virðist.

appearance *m.* svipur (*look, face*); *n.* útlit (*look*); koma; útkoma (*of book*).

appetite f. matarlyst, lyst.

apple n. epli; *apple of the eye*, augasteinn.

arm m. handleggur; m.

around prep. í kringum, umhverfis; adv. í kring.

arrive v.i. koma (til).

art f. list; *the fine arts*, fagrar listir.

artist m. listamaður; m. listmálari.

as adv. & conj. eins, svo; *as . . . as . . .* (eins) . . . eins og; *as soon as*, jafnskjótt sem; *as yet*, enn; *as long as*, svo lengi sem; *as far as*, allt til.

ask v.i. & t. spyrja (*a person, a question*), biðja (um); *ask for*, krefjast (*demand*); bjóða (*invite*).

asleep adv. í svefni, sofandi; *fall asleep*, sofna.

at prep. á, að, hjá, í, til, um, við.; *at first*, í fyrstu; *at last*, loks, að lokum; *at home*, heima; *at school*, í skóla; *at once*, strax; *at work*, við vinnu; *at a low price*, við lágu verði.

aunt f. föður (*or*) móðursystir.

average n. meðaltal; *on an average*, að meðaltali.

avoid v.t. forðast, komast undan.

away adv. í burtu, af stað; *away from home*, að heiman; *go away*, fara í burtu; *throw away*, fleygja burt; *straight away*, tafarlaust.

awkward adj. klaufalegur, klunnalegur, ófimur.

B

baby n. brjóstbarn, ungbarn.

back n. bak m. (-jar, -ir) hryggur; n. stólbak (*of chair*); m. kjölur (*book*); *turn one's back on*, snúa baki við; *back of the hand*, handarbak. adv. aftur, aftur á bak, til baka.

bad adj. slæmur, vondur, illur.

bag m. poki; m. (-a, -ar) sekkur;

f. taska; *travelling-bag*, ferðataska.

bake v.i. & t. baka, bakast.

bald adj. sköllóttur.

ball m. hnöttur (hnattar, hnettir) (*globe, sphere*); f. kúla; m. dansleikur, ball (*dance*); *football*, fótbolti, fóthnöttur.

bank m. banki; m. bakki (*of river*); *banknote*, m. bankaseðill.

bar v.t. loka; banna (*forbid*). f. (málm) stöng; n. sker (*in sea*); n. drykkjarsöluborð; *barman*, veitingamaður.

bare adj. ber, nakinn.

bath n. bað; f. laug; n. baðker.

bay m. fjörður, flói.

be v. aux. vera; verða; *that's to say*, það er að segja; *I am writing*, ég er að skrifa.

beach f. strönd; f. fjara (fjöru, fjörur).

bear m. björn. v.t. bera; þola (*stand*); fæða (*a child*); *be born*, fæðast; *bear in mind*, hafa í huga; *bear up*, harka af sér.

beard n. skegg.

beat v.t. sigra (*sport, etc.*); berja (*drum, carpet, etc.*); slá (*time, etc.*); *beat about the bush*, vera með vafninga.

beautiful adj. fagur, fallegur.

because conj. af því að, vegna, sakir, sökum.

become v. aux. verða.

bed n. rúm; n. beð (*garden*); *go to bed*, fara í rúmið; *bedroom* n. svefnherbergi.

beef n. nautakjöt.

beer n. öl.

before prep. fyrir, fram fyrir, fyrir framan; *before long*, fyrr en síðar; adv. áður, fyrr, á undan; conj. áður en, fyrr en.

begin v.i. & t. byrja (á), hefja; *beginning* n. byrjun.

behind prep. bakvið, á eftir, eftir; adv. á eftir, of seinn; *far behind*, langt að baki.

142 ICELANDIC

believe *v.i. & t.* trúa (á); hyggja (*think*).
belong *v.t.* heyra til; *it belongs to him*, hann á það.
bend *v.t.* beygja, benda.
best *adj.* beztur; *best man*, svaramaður; *at best*, í mesta lagi.
bet *n.* veðmál; *f.* veðjun (-anir); *v.i. & t.* veðja.
better *adv.* betri, betur; *better late than never*, betra seint en aldrei.
between *adv. & prep.* (á) milli.
bicycle *n.* reiðhjól; *v.i.* fara á hjóli.
big *adj.* stór; digur, þykkur.
bird *m.* fugl.
bit *m.* biti; *m.* munnbiti; *f* ögn (agnar, agnir); *bit by bit*, smámsaman; *every bit as*, alveg eins og.
bite *v.t.* bíta.
black *adj.* svartur.
blind *adj.* blindur.
blood *n.* blóð; *in cold blood*, af ásettu ráði.
blue, *adj.* blár; *once in a blue moon*, örsjaldan.
boast *v.i.* gorta, raupa, grobba; *boastful*, montinn, montandi.
boat *m.* bátur.
body *m.* líkami; *n.* lík (*corpse*).
boil *v.i. & t.* sjóða, ólga.
bone *n.* bein.
book *f.* bók; *bookcase*, *m.* bókaskápur.
both *pron.* báðir, bæði; *conj. both . . . and . . .*, bæði . . . og . . .
bottle *f.* flaska.
boy *m.* drengur; *m.* piltur.
branch *f.* grein; *f.* kvísl.
brave *adj.* hugaður, hraustur.
bread brauð.
break *v.i. & t.* brjóta; brotna; slíta; slitna.
breath *m.* andi, andardráttur (-ar, -drættir).
bridge *f.* brú; *bridge* (*card game*).

bright *adj.* bjartur, skær; gáfaður (*clever*).
bring *v.t.* færa; flytja; koma með; *bring up*, ala upp.
brother *m.* bróðir.
brown *adj.* brúnn.
build *v.t.* byggja.
burn *v.i. & t.* brenna.
business *n.* starf; *m.* starfi; *f.* atvinna; *f.* iðn (*work, job*); *m.* kaupskapur (-ar); *f.* kaupsýsla; *businessman*, kaupsýslumaður; *n.* erindi (*errand*); *f.* verzlun (*commerce*); *business deal, n.* kaup.
busy *adj.* starfsamur, önnum kafinn; *be busy*, eiga annríkt.
but *conj.* en; nema (*except*); aðeins (*only*); án (*but for*).
butcher *m.* slátrari.
butter *n.* smjör.
buy *v.t.* kaupa.
by *prep. & adv.* á (*by day, etc.*); af (*written by*); ekki seinna en (*not later than*); að nafni (*by the name of*); með; hjá; eftir.

C

cake *f.* kaka.
calf *m.* kálfur; *m.* kálfi (*of the leg*).
call *n.* kall. *v.i. & t.* kalla; kalla á; nefna (*name*); heimsækja (*call on*).
calm *adj.* rólegur.
camera *f.* ljósmyndavél.
can *f.* kanna; *f.* dós; *aux. v.* geta.
capable *adj.* fær um (*of*).
capital *f.* höfuðborg (*town*); *m.* upphafsstafur (*letter*).
captain *m.* skipstjóri, kapteinn.
car *m.* bíll; *f.* bifreið.
care *f.* umhyggja; *f.* umsjón; *take care of*, annast. *v.i.* kæra sig (*um, about*); *care for*, þykja vænt um.
carpet *n.* gólfteppi.
carry *v.t.* bera; flytja.

cat *m.* köttur; *rain cats and dogs*, hellirigning.
catch *v.t.* grípa, taka til fanga (*arrest*); ná í (*train, etc.*); ná tökum á (*catch hold of*); sýkjast (*illness*).
ceiling *n.* loft í húsi.
centre *f.* miðja; *m.* miðpunktur; þungamiðja (*centre of gravity*).
certain *adj.* viss; ákveðinn; *to a certain extent*, að vissu leyti.
certainly *adv.* vissulega.
chair, *m.* stóll.
chance *f.* tilviljun; *n.* tækifæri (*opportunity*); af tilviljun, *by chance*.
change *f.* breyting (-ar); *n.* skipti; *m.pl.* smápeningar (*money*). *v.t.* breyta; breytast.
cheap *adj.* ódýr.
cheese *m.* ostur.
chief *m.* foringi, höfðingi; *adj.* fremstur; helztur; aðal-, megin-.
child *n.* barn.
choose, *v.t.* velja, kjósa.
Christmas *n.* jól.
church *f.* kirkja.
cigarette *m.* vindlingur, (-s, -ar); sígaretta.
cinema *m.* bíó.
class *m.* flokkur; *f.* stétt (*people*); *m.* bekkur (*of school*); *in a class by itself*, sér í flokki.
clean *adj.* hreinn; hreinlegur; þrifinn. *v.t.* hreinsa; fága; bursta.
clear *adj.* bjartur; skír; skýr; ljós. *v.t.* hreinsa; taka af borði (*table*); *clear the throat*, ræskja sig.
clever *adj.* duglegur; röskur; gáfaður.
climate *n.* loftslag, veðurlag.
climb *v.t. & i.* klífa.
clock *f.* klukka.
close *adj.* nálægt; náinn (*friend*); nízkur; nákvæmur; *m.* endir, endi; *v.t.* loka; ljúka við; gera enda á.

clothes *n.pl.* föt; *n.pl.* klæði.
cloud *n.* ský.
coast *f.* strönd.
coat *m.* frakki.
coffee *n.* kaffi.
cold *adj.* kaldur; mér er kalt, *I feel cold*; *m.* kuldi (*weather*); *n.* kvef (*chill*).
colour *m.* litur.
come *v.i.* koma; komast; heimsækja (*visit*); *come to an end*, hætta; *come to nothing*, verða að engu.
comfortable *adj.* þægilegur.
common *adj.* vanalegur, hversdagslegur (*usual, ordinary*); almennur; sameiginlegur (*belonging to each*); *common sense*; *f.* heilbrigð skynsemi; venjulegur; dónalegur (*vulgar*).
company *n.* félag; *m.* félagsskapur.
complete *adj.* fullkominn, heill, allur.
condition *m.* skilmáli; *n.* skilyrði; *n.* ástand (*state*); *on condition that*, með því skilyrði.
continue *v.t. & i.* halda áfram.
conversation *n.* samtal.
cook *m. & f.* matreiðslu/maður, kona; *f.* eldastúlka. *v.i.* elda, matbúa, matreiða.
cost *n.* verð; *m.* kostnaður. *v.i.* kosta.
cough *m.* hósti; *v.i.* hósta.
count *v.t. & v.i.* telja; reikna.
country *n.* land; *n.* hérað; *f.* sveit (*countryside*).
cow *f.* kýr.
crew *f.* áhöfn (áhafnar, áhafnir).
cry *n.* kall; *m.* grátur (-s); *v.i.* kalla; æpa (i) (*shout*); gráta (*weep*).
cup *m.* bolli.
cut *v.t.* skera; klippa (i).

D

dance *m.* dans; *v.i.* dansa (a).
danger *f.* hætta.
dangerous *adj.* hættulegur.

dark *adj.* dimmur, myrkur.
daughter *f.* dóttir.
day *m.* dagur.
dead *adj.* dauður, dáinn.
deaf *adj.* daufur.
dear *adj.* dýr (*expensive*); kær.
deep *adj.* djúpur; dimmur (*colour, voice*).
Denmark *f.* Danmörk.
destroy *v.t.* eyða (i).
develop *v.t.* láta þróast; framkalla (*photo*); *develop into,* verða.
die *v.i.* deyja.
different *adj.* ólíkur.
dinner *m.* miðdegisverður (-ar, ir).
dirty *adj.* óhreinn.
disappear *v.i.* hverfa.
disappointment *n.pl.* vonbrigði.
discover *v.t.* finna.
dish *m.* diskur; *n.* fat; *m.* réttur (-ar, -ir) (*food*).
district *n.* hérað; *f.* sveit.
do *v.t.* gera.
doctor *m.* læknir.
dog *m.* hundur.
door *f.pl.* dyr.
doubt *m.* efi; *be in doubt,* vera í efa; *doubtless,* efalaust.
down *adv.* niður.
draw *v.t.* teikna (a); draga.
dream *m.* draumur; *v.i.* dreyma.
dress *v.t.* klæða; *v.i.* klæða sig.
drink *v.t.* drekka.
drop *v.t.* láta falla; missa.
drown *v.t.* drekkja; *be drowned,* drukkna.
drunk *adj.* drukkinn, fullur; *dead drunk,* blindfullur.
dry *adj.* þurr.

E

each *pron.* hver; *each other,* hver annan.
ear *n.* eyra.
early *adv.* snemma.
east *n.* austur.
easy *adj.* auðveldur.
eat *v.i.* & *v.t.* éta, eta.

edge *f.* rönd (randar, rendur); *f.* brún (-ir); *f.* egg.
electric *prefix* rafmagns-.
else *adv.* annars; (*otherwise*) að öðrum kosti; *elsewhere,* annars staðar.
empty *adj.* tómur; auður.
end *m.* endi; *v.t.* & *v.i.* enda.
enemy *m.* óvinur.
England *n.* England.
English *adj.* enskur.
enough *adv.* nógu; *adj.* nógu sb nóg.
enter *v.i.* & *v.t.* ganga inn í.
envelope *n.* bréfumslag.
especially *adv.* einkum; sérstaklega.
Europe *f.* Evrópa.
even *adj.* jafn, flatur, sléttur; *adv.* jafnvel; *v.t.* jafna (a).
evening *n.* kvöld; *this evening,* í kvöld.
ever *adv.* ávallt; alltaf; (*some time*) nokkurn tíma.
exact *adj.* nákvæmur.
example *n.* dæmi; *for example,* til dæmis.
excellent *adj.* ágætur.
except *prep.* nema; *v.t.* undanskilja.
excite *v.t.* æsa.
explain *v.t.* skýra.
export *m.* útflutningur (-s, -ar); *v.t.* flytja út vöru.
eye *n.* auga; *eyesight, f.* sjón.

F

face *n.* andlit; *m.* svipur; *face to face,* augliti til auglitis.
fair *adj.* fagur, bjartur; ljós (*light*); hreinn.
fall *v.i.* detta; falla; *fall asleep,* sofna; *fall in love,* verða ástfanginn.
family *f.* fjölskylda; *a large family,* stór barnahópur.
far *adv.* langt; *far away,* langt í burtu; *adj.* fjarlægur.
farm *f.* jörð; *n.* býli; *m.* bær.
fast *adj.* fljótur.

fat *adj.* feitur.
father *m.* faðir.
few *adj.* fáir; nokkrir.
field *n.* tún; *m.* völlur.
fight *v. reflex.* berjast við e-n, *against someone.*
fill *v.t.* fylla.
film *m.* bíóleikur.
find *v.t.* finna, hitta.
finger *m.* fingur.
finish *v.i. & v.t.* enda (a); *v.t.* ljúka við að gera e-ð.
fire *m.* eldur.
first *adj.* fyrstur; fremstur; *first-rate,* fyrsta flokks.
fish *m.* fiskur; *v.t. & v.i.* fiska (a).
flat *f.* íbúð; *adj.* flatur.
floor *n.* gólf; *(storey) n.* loft, *f.* hæð.
flower *n.* blóm.
fly *f.* fluga; *v.i.* fljúga.
fog *f.* þoka.
fond *be fond of,* þykja gott að gera e-ð; þykja vænt um.
fool *m.* bjáni; *n.* flón; *foolish,* fíflslegur.
foot *m.* fótur; *(measure) n.* fet.
for *prep.* fyrir; *for five years,* í fimm ár; *for sale,* til sölu.
foreign *adj.* erlendur; *Foreign Minister,* utanríkisráðherra.
forget *v.t.* gleyma.
forgive *v.t.* fyrirgefa.
France *n.* Frakkland.
French *adj.* franskur; *f.* franska *(language).*
fresh *adj.* ferskur; nýr.
friend *m.* vinur; *f.* vinkona; *friendly, adj.* vingjarnlegur.
from *prep.* frá.
front *f.* framhlið; *in front of,* fyrir framan.
fruit *n.* aldin.
full *adj.* fullur.
funny *adj.* kátlegur, skringilegur; *(odd)* skrítinn.

G

game *m.* leikur; *(cards) n.* spil.
garden *m.* garður.

general *m.* hershöfðingi; *adj.* almennur, algengur; *in general,* yfirleitt.
German *adj.* þýzkur; *(language) f.* þýzka.
Germany *n.* Þýzkaland.
get *v.t.* fá; *(become)* verða; *get up,* fara á fætur.
girl *f.* stúlka.
give *v.t.* gefa.
glass *n.* glas; *n.* gler; *(mirror), m.* spegill; *(spectacles), n.pl.* gleraugu.
glove *m.* hanzki.
go *v.i.* fara; *(become)* verða; *(leave)* fara burtu.
God *m.* Guð.
gold *n.* gull; *adj.* úr gulli.
good *adj.* góður.
government *f.* landstjórn.
grandfather *m.* afi.
grandmother *f.* amma.
grass *n.* gras.
great *adj.* stór; mikill.
green *adj.* grænn.
grey *adj.* grár.
ground *n.* jarðvegur *(soil); n.* land; *f.* jörð.
grow *v.i.* vaxa, gróa; *v.t.* rækta (a).

H

habit *m.* vani.
hair *n.* hár.
half *m. & adj.* hálfur.
hand *f.* hönd; *handkerchief,* m. klútur.
happen *v.i.* henda; vilja til.
happy *adj.* sæll; glaður.
hard *adj.* harður; *(difficult)* erfiður, örðugur.
hardly *adv.* varla, tæplega.
have *v.i.* eiga; *v. aux.* hafa; *have s.t. done,* láta gera e-ð.
he *pron.* hann; *he who;* sá, sem.
head *n.* höfuð.
hear *v.t.* heyra; hlusta á.
heart *n.* hjarta.
heavy *adj.* þungur.
help *v.t.* hjálpa; *helpful, adj.* hjálpsamur.

her *pron.* hana, henni, hennar.
here *adv.* hér; (*to*) *here*, hingað.
high *adj.* hár.
hill *f.* hæð.
hit *v.t.* hitta, slá; *n.* högg.
hold *v.i.* & *v.t.* halda, halda á; hafa á hendi.
holiday *m.* helgidagur; frídagur.
home *n.* heimili; *adv.* heim; *at home*, heima.
honest *adj.* ráðvandur.
hope *v.i.* vona; *f.* von; *hopeless*, *adj.* vonlaus.
horse *m.* hestur; *n.* hross.
hot *adj.* heitur.
hour *f.* klukkustund; *m.* tími.
house *n.* hús.
how *adv.* hvernig; *however*, samt sem áður.
hunger *n.* hungur; *m.* sultur (-ar); *hungry*, hungraður, soltinn; mig hungrar, *I'm hungry*.
husband *m.* bóndi, eiginmaður; *husband and wife*, *n.pl.* hjón.

I

I *pron.* ég.
ice *m.* ís; *ice-cream*, rjómaís.
Iceland *n.* Ísland; *Icelander*, *m.* Íslendingur; *Icelandic* *adj.* íslenzkur; *f.* íslenzka (*language*).
idea *f.* hugmynd.
if *conj.* ef.
ill *adj.* veikur; sjúkur.
in *prep.* í; á; *in Icelandic*, á íslenzku; *adv.* inni í, inni, heima (*at home*).
inhabitant *m.* íbúi.
instead *adv.* í staðinn; *instead of doing*, *s.t.*, í staðinn fyrir að gera e-ð.
intelligent *adj.* skynugur.
iron *n.* járn; (*for ironing*) pressu-járn; *v.i.* & *v.t.* pressa.
island *f.* ey.
Italian *adj.* ítalskur; ítalska *f.* (*language*).
Italy *f.* Ítalía

J

job *f.* vinna, atvinna; lausa-vinna; *n.* viðvik.
jolly *adj.* glaður, kátur; *adv.* mjög, ákaflega.
jump *v.i.* & *v.t.* hoppa; stökkva.
just *adj.* réttvís, réttlátur; *adv.* aðeins, alveg, einmitt; *just now*, rétt áðan.

K

key *m.* lykill.
kind *f.* tegund; *all kinds of*, alls konar; *this kind of*, þess konar; *adj.* góður, vingjarnlegur.
king *m.* konungur.
kiss *v.t.* kyssa; *v. reflex.* kyssast; *m.* koss (*pl.* -ar).
kitchen *n.* eldhús.
knee *n.* hné; kné.
knife *m.* hnífur.
knock *v.t.* slá; berja að dyrum, *knock at the door*.
know *v.i.* & *v.t.* vita; þekkja; kunna (*how to do s.t.*).
knowledge *f.* þekking.

L

lady *f.* kona; frú.
lamp *m.* lampi.
land *n.* land; *f.* jörð (*earth*).
language *n.* mál, tungumál.
large *adj.* stór.
last *adj.* síðastur; yztur; *last night*, í gærkvöldi; *v.i.* haldast, standa.
late *adj.* seinn; of seinn.
laugh *m.* hlátur; *v.i.* hlæja (að, at).
lay *v.t.* leggja, setja.
lazy *adj.* latur.
learn *v.t.* læra; (*get to know*) frétta, fá að vita.
least *adj.* minnstur; *at least*, að minnsta kosti; *adv.* sízt, minnst.
leave *v.t.* skilja eftir, skilja við, fara frá; hætta, (*leave off*); fara af stað (*depart*).

left *adj.* vinstri; *v. be left*, vera eftir.

leg *m.* leggur.

length *f.* lengd.

let *v.t.* láta, leyfa; (*rooms*) leigja út.

letter *m.* bókstafur (-s, -ir); *n.* bréf.

lie *f.* lygi; *v.i.* ljúga (*untruth*); *v.i.* liggja.

life *n.* líf; *f.* æfi; *f.* æfisaga (*lifetime, biography*).

light *n.* ljós; *f.* birta; *adj.* ljós, bjartur; léttur; *v.t. & v.i.* kveikja (i); lýsa (*a lamp*).

like *adj.* líkur; *v.t.* líka; *v. reflex.* geðjast (a); mér geðjast að e-u, *I like s.t.*

live *v.i.* lifa; (*dwell*) búa.

long *adj.* langur.

look *m.* svipur; útlit; *v.i.* horfa, sjá, líta.

lose *v.t.* tapa, missa.

love *f.* ást; *m.* kærleikur; *f.* elska; *v.t.* elska.

low *adj.* lágur.

M

mad *adj.* vitlaus; óður.

make *v.t.* gera; búa til; skapa; *make fun of*, gera gys að; *make money*, græða fé.

man *m.* maður.

many *adj.* margir.

marry *v.i.* giftast.

matter *n.* efni; *it doesn't matter*, það skiptir engu; *what's the matter?*, hvað gengur að?

may *v. aux.* má; *maybe*, kannske, ef til vill.

mean *v.t.* (*intend*) ætla; meina (*signify*); *adj.* (*stingy*) nízkur; *by this means*, þannig; *by no means*, alls ekki; *by means of*, með tilstyrk; hjálp.

meat *n.* kjöt.

milk *f.* mjólk; *it's no use crying over spilt milk*, ekki tjáir að sakast um orðinn hlut.

mind *m.* hugur; *n.* skap; *f.* lund;

f. (*opinion*) skoðun; *change one's mind*, skipta um skoðun; *I have half a mind to* ... mig hálflangar að ...; *be out of one's mind*, vera ekki með öllum mjalla; *make up one's mind*, ákveða sig; *to my mind*, að mínu áliti; *v.t.* (*be against*) vera á móti.

mine *pron.* minn. mín, mitt; *f.* náma (*mineral-mine*).

minute *f.* mínúta; *adj.* smár.

miss *f.* ungfrú; *v.t.* missa e-s, ná ekki í; sakna (*feel the lack of, absence of*); *be missing*, vanta, finnast ekki.

mistake *n.pl.* mistök; *v.t.* villast, misskilja.

modern *adj.* prefix, nútíðar-.

moment *n.* augabragð, augnablik.

money *m.pl.* peningar.

month *m.* mánuður.

moon *n.* tungl.

more *adj.* meiri, meira; fleiri; *adv.* meir, framar, fremur.

morning *m.* morgunn; *good morning*, góðan dag.

most *adj.* mestur; flestir; *adv.* mest; *most of all*, allra helzt; *most of us*, flest okkar.

mother *f.* móðir.

mountain *n.* fjall.

mouth *m.* munnur.

move *v.t.* hreyfa; hreyfast; flytja; flytjast.

much *adj.* mikill; *adv.* mjög.

music *f.* tónlist; *f.* sönglist.

must *v. aux.* (ég) verð, hlýt.

my *pron. poss.* minn, mín, mitt.

mysterious *adj.* leyndardómsfullur, dularfullur.

N

name *n.* nafn.

narrow *adj.* þröngur.

near *adj.* nálægur; nákominn; ná-; *v.t.* nálgast, koma nær.

necessary *adj.* nauðsynlegur.

neck *m.* háls.
need *f.* nauðsyn (-synjar); *if need be,* ef nauðsyn krefur; *v.t.* þurfa.
neither *adv. & conj.* hvorugur; *neither . . . nor . . .,* hvorki . . . né . . .
nervous *adj.* taugaveiklaður, taugaóstyrkur.
never *adv.* aldrei; *never before,* aldrei fyrr; *never more,* aldrei framar.
nevertheless *adv.* eigi (engu) að síður.
new *adj.* nýr; ferskur
news *f.* frétt.
newspaper *n.* dagblað.
next *adj.* næstur.
night *f.* nótt; *n.* kvöld.
no *adv.* nei; *adj.* enginn, ekkert; *no one,* enginn.
noise *m.* hávaði.
noisy *adj.* hávær.
north *n.* norður; *adj.* norður; *adv.* í norður.
Norway *m.* Noregur (-s).
Norwegian *adj.* norskur; *m.* Norðmaður; *f.* norska (*language*).
nose *n.* nef.
not *adv.* ekki.
nothing *pron.* ekkert; *next to nothing,* varla nokkuð; *nothing but,* ekkert nema, ekki annað en.
now *adv.* nú; núna.
number *f.* tala.

O

occasionally *adv.* öðru hverju.
ocean *n.* haf.
of *pron.* af; um; úr; eftir; frá; *the battle of* (við).
off *adv.* burt.
often *adv.* oft.
old *adj.* gamall.
on *prep.* á; við; um; *on foot,* á fæti; *on purpose,* af ásettu raði; *later on,* síðar.
once *adv.* einu sinni; *all at once,*

allt í einu; *once again,* einu sinni enn.
one *pron.* einn; nokkur; einhver; maður, menn (*people*); *one another,* hvor (hver) annan; *everyone,* hver og einn.
only *adv.* aðeins; einungis; bara.
open *adj.* opinn; *v.t.* opna.
or *conj.* eða; *either . . . or . . .,* annaðhvort . . . eða . . .
other *adj.* annar; hinn; *otherwise,* annars.
out *adv.* út, úti; *be out,* vera úti; slokknaður (*not alight*); úr (*out of*); *out of breath,* móður; *out of sight, out of mind,* gleymt er, þá gleypt er.
over *prep.* yfir; ofan á; fyrir ofan; (*higher than*) hærra en; *all over the world,* um allan heim; *adv.* yfir um, úti; *over again,* á ný, einu sinni enn.
overcoat *m.* yfirfrakki.
own *pron.* eiginn; *v.t.* eiga; *own up,* játa.

P

page *f.* blaðsíða (*of book*).
paper *m.* pappír; (*sheet of paper*) pappírsblað; dagblað (*daily*).
parliament *n.* þing; (*Iceland*) Alþing; (*G.B.*) þjóðþing Breta.
part *m.* partur (-s, -ar); *m.* hluti; *v.t.* skipta; *part from someone,* skilja við e-n.
particular *adj.* sérstakur.
partly *adv.* sumpart, sumt.
pass *v.t. & v.i.* fara (ganga, aka) framhjá, yfir, áfram; (*of time*) líða (burt); (*exam*) standast (próf); *n.* (fjall-) skarð.
past *adj.* liðinn; fyrri; *prep.* úr, yfir, framhjá.
pay *v.t. & v.i.* borga, gjalda, greiða; *pay a call,* heimsækja; *pay a compliment,* hrósa.
pen *m.* penni.
people *n.* fólk; *f.* þjóð; *people say,* fólk segir.

person m. maður; f. persóna.

photograph f. ljósmynd, mynd.

pick v.t. plokka; reyta (i); pick up, taka upp; (gather) tína (i); pick pockets, stela úr vösum; pick out, velja.

picture f. mynd; n. málverk (painting); pl kvikmyndir; bíó.

piece m. moli; m. hluti; m. biti; n. stykki; break to pieces, brjóta sundur; piece of paper, n. pappírsblað; piece of advice, ráð.

place m. staður; in the first place, í fyrsta lagi; in place of, í staðinn fyrir; take place, eiga sér stað, bera við. v.t. setja, leggja.

plain f. slétta; adj. sléttur; (clear) augljós; (distinct) skýr; (colour) einlitur; (looks) ólaglegur.

plate m. diskur.

play v.i. leika; play the piano, leika á píanó; play cards, spila á spil; play for money, spila um peninga; play the fool, haga sér eins og flón; m. leikur, sjónleikur.

pleasant adj. skemmtilegur, gamansamur.

please v.t. gera e-m til geðs; geðjast; please do that, gerðu svo vel að gera það; yes, please; já, þakka þér fyrir.

pocket m. vasi.

point m. oddur (-s, -ar); point of view, n. sjónarmið; keep to the point, halda sér við efnið; in point of fact, satt að segja; be on the point of, vera rétt að því kominn; that is just the point, það er lóðið; v.t. benda (i)

policeman m. lögregluþjónn; police-station, f. lögreglustöð.

polite adj. hæverskur, hæversklegur; kurteis.

poor adj. fátækur; aumur (sore; unhappy); vesall (unhappy).

port m. hafnarbær; f. höfn; (side) bakborð (í skipi).

position f. staða (stöðu, stöður); afstaða; n. ástand.

possible adj. mögulegur.

post m. stólpi; (mail) m. póstur, v.t. setja bréf í póstinn; go to the post, fara með bréf í póstinn.

pound n. pund (weight and sterling).

prefer v.t. vilja eitt öðru fremur.

president m. forseti.

pretty adj. snotur; laglegur; adv. fremur, dável.

prevent v.t. hindra.

price n. verð; at a low price, lágu verði.

proud adj. dramblátur; stoltur; hreykinn.

pull v.t. draga; pull the leg, gera gys að; pull oneself together jafna sig.

push v.t. ýta (i), with dat.; hrinda (hrindi; hratt, hrundum; hrundið).

put v.t. setja, leggja, láta; put on, fara í föt; put on weight, fitna; put out the light, slökkva ljósið.

Q

queen f. drottning.

question f. spurning; ask a question, spyrja spurningar.

queue f. biðröð; v.i. queue up, skipa sér í biðröð.

quick adj. fljótur.

quiet adj. kyrr, kyrrlátur; rólegur, spakur; hægur; (peaceful) friðsamlegur.

quite adv. alveg.

R

radio n. útvarp.

railway f. járnbraut.

rain n. regn; f. rigning (-ar); v.i. rigna.

raincoat f. regnkápa.

raise v.t. reisa, lyfta, hefja.

rather *adv.* fremur, heldur.
reach *v.t.* rétta; ná í; komast (*arrive*).
read *v.i. & v.t.* lesa.
ready *adj.* tilbúinn, búinn til e-s; *get oneself ready*, búa sig.
real *adj.* raunverulegur, sannur (*true*); ekta (*genuine*).
really *adv.* sannarlega; í raun og veru.
reason *n.* vit; *lose one's reason*, missa vitið; *f.* skynsemd; *it stands to reason that*, það er augljóst að; *f.* ástæða, *f.* orsök.
receive *v.t.* taka á móti; fá; meðtaka.
recent *adj.* nýlegur.
record *f.* hljómplata (plötu, plötur) (*gramophone*); *f.* skrá (-r, -r); *have a good record*, hafa gott orð á sér.
red *adj.* rauður.
religion *f.* trú.
remain *v.i.* vera kyrr (*stay*); vera eftir (*be left over*).
remember *v.t.* muna, muna eftir; minnast.
reply *v.i.* svara; *n.* svar.
rest *m.* afgangur (*remainder*); *the rest*; það, sem eftir er; *the rest* (*people*); þeir, sem eftir eru; hinir; *f.* hvíld; *f.* ró; *at rest*, í ró; *v.i.* hvíla sig. hvílast.
return *v.i.* koma aftur; snúa aftur; *f.* afturkoma.
rich *adj.* ríkur.
ride *v.i. & v.t.* ríða, aka; fara (í lest, *by train*); *f.* reið.
right *adj.* réttur, beinn (*straight*); hægri (*side*); *be right*, hafa rétt; *adv.* rétt; *right away*, þegar í stað; *by rights*, með réttu.
ring *v.t.* hringja klukku; hljóma; *ring up*, hringja upp (í síma); *ring off*, hringja af (síma); *f.* hringing (-ar); *m.* hringur; *m.* baugur.

rise *v.i.* rísa upp; stíga upp, standa upp, fara á fætur.
river *f.* á.
road *m.* vegur.
rob *v.t.* ræna; stela frá; stela e-u frá e-m.
rock *m.* klettur; *n.* sker.
room *n.* herbergi; *dining-room*, borðstofa; *bedroom*, svefnherbergi; *n.* rúm (*space*).
rudder *n.* stýri.
run *v.i.* hlaupa; *run away*, strjúka; *run after*, hlaupa eftir; *run off*, hlaupa burt; *n.* hlaup.

S

sad *adj.* hnugginn, dapur; sorglegur (*unfortunate*).
safe *adj.* öruggur; *safe and sound*, óskaddaður.
sail *n.* segl; *v.i.* sigla; fara a stað.
sailor *m.* sjómaður.
salt *n.* salt; *adj.* saltur.
same *adj.* samur; *at the same time*, jafnframt.
sand *m.* sandur.
save *v.t. with dat.* bjarga; (*w.acc.*) frelsa; (*money*) spara, leggja peninga fyrir; *conj.* nema.
say *v.t.* segja; *that's to say*, það er að segja.
Scandinavian *adj.* skandinaviskur, norrænn.
school *m.* skóli; *go to school*, fara í skóla.
schoolteacher *m.* skólakennari; *f.* skólakennslukona.
Scottish *adj.* skozkur; (*language*) skozka.
sea *n.* haf; *m.* sjór; *at sea*, úti á sjó.
season *f.* árstíð.
seat *n.* sæti.
second *adj.* annar; *second class*, annars flokks; *f.* sekúnda (*of time*); *second-hand*, notaður.
see *v.t. & v.i.* sjá, skilja; *see to*,

líta eftir, sjá um; *I see*, ég skil.

seem *v. reflex.* sýnast, virðast; *it seems to me*, mér virðist.

seldom *adv.* sjaldan.

self *pron. dem.* sjálfur, *prefix*, sjálf-, sjálfs-.

sell *v.t.* selja.

send *v.t.* senda.

sense *n.* skyn, vit; *f.* greind; *f.* þýðing (-ar) (*meaning*); *common sense*, heilbrigð skynsemi; *in a sense*, að vissu leyti; *sensible, adj.* greindur, skynsamur.

separate *adj.* aðskilinn; sérstakur; *v.t.* greina í sundur; skilja.

set *v.t.* setja; *set eyes on*, sjá; *set in motion*, setja í hreyfingu; *set the fashion*, setja tízku; *the sun has set*, sólin er setzt; *set about* (*doing*), fara að; *set in*, byrja; *set out*, leggja af stað; *adj.* fastur; (*serious*) alvarlegur.

sex *n.* kyn; *sex-appeal, m.* kynþokki.

shall *v. aux.* munu, skulu.

shame *f.* skömm.

shape *f.* lögun; *m.* skapnaður (-ar); *n.* snið (*cut, pattern*).

sharp *adj.* hvass; beittur (*sharp-edged*).

she *pron. pers.* hún; *she who*; sú, sem.

sheep *f.* kind.

shine *v.i.* skína, ljóma.

ship *n.* skip.

shirt *f.* skyrta.

shoe *m.* skór.

shop *f.* búð.

shore *f.* strönd; *come ashore*, koma í land.

short *adj.* stuttur; skammur; (*in height*) lágur.

shorthand *f.* hraðritun.

shortly *adv.* bráðum, innan skamms; (*in few words*) í stuttu máli.

show *v.t.* sýna; *show off*, monta.

shut *v.t.* loka.

shy *adj.* fælinn; feiminn.

sick *adj.* sjúkur; *seasick*, sjósjúkur, sjóveikur; *be* (*feel*) *sick*, vera flökurt; *sick of doing s.t.*, leiður á að gera e-ð.

side *f.* hlið; *adv.* sideways, til hliðar; *adj.* frá hliðinni.

silver *n.* silfur; *adj.* úr silfri, silfur-.

since *adv. & conj.* úr því að, með því að (*seeing that, as*); *long since*, fyrir löngu; *since last year*, síðan í fyrra.

sing *v.t. & v.i.* syngja.

sink *v.i.* sökka; *v. reflex.* setjast (*sun*).

sister *f.* systir; *sister-in-law*, mágkona.

sit *v.i.* sitja; *sit down*, setjast.

skin *n.* skinn; *f.* húð.

skirt *n.* pils.

sky *n.* loft; *m.* himinn.

sleep *m.* svefn; *v.i.* sofa.

slow *adj.* hægur, seinn.

small *adj.* lítill, smár.

smile *v.i.* brosa; *n.* bros.

smoke *m.* reykur; *v.i.* reykja.

snobbish *adj.* montinn.

snow *m.* snjór; *v.i.* snjóa.

so *adv., conj.* svo; (*thus*) þannig; *so that*, svo að; *I hope so*, ég vona það; *so as to*, til þess að; *and so on*, o.s.frv.

soap *f.* sápa.

soft *adj.* mjúkur.

some *pron.* nokkur; einhver; *some* (*people*), sumir.

someone *pron.* einhver.

something *pron.* eitthvað, nokkuð.

sometimes *adv.* stundum.

son *m.* sonur.

song *m.* söngur; *n.* kvæði.

soon *adv.* bráðum, bráðlega; fljótt; *as soon as*, jafnskjótt sem.

sorry *adj.* hryggur, hryggilegur; *sorry* (*excuse me*), afsakið; *I*

am sorry (to hear) that ...,
það hryggir mig, að ...
sort *m.* flokkur; *nothing of the
sort*, ekkert því líkt; *all sorts
of*, alls konar; *that sort of, þess*
konar.
south *n.* suður; *adj.* suður-, suð-
lægur; *south-east*, suðaustur;
adj. suðaustur-; *south-west*,
suðvestur; *adj.* suðvestur-.
speak *v.i.* tala.
special *adj.* sérstakur.
speed *m.* hraði; *at full speed*, með
fullum hraða.
spell *v.t. & v.i.* stafa (a).
spend *v.t.* verja (peningum,
tíma).
spoon *f.* skeið; *tea-spoon*, teskeið;
dessert-spoon, ábætisskeið;
egg-spoon, eggjaskeið; *table-
spoon*, matskeið.
sport *f.* íþrótt; *sportsman*, íþróttamaður.
spring *v.i.* stökkva; *spring to the
feet*, stökkva á fætur; *n.* vor;
(jump) n. stökk; *(of machine)*,
f. fjöður (fjaðrar, fjaðrir).
square *n.* torg *(market-place, etc.)*;
adj. ferstrendur, ferhyrndur,
ferhyrnings-, fernings-, fer-.
stamp *n.* frímerki *(postage-
stamp)*; *v.i.* stappa *(with foot)*;
frímerkja.
stand *v.i.* standa; *v.t. (bear)* þola;
I can't stand him, ég þoli hann
ekki.
star *f.* stjarna (stjörnu, stjörnur);
(of screen) aðalleikari.
start *v.i.* leggja af stað; *v.t. & v.i.*
byrja; *start work*, hefja vinnu;
start up an engine, koma vél af
stað; *f.* byrjun.
stay *v.i.* dveljast; bíða; vera
kyrr *(stay behind)*.
steal *v.t.* stela.
steam *f.* gufa; *v.i.* gufa, rjúka.
steel *n.* stál.
steep *adj.* brattur.
steer *v.t. & v.i.* stýra, (i). *(v.t.
with dat.)*

step *n.* skref *(pace)*; *n.* stig; *step
by step*, skref fyrir skref; *flight
of steps*, *m.* stigi; *v.i.* stiga
skref; *step forward*, stíga fram;
step back, stíga aftur á bak.
stick *m.* stafur (-s, -ir); *v.t.* líma;
(bear) þola.
stone *m.* steinn.
stop *v.t.* stöðva (a); *stop work*,
hætta vinnu; *come to a stop*,
stanza; *full stop*, *m.* punktur
(-s, -ar).
storm *m.* stormur; *n.* óveður.
story *f.* saga.
straight *adj.* beinn.
street *f.* gata.
strike *v.t.* slá; *something strikes
me*, mér dettur nokkuð í hug;
v.i. gera verkfall; *n.* verkfall
(stoppage of work).
strong *adj.* sterkur.
study *n.* nám; *study of languages*,
tungumálanám; *f.* lesstofa *(of
headmaster, etc.)*; skrifstofa; *v.t.*
læra, nema; hugsa um e-ð;
study history, læra sögu.
stupid *adj.* heimskur; bjánalegur.
succeed *v.i.* koma á eftir *(come
after)*; takast, heppnast (að
gera e-ð, *in doing s.t.*).
such *adj.* slíkur; *such as*; sá sem,
þeir sem, slíkir sem; *pron.*
þvílíkur.
sudden *adj.* skyndilegur; snöggur.
sugar *m. & n.* sykur.
sun *m.* sól; *sun oneself*, sóla sig;
sunlight, sólarljós; *sunrise*,
sólaruppkoma; *sunset*, sól-
setur; *sunshine*, sólskin.
sure *adj.* viss; *feel sure*, þykjast
viss um; *be sure of*, vera viss
um; *surely*; sannarlega, vafalaust.
Sweden *f.* Svíþjóð.
Swedish *adj.* sænskur; *f.* sænska
(language).
sweet *adj.* sætur; *sweets*, *n.pl.*
sætindi; *sweetheart*, *m.* unnusti;
f. unnusta.
swim *v.i.* synda; *swim the Chan-*

nel, synda yfir Ermarsund; *n.* sund; *go for a swim*, fara að synda; *swimming-pool*, *f.* sundlaug (-ar).

T

table, *n.* borð.
take, *v.t.* taka; fara með (*go with*); grípa, fanga (*in hand*).
talk *v.i.* tala; *n.* tal, samtal.
tall *adj.* hár.
taste *v.t.* bragða, smakka; *v.i.* smakkast; *n.* bragð.
taxi *m.* leigubíll.
tea *n.* te; *teacup*, *m.* tebolli.
teach *v.t.* & *v.i.* kenna; *teacher*, *m.* kennari; *f.* kennslukona.
tear *n.* tár; *v.t.* rífa (slíta) í sundur.
telephone *m.* talsími, sími; *v.i.* tala í síma.
television *n.* sjónvarp.
tell *v.t.* segja, segja frá.
than *conj.* en, heldur en.
thank *v.t.* þakka; *no, thanks*; nei, þökk fyrir; *thanks*, *f.* þökk.
that *conj.* að, svo að; *adv.* það, svo; *pron. rel.* sem, er; *pron. demons.* sá (sú, það); þetta.
the *art.* hinn, hin, hið; (*after nouns*) -(i)nn, -(i)n, -(i)ð; the . . . the . . ., því . . . því . . . .
theatre *n.* leikhús.
then *adv.* þá; *now and then*, öðru hverju; *adj.* þáverandi.
there *adv.* þar, þarna; (*to there*) þangað; *there is*, það er.
therefore *adv.* þess vegna; fyrir því.
thick *adj.* þykkur, digur.
thin *adj.* þunnur; magur.
thing *m.* hlutur.
think *v.t.* (*intend*) ætla, hyggja; hugsa (um) (*about*).
thirsty *adj.* þyrstur; *I'm thirsty*, mig þyrstir.
this *pron.* þessi; *this morning*, í morgun.
thousand *f.* & *n.* þúsund.
through *prep.* gegnum; um;

fyrir; yfir; vegna (*by means of*).
tie *v.t.* binda, hnýta; *n.* slifsi, hálsbindi (wear); band.
till *prep.* til.
time *m.* tími; *f.* tíð; *what's the time?* hvað er klukkan?; *n.* sinn; *four times*, fjórum sinnum.
tin *f.* dós af (*of*); *n.* tin, blikk.
tip *m.* broddur (-s, -ar); *m.* oddur (-s, -ar); *finger-tip*, *m.* gómur (-s, -ar); *n.* þjórfé (*gratuity*); *give a tip*, gefa þjórfé; *v.t. with dat.* (*tilt*) halla; *v.t.* (*tip out*) hella (úr).
to *prep.* til; *to be*, að vera; *in order to*, til þess að.
today *adv.* í dag; (*nowadays*) nú á dögum.
toe *f.* tá.
together *adv.* saman; í senn (*at the same time*); ásamt (*together with*).
tomorrow *adv.* á morgun.
tongue *f.* tunga; *n.* tungumál.
tonight *adv.* í nótt; í kvöld.
too *adv.* of; (*also*) líka.
tooth *f.* tönn; *toothbrush*, *m.* tannbursti.
top *m.* toppur (-s, -ar).
towards *adv.* í áttina til, til.
town *m.* bær; *f.* borg.
tractor *f.* dráttarvél.
train *f.* lest.
translate *v.t.* þýða.
travel *v.i.* ferðast; *traveller*, *m.* ferðamaður.
trawler *m.* togari.
tree *n.* tré.
trouble *n.pl.* vandræði; *n.* ónæði; *f.* fyrirhöfn; *v.t.* gera ónæði, trufla, ónáða; *in trouble*, í vandræðum.
trousers *f.pl.* buxur; *a pair of trousers*, einar buxur.
true *adj.* sannur.
truth *m.* sannleikur (-s, -ar).
try *v.t.* & *v.i.* reyna; (*a case*)

rannsaka (mál); (a criminal)
yfirheyra (glæpamann); try on,
máta.
turn v.t. with dat & v.i. snúa;
turn a corner, fara fyrir horn;
(become) gerast; turn out (light)
slökkva.
twice adv. tvisvar.
typewriter f. ritvél.

U

ugly adj. ljótur.
umbrella f. regnhlíf (-ar).
un- prefix ó-.
uncle m. föður- (eða) móður-
bróðir.
under prep. undir; under the circumstances, eins og ástatt er;
under age, undir lögaldri.
understand v.t. skilja.
university m. háskóli.
unless conj. ef . . . ekki; nema.
up adv. upp; look up, líta upp;
get up, fara á fætur; come up to
s.o., koma til e-s; speak up,
tala hátt.
upstairs adv. uppi.
use f. notkun (-anir); n. gagn
(advantage); be of use, vera til
gagns; v.t. nota, beita; be used
to, vera vanur.
useless adj. gagnslaus.
usual adj. venjulegur.

V

vain adj. hégómlegur; (useless)
árangurslaus, fánýtur; in vain,
árangurslaust.
valley m. dalur.
various adj. ýmislegur.
vegetable n. grænmeti.
very adv. mjög.
view f. útsýn; (opinion) skoðun.
village n. þorp.
visit v.t. heimsækja, vitja; f.
heimsókn; pay a visit, heimsækja e-n.
visitor m. gestur.
voice f. rödd.
voyage f. ferð á sjó.

W

waist f. miðja.
wait v.i. bíða; keep waiting, láta
bíða.
wake v.t. vekja; v.i. vakna.
walk v.i. ganga.
wall m. veggur.
want v.t. vilja, vilja fá; (need)
þurfa.
warm adj. hlýr.
wash v.t. þvo; have a wash, þvo
sér.
watch v.t. horfa á; gæta e-s; n.
úr (clock).
water n. vatn.
wave f. bylgja; f. bára; f. alda;
v.i. veifa.
way f. leið; m. vegur; show the
way, vísa e-m leið.
weak adj. veikur; óstyrkur.
wear v.t. vera í fötum; (out)
slíta.
weather n. veður.
weak f. vika.
weigh v.t. vega; v.i. vera að
þyngd.
weight f. þyngd; in weight, að
þyngd.
well m. brunnur; adv. vel.
west n. vestur; adj. vestur-.
wet adj. votur.
what pron. hvað.
wheel n. hjól.
when adv. hvenær; conj. þegar.
where adv. hvar; (whither) hvert.
whether conj. hvort.
which pron. hver, hvor, hvort;
relative, sem; (and that) og það.
while conj. á meðan.
white adj. hvítur.
who pron. hver; relative, sem,
er.
whole adj. heill.
why adv. hvers vegna; hví.
wide adj. víður.
wife f. kona.
will v. aux. munu; skulu; ætla;
(desire) vilja; m. vilji.
win v.i. vinna, sigra; (get) fá.

wind *m.* vindur.
window *m.* gluggi.
wing *m.* vængur (-s, -ir).
wish *f.* ósk; *v.t.* óska (*with dat. & gen.*)
with *prep.* með.
without *prep.* án.
woman *m.* kvennmaður.
wonderful *adj.* dásamlegur.
wood *m.* skógur (*forest*); *n.* tré.
wool *f.* ull; *of wool*, úr ull.
word *n.* orð; *keep one's word*, halda loforð sitt.
work *n.* verk; *f.* vinna; *n.* starf; *v.i.* vinna.
world *m.* heimur.

worse *adj.* verri; *worst*, verstur; *adv.* ver.
worth *adj.* verður; *it's worth* . . . *ing*, það er þess vert að . . .
write *v.t. & v.i.* skrifa.
wrong *adj.* rangur.

Y

year *n.* ár; *leap year*, hlaupár; *this year*, þetta ár.
yellow *adj.* gulur.
yes *adv.* já; jú (*after a negative*).
yesterday *adv.* í gær.
yet *adv.* enn, ennþá.
young *adj.* ungur.
youth *f.* æska.

ICELANDIC–ENGLISH VOCABULARY

A

á *prep. with acc. & dat.* on, upon; in; at; by; of; about.
á (-r, -r) *f.* river, stream.
ábyrgð *f.* responsibility; liability; insurance; *á mína ábyrgð*, at my risk.
að *conj.* that; *þó að*, although; *því að*, for; *af því að*; as, because; *til þess að*, in order that; *svo að*, so that; *að skrifa*, to write; *það er að skilja*, that is to say; *með því að skrifa*, by writing.
að *prep. with dat.* to, up to; at; towards; against.
aðal- *prefix* main, principal, chief. *-áherzla*, main stress; *stræti*, main street.
aðallega *adv.* mainly, chiefly.
áðan *adv.* just now, a short time ago.
aðeins *adv.* only, just; but; merely.
aðfall *n.* flood tide, rising tide; *aðfall og útfall*, ebb and flow;

það er aðfall, the tide is coming in.
aðferð (-ar, -ir) *f.* conduct; method.
aðgreina (i) *v.t.* separate, distinguish (*e-ð frá e-u*, something from s.t.)
aðgæta (i) *v.t.* observe.
aðgætinn *adj.* careful, attentive; observant.
aðgæzla *f.* care, attention.
aðgæzlulaus *adj.* careless, negligent.
aðkall *n.* claim; *gera aðkall til e-s*, lay claim to s.t.
aðkoma *f.* arrival.
aðkominn *p.p.* from afar, alien.
aðkomumaður *m.* stranger.
aðsjáll *adj.* stingy, close-fisted.
aðstoð *f.* aid, help, assistance.
aðstoða (a) *v.t.* to assist, help; back up.
aðstoðarlaus *adj.* helpless.
áður *adv.* before, formerly, once; *áður en*, before; *áður en langt um líður*, before long.

af *prep.* *with dat;* by; off; of; with; from.

áfall *n.* heavy sea; damage; disaster, calamity; dew.

áfangi *m.* one day's journey; stage (of a journey).

afar- *prefix* very; *afarlítill;* tiny, very small.

áfátt *adj.* missing, wanting, deficient; *mikils er áfátt,* there is much lacking.

afbragð *n.* model, paragon.

afbragðsgóður *adj.* excellent; extremely good.

afbragðslegur *adj.* exceptional.

afbrigði *n.* exception; variation; variety (animals, plants).

afbrigðilegur *adj.* irregular.

afbrýði *n.* jealousy.

afbrýðissamur *adj.* jealous.

áfengi *n.* spirits, liquor; alcohol; strong drink.

áfengur *adj.* intoxicating; *áfengir drykkir,* alcoholic drinks.

affall *n.* outlet; *pl.* discount; *selja með afföllum,* sell at a discount.

afferma (i) *v.t.* unload.

afhenda (i) *v.t.* deliver.

afi *m.* grandfather.

afkasta (a) *v.t. with dat.* accomplish; perform; carry out, do.

afklæða (i) *v.t.* undress.

afkvæmi *n.* offspring.

afl *n.* physical strength; power, might.

afla (a) *v.t. with gen.* earn; gain; acquire. *v.t. with acc.* fish; *afla sér fjár og frægðar,* earn fame and fortune.

aflaga *f.* surplus; *hafa e-ð aflögu,* have a surplus of s.t., have s.t. to spare.

aflát *n.* stop, cessation; *án afláts;* non-stop, continuously.

afleggja *v.t.* leave off, abandon.

afleiðing *f.* result, consequence; *orsök og afleiðing,* cause and effect.

afleiðis *adv.* astray; *snúa e-m afleiðis,* lead s.o. astray.

afllaus *adj.* powerless; weak; faint.

aflóga *adj. indec.* worn out.

aflvana *adj. indec.* powerless; impotent.

afmæli *n.* anniversary; birthday.

afmælisdagur *m.* birthday.

afneita (a) *v.t. with dat.* deny; denounce.

áform *n.* intention; purpose, aim; project.

áforma (a) *v.t.* intend, propose, contemplate.

afráða *v.t.* decide; make up one's mind.

áfram *adv.* forward/s; *halda áfram;* keep on, go on, continue.

aftan (-s, aftnar) *m.* evening.

aftan *adv.* (from) behind; *aftan að,* from behind.

aftar *adv.* farther back.

aftari *adj.* back, after, hind.

aftna (a) *v. impers.* become evening.

aftur *adv.* back, again, back again; *aftur á bak,* backwards; *aftur á móti,* on the other hand; *fram og aftur,* to and fro; *kalla aftur,* call back; *koma aftur,* come back.

afturstafn *m.* stern (ship).

aga (a) *v.t.* punish.

agi *m.* discipline.

ágizkun (-anir) *f.* guess.

ágjöf *f.* heavy sea.

agn *n.* bait; *ganga á agnið,* swallow the bait.

agndofa *adj. indec.* thunderstruck, astounded.

agnúi *m.* drawback, snag, disadvantage; *það er aðeins einn agnúi á því,* there is just one snag.

ágóði *m.* profit; benefit; gain.

ágúst (-s) *m.* August.

ágæta (i) *v.t.* praise.

ágæti *n.* excellence; worth.

ágætlega adv. excellently.

ágætur adj. excellent, first-class, first-rate.

áhald n. instrument; tool; utensil.

áherzla f. stress, emphasis, accent; leggja áherzlu á, stress.

áherzlulaus adj. unstressed.

áhorfandi (-endur) m. onlooker, spectator.

áhrif n.pl. influence, effect.

áhrifssögn f. transitive verb.

áhugi m. zeal, eagerness, enthusiasm.

áhyggja f. anxiety; care; concern.

áhyggjufullur adj. anxious, worried (um, about).

aka (ek; ók; ekið) v.i. & t. with dat. drive, ride; aka seglum eftir vindi, sail with the wind; aka sér, shake oneself.

ákafast (a) v. reflex. be very angry, furious; be excited.

ákafi m. violence; zeal, enthusiasm.

ákafur adj. violent; hot; vehement; severe.

akkeri n. anchor; liggja við akkeri, be at anchor.

akur (-rs, -rar) m. field.

ákveðinn p.p. fixed, definite; ákveðni greinirinn, the definite article.

ákæra f. charge, accusation.

ákæra (i) v.t. charge, accuse.

ala (el; ól; alinn) v.t. give birth to, bear; feed, support; ala upp, bring up; v. reflex. alast upp, be brought up.

alblindur adj. blind as a bat.

alda f. wave.

aldin n. fruit.

aldrei adv. never; aldrei framar, never again.

aldur (-rs) m. age; að aldri, of age.

algengur adj. ordinary, common, commonplace.

algert adv. quite, completely.

algjörlegur adj. perfect, absolute.

álit n. appearance, look, aspect; opinion, view; koma til álita, be taken into consideration.

alkunnugur adj. generally or widely known.

allrabeztur adj. the very best.

allrahelzt adv. most of all, especially, particularly.

alls adv. altogether; alls ekki, not at all; alls enginn, none at all; alls ekkert, nothing at all.

allskonar all kinds of.

allt pron. everything.

alltaf adv. always.

allur adj. all; whole; entire; með öllu, completely; allt að einu, allt um það; nevertheless.

almennur adj. common, general; public.

almennt adv. commonly, generally.

alstaðar adv. everywhere.

alúð f. affection; sincerity.

alvara f. seriousness, earnestness.

alvarlegur adj. serious.

alveg adv. quite, completely, altogether.

alþing/i n. Icelandic Legislative Assembly.

alþjóð f. people, the general public.

alþýða f. the common people.

alþýðlegur adj. common; general; popular.

amalegur adj. annoying, tiresome.

ameriskur adj. American.

ami m. annoyance.

amma (ömmu, ömmur) f. grandmother.

anda (a) v.i. & t. with dat. breathe.

andast v. reflex. die, breathe one's last.

andi m. breath, breathing; ghost, spirit; draga andann, take a breath.

andlit n. face.

andlitslitur *m.* complexion.
andlitssvipur *m.* facial expression.
andmæla (i) *v.t. with dat.* contradict.
andspænis *prep. with dat.* (directly) opposite.
andstuttur *adj.* short of breath; asthmatic.
angan *f.* fragrance, scent.
angur *n.* sorrow, grief.
angurblíður *adj.* sad, sorrowful.
angurvær *adj.* sad, depressed, down in the dumps.
annar *adj.* one, other, another, one of two; second; different; *í annað sinn*, for the second time; *í öðru lagi*, secondly; *með öðrum orðum*, in other words; *hvorannan*, each other; *enginn annar (en)*, no other (than); *pl. aðrir*, others; *allir aðrir*, everyone else.
annarhver *pron.* each other; every other.
annarhvor *pron.* either, one or other of two.
annaðhvort *pron.* either (*eða*, or).
annars *adv.* (or) else, otherwise.
annarstaðar *adv.* somewhere else.
annast (a) *v. reflex.* take care of.
annríkur *adj.* busy.
anza (a) *v.t. with dat.* heed, take notice of; reply, answer.
ánægður *adj.* content, contented, pleased.
ánægja *f.* contentment, pleasure.
ánægjulegur *adj.* pleasant.
appelsína *f.* orange (fruit).
api *m.* monkey, ape.
apríl (-s) *m.* April.
ár *n.* year; *árið, sem leið*; last year; *ár frá ári*, year after year.
ár (ar) *f.* oar; *leggja árar í bát*, throw up the sponge.
áreiðanlega *adv.* certainly, without doubt.
áreiðanlegur *adj.* reliable, trustworthy.

áreita (i) *v.t.* tease, molest, irritate; offend.
arfur (-s, -ar) *m.* inheritance.
ári *m.* fiend, demon; *ári góður (slæmur)*, awfully good (bad).
árla *adv.* early.
árlegur *adj.* yearly, annual.
armleggur *m.* arm.
armur (-s, -ar) *m.* arm; wing.
áræða (i) *v.t.* dare, venture.
áræði *n.* daring, pluck.
ásamt *adv.* together; *prep. with dat.*, (*með*), together with.
áskilja *v.t.* to stipulate, specify.
askja *f.* small box.
ást *f.* love, affection; *ástin mín*, my love; *fá ást á e-m*, fall in love with someone.
ástand *n.* state, condition; position; habit.
ástarbréf *n.* love-letter.
ástarljóð *n.* love-poem.
ástfanginn *adj.* in love (*í*, with).
ástæðulaust *adv.* without reason.
ásýn *f.* sight, presence; face.
atburður (-ar, -ir) *m.* occurrence, incident; *af atburð*, by chance.
athugasamur *adj.* thoughtful; attentive; considerate.
athugi *m.* care, attention.
atviksorð *n.* adverb.
atvinna *f.* livelihood; trade; employment.
atvinnugrein *f.* trade, line, branch of business.
atvinnulaus *adj.* unemployed.
auð- *suffix* easily.
auðfenginn *adj.* easy to obtain.
auðfluttur *adj.* easily moved.
auðkenna (i) *v.t.* distinguish, make out.
auðskiljanlegur *adj.* very understandable.
auður *adj.* empty, desolate; uninhabited; *m.* (-s) wealth, riches.
auðvitað *p.p.* easy to see, easy to understand, clear, obvious. *adv.* of course, obviously, naturally.

auga *n.* eye; *með berum augum*, with the naked eye.

augabrún (-ir) *f.* eyebrow.

augahvarmur (-s, -ar) *m.* eyelid.

auglýsa (i) *v.t.* publish, advertise, announce.

auglýsing (-ar) *f.* advertisement, announcement.

auk *adv.* besides; *prep.* with *gen.*, besides, in addition to.

auka (eyk; jók, jukum; aukinn) *v.t.* increase, augment.

auma *f.* pity; *það er auman*, what a pity.

aumk(v)a (a) *v.t.* pity, have pity on.

aumk(v)ast (yfir) *v.t.* take pity (on).

aumk(v)un *f.* pity.

aumlegur *adj.* wretched, miserable.

aurugur *adj.* muddy.

austan *adv.* from the east; *fyrir austan*, in the east of the land.

austarlegur *adj.* easterly.

austur *n.* East.

ávarp *n.* address.

ávinna *v.t.* gain, achieve, get.

B

baða (a) *v.t.* bathe.

báðir *adj.* both.

bágur *adj.* difficult, hard; awkward; *eiga bágt*, be hard up, be hard put to.

bak *n.* back; *að fjallabaki*, behind the mountains; *fara á bak (hesti)*, mount a horse; *fara af baki*, dismount.

baka (a) *v.t. & i.* bake.

bakari *m.* baker.

bakborði *m.* port (side).

bakki *m.* bank (river, lake); ridge; tray.

band *n.* ribbon; band; string, cord; hyphen; volume (book); *pl. (bönd)*, bonds.

Bandaríki *n.pl.* the United States.

bankareikningur *m.* bank account.

bankari *m.* banker.

banki *m.* bank.

banna (a) *v.t.* forbid.

bara *adv.* only, just, but.

bára *f.* wave (sea); *sjaldan er ein báran stök*, misfortunes never come singly; *sigla milli skers og báru*, to be between the devil and the deep blue sea.

barátta *f.* fight, struggle.

barn *n.* child.

barnalegur *adj.* childish, puerile.

barndómur *m.* childhood.

batna (a) *v.i.* improve, get better *(veðrið batnar)*, it's clearing up).

bátur (-s, -ar) *m.* boat.

baugur (-s, -ar) *m.* ring.

baun *f.* bean.

beiða (i) *v.t.* ask, request.

beiðast e-s af e-m ask something of someone.

bein *n.* bone; *hafa bein í hendi*, be well off.

beinn *adj.* straight, direct.

beint *adv.* straight, right; just, precisely.

beiskur *adj.* bitter, sharp.

bekkur (-jar, -ir) *m.* bench; class, form.

benda (i) *v.t.* with *dat. & v.i.*, beckon, point.

ber *adj.* bare, naked; clear, obvious; *undir berum himni*, under the bare sky.

bera (ber; bar, bárum; borinn) *v.t.* carry; wear clothes; bear, endure, stand; *bera á borð*, lay the table; *bera af borði*, clear the table.

berja (ber; barði barinn) *v.t.* thrash, beat; *berja á dyr*, knock at the door.

betla (a) *v.i.* beg.

betra (a) *v.t.* improve.

betur *adv.* better.

beygja (i) *v.t.* bend; *v.i. beygja af*, turn off.

bíða (bíð; beið, biðum; beðið) *v.i.* wait, stay; *bíða eftir e-m*, wait for s.o.; *v.t.* suffer, sustain.

biðja (bið; bað, báðum; beðinn) *v.t.* ask, request; beg; pray; *biðja um e-ð*, ask for something.

biðjast fyrir *v. reflex.* pray; say one's prayers.

bifreið (-ar) *f.* motor-car.

bil *n.* interval, space, period; moment; *í því bili*, just at that moment; *hér um bil*, approximately.

bíll (bíls, bílar) *m.* motor-car.

bílstjóri *m.* chauffeur.

binda (bind; batt, bundum; bundinn) *v.t.* tie; fasten; bind; *binda enda á e-ð*, finish something (off).

bindast e-s *v. reflex.* refrain from.

bíta (bít; beit, bitum; bitinn) *v.i. & v.t.*, bite; *bíta á*, have an effect on.

bíti *n.* the early morning; *í bítið*, very early.

bjáni *m.* fool, dolt.

bjartur *adj.* bright, clear (weather, air).

bjóða (býð; bauð, buðum; boðinn) *v.t. bjóða e-m e-ð*, offer someone something; bid, invite.

bjóðast *v. reflex. bjóðast til að gera e-ð*, offer to do something.

björn (bjarnar, birnir) *m.* bear.

blað *n.* leaf (plant, book); blade (knife, oar); newspaper.

blaðamaður *m.* newspaperman, reporter.

blakta (blakti; blaktaði; blaktað) *v.i.* flutter, wave; flicker (light).

blanda (a) *v.t.* mix; blend; *blanda e-u saman við e-ð*, mix one thing up with another; *blandast, v. reflex.*, get mixed, mix.

blár *adj.* blue; stupid; *blár af kulda*, blue with cold; *blátt áfram*, openly, frankly.

blása (blæs; blés; blásinn) *v.i. & v.t. with dat.*, blow (wind); pant, breathe hard; *v. impers.*, swell (limbs, wounds).

blautur *adj.* soft; wet, sodden; *blautur fiskur*, fresh fish.

blekkja (i) *v.t.* deceive, delude.

bleyði *f.* cowardice; *-skapur (-ar) m.* cowardice.

blíður *adj.* mild, gentle.

blína (i) *v.t.* stare, gaze.

blindfullur *adj.* dead drunk.

blindur *adj.* blind; *blindur á öðru auga*, blind in one eye.

bljúgur *adj.* shy; modest.

blóð *n.* blood; *á líf og blóð*, with all one's strength.

blóm *n.* flower; blossom.

blómgast (a) *v.i.* flower, blossom; flourish, thrive, prosper.

blómstra (a) *v.i.* flower, blossom.

blý *n.* lead (metal).

blýantur (-s, -ar) *m.* lead-pencil.

blygð *f.* shame.

blygðast (a) *v. reflex. (sín) (fyrir e-ð)*, be ashamed (about s.t.).

blæða (i) *v.i.* bleed.

boð *n.* offer; bid; invitation; party, feast; order, command; message; *gera boð eftir e-m*, send for s.o.

boginn *p.p.* bent; curved.

bógur (-s, -ar) *m.* shoulder (animals); bow (ship); side; *á báða bóga*, on both sides; *á hinn bóginn*, on the other hand.

bók (-ar, bækur) *f.* book.

bókari *m.* book-keeper, accountant.

bókhald *n.* book-keeping, accountancy.

bókhaldari *m.* book-keeper, accountant.

bókhlaða *f.* bookseller's, bookshop.

bókmentir *f.pl.* literature.

bókstaflega *adv.* literally, word for word, to the letter.

bolli *m.* cup.

bón *f.* request; *gera bón e-s*, do

s.o. a favour; *biðja e-n bónar*, ask a favour of s.o.

bóndi (*pl.* **bændur**) *m.* farmer; peasant, farm-labourer; husband.

borð *n.* table; board; plank; desk; side of ship; *sitja yfir borðum*, sit at table; *standa upp frá borðum*, get up from the table; *á borði*, in reality.

borða (a) *v.t.* eat; *borða sig saddan*, eat one's fill; *borða yfir sig*, over-eat.

borðdúkur *m.* tablecloth.

borðsalur (**-s, -ir**) *m.* dining-room.

borðstofa *f.* dining-room.

borg *f.* town; city; castle, fortification; rocky hill.

borga (a) *v.t.* pay; *borga e-m e-ð*, pay s.o. s.t.

bót (*pl.* **bætur**) *f.* cure, remedy; compensation; patch (clothes); *taka bótum*, change for the better.

botn (**-s, -ar**) *m.* bottom; *þegar öllu er á botninn hvolft*, when all is said and done, after all.

bráð *f.* flesh; prey; moment; *í bráðina*, at the present moment; *í bráð og lengd*, for ever and ever.

bráðan *adv.* suddenly, all at once.

bráðlega *adv.* soon, shortly, presently.

bráðum *adv.* soon, shortly, presently.

bráður *adj.* sudden; quick-tempered; rash, impatient.

bragð *n.* taste; quick movement; trick; look, expression; *dapur í bragði*, downcast, dejected; *í fyrsta bragði*, at first sight.

bragða (a) *v.i. & v.t.* taste; *v.i.* move, stir.

brátt *adv.* soon; *sem bráðast*, as soon as possible; *von bráðara*, very soon.

brattur *adj.* steep.

brauð *n.* bread; loaf.

braut *f.* road; path; track.

bregða (**bregð; brá, brugðum; brugðinn**) *v.t. with dat.*, move quickly; twist; change; leave off; *bregða heiti*, break one's promise; *bregða lit*, turn pale; *v.i. bregða út af e-u*, depart from, deviate from; *bregðast*, *v. reflex.* fail, disappoint s.o.

breiða (i) *v.t.* spread.

breidd *f.* breadth, width.

breiður *adj.* broad, wide.

brenna (**brenn; brann, brunnum; brunninn**) *v.i.* burn, be on fire; *brenna af löngun*, burn with desire.

brenna (i) *v.t.* burn, scorch; roast (coffee).

bresta (**brest; brast, brustum; brostinn**) *v.i.* break burst; snap, crack.

Bretland *n.* Britain.

bretta (i) *v.t.* turn upwards; *bretta brýnnar*, frown; *bretta eyrun*, prick up one's ears; *bretta upp ermarnar*, roll up sleeves.

breyta (i) *v.i. & v.t. with dat.*, change, alter; behave; *breyta eftir e-m*, imitate s.o.; *breyta eftir e-u*, act on; *breyta til*, make a change.

breytilegur *adj.* changeable.

brezkur *adj.* British.

bréf *n.* letter.

brjóst *n.* breast; chest; mind; *hafa ekki brjóst til e-s*, not to have the heart to do something.

brjóta (**brýt; braut, brutum; brotinn**) *v.t.* break; destroy; fold; *brjóta heilann um e-ð*, rack one's brains about something.

bróðir (**bróður, bræður**) *m.* brother.

bros *n.* smile.

brosa (**brosi; brosti; brosað**) *v.i.* smile.

brú (**-ar, brýr**) *f.* bridge.

brúðkaup *n.* wedding.
brúðkaupsdagur *m.* wedding day.
brúður (-ar, -ir) *f.* bride.
brúka (a) *v.t.* use.
brúnn *adj.* brown.
brunnur(-s, -ar) *m.* spring; well.
bræði *f.* anger.
búa (bý; bjó, bjuggum; búið) *v.i. & v.t.* live; equip; farm; rig out; dress; prepare; *búa um böggul*, tie up a parcel; *búa um rúm*, make the bed.
búast *v. reflex.*, get something ready.
búinn *p.p.* ready; rigged out, prepared, equipped; decorated with; *vera búinn að gera e-ð*, have (just) done something.
búr *n.* pantry; larder; (bird) cage.
burt/u *adv.* away, off.
byrja (a) *v.t.* begin, start, commence.
byrjun (-anir) *f.* beginning.
býti *n.pl.* exchange.
bæði *conj.* both; *bæði . . . og . . .*, both . . . and . . .
bæn *f.* prayer; request; *í öllum bænum*, for goodness' sake (colloq.).
bær (-jar, -ir) *m.* town; farmstead, farmhouse, farm.
bæta (i) *v.t.* improve; mend.
bölva (a) *v.i. & v.t. with dat.* curse, swear; *bölvaður*, damned, cursed.

D

dáð *f.* deed, exploit; *af sjálfs dáðum*, of one's own accord.
daga *v. impers.* dawn.
dagblað *n.* daily newspaper.
daglega *adv.* daily.
dagur (-s, -ar) *m.* day; *allan daginn*, all day; *í dag*, today; *á daginn*, during the day; *dögum saman*, for days on end; *um daginn*, the other day.
dáinn *p.p.* dead.

dálítill *adj.* little, small; *dálítið*, a little.
dalur (-s, -ar) *m.* valley.
dans *m.* dance.
dansa *v.i.* dance.
danska *f.* Danish (language).
danskur *adj.* Danish.
dapur (-ran) *adj.* sad, downcast; dreary; faint, dim (light).
dár *n. draga dár að e-m*, scoff at, mock at.
dáraskapur (-ar) *m.* foolishness.
dásamlegur *adj.* wonderful, marvellous.
dauði *m.* death.
dauðleiðast (i) *v. reflex. impers. mér dauðleiðist*, I'm bored to tears.
dauður *adj.* dead.
deila (i) *v.t.* divide, separate; deal out; distinguish; quarrel.
detta (dett; datt, duttum; dottinn) *v.i.* fall, drop; *detta á*, come on suddenly; *detta í stafi*, be flabbergasted, staggered; *mér dettur . . . í hug*, . . . it occurs to me; *detta út af*, fall asleep.
deyja (dey; dó; dáinn) *v.i.* die.
diskur (-s, -ar) *m.* plate.
djúpur *adj.* deep.
djöfull (-s, djöflar) *m.* devil; fiend, demon.
dómur (-s, -ar) *m.* judgement, sentence; opinion; *segja upp dóm*, pass sentence.
dóttir (dóttir, dætur) *f.* daughter.
dótturdóttir *f.* grand-daughter (by a daughter).
dóttursonur *m.* grandson (by a daughter).
draga (dreg; dró, drógum; dreginn) *v.t.* pull; drag; draw; delay; *v.i.* carry a gun; *draga fisk*, catch fish; *draga sig í hlé*, withdraw; *draga að sér*, gather, collect; *draga upp segl*, hoist sail; *draga upp akkeri*, weigh anchor.
drap *n.* murder.
dráttarvél *f.* tractor.

draumur (-s, -ar) *m.* dream.

drekka (drekk; drakk, drukkum; drukkinn) *v.t.* drink.

drekkja (i) *v.t. with dat. drekkja sér,* drown; submerge.

drengilegur *adj.* brave.

drengur (-s, -ir) *m.* boy.

drepa (drep; drap, drápum; drepinn) *v.t.* kill, murder; slay; *with dat., drepa (hendi) í vatn,* dip (the hand) in water; *v.i. drepa á dyr,* knock; *drepa á e-ð,* knock something.

dreyma (i) *v. impers.* dream; *mig dreymir (um),* I dream (about).

drotning (-ar) *f.* queen.

drottinn (-s, drotnar) *m.* king; ruler; the Lord.

drykkur (-jar, -ar) *m.* drink.

duga (dugi; dugði; dugað) *v.t. with dat.* help, assist; be enough, suffice.

duglegur *adj.* clever, capable.

dúkur (-s, -ar) *m.* cloth, fabric; table-cloth.

dvelja (dvel; dvaldi; dvalið) *v.i.* stay, wait; delay; *v.t.* delay.

dygð *f.* virtue.

dygðugur *adj.* virtuous.

dylja (dyl; duldi; duldur, dulinn) *v.t.* hide; conceal; *dyljast, reflex.* hide oneself.

dýpi *n.* depth.

dyr *f.pl.* door; *berja á dyr,* knock at the door.

dýr *adj.* dear, expensive.

dýr *n.* animal; fox.

dýrindis *adj. indec.* precious.

dýrka (a) *v.t.* worship.

dæll *adj.* gentle, easy; genial, familiar.

dæma (i) *v.t. & i.* judge; pass sentence; *dæma e-n sýknan (sekan),* acquit (find guilty); *dæma e-n af lífi,* sentence to death; *dæma e-m sekt,* fine.

dæmi *n.* example; instance; *til dæmis,* for example.

dögg (daggar, daggir) *f.* dew.

dökkur *adj.* dark.

E

eða *conj.* or; *annaðhvort . . . eða . . .,* either . . . or. . . .

eðli *n.* nature.

eðlilega *adv.* naturally, of course.

ef *conj.* if; in case; *ef til vill,* perhaps.

efa (a) *v.t.* doubt.

efast um e-ð *v. reflex.* doubt, question something.

efi *m.* doubt; *vera í efa,* be in doubt (*um,* about).

efnaður *adj.* wealthy, well-off.

efni *n.* material; stuff; subject, subject-matter, topic; *pl.* wealth; means; *ég hef ekki efni á því,* I cannot afford it.

eftir *pron. with dat.* after; according to; along; for, etc.

ég *pron.* I.

egg *n.* egg; *verpa eggjum,* lay eggs.

egg (-jar, -jar) *f.* edge.

eiga (á; átti; áttur) *v.t.* own, possess, have; *eiga heima,* live; *eiga börn, vini;* have children, friends; *eiga von á e-u,* expect; *eiga hlut í e-u,* have a share (hand) in something; *eiga kost á e-u,* have a chance of something; *eiga rétt á e-u,* have a right to s.t.; *eiga við e-ð (e-n),* refer to s.t., (someone); *eiga vel saman;* match, be well suited; *eiga ekki við,* not suit; *eiga að gera e-ð,* ought to do s.t.

eigin *adj. indec.* own; *með eigin augum,* with one's own eyes.

eigingjarn *adj.* selfish.

eiginlegur *adj.* proper, real.

eignarfall *n.* genitive case.

eignarfornafn *n.* personal pronoun.

eilíflega *adv.* eternally, for ever.

eimur (-s) *m.* steam; vapour.

einfaldur *adj.* simple; single; silly, foolish.

einhver *pron.* some; someone.

einhverstaðar *adv.* somewhere.

einkar *adv.* very, exceedingly.

einkenna (i) *v.t.* characterize, stamp, mark.

einkennilegur *adj.* characteristic, special.

einlæglega *adv.* sincerely.

einlægni *f.* sincerity, openness, frankness.

einn *pron. & num.* one; alone; *einn og einn*, one by one.

einnig *conj.* also; too.

einræðisherra *m.* dictator.

eins *adv.* as, so; *eins og*, as; as if; *eins fagur og* . . ., as beautiful as. . . .

einstaklega *adv.* extraordinarily.

einsær *adj.* clear, evident.

einungis *adv.* only, but.

eir (-rs) *m.* brass; copper.

eitur *n.* poison.

ekkert *pron.* no; nothing; *adv.* nowhere.

ekki *adv.* not; nothing; *koma fyrir ekki*, come to nothing.

ekta *adj. indec.* real, genuine.

elda (i) *v.i.* light a fire; *v.t.* heat, warm up, cook.

eldhús *n.* kitchen.

eldri *adj. comp.* older; elder.

eldur, (-s, -ar) *m.* fire.

ellefu *num.* eleven.

elska (a) *v.t.* love; *elskast, v. reflex.*, love one another.

elska *f.* love; affection.

elskur *adj. elskur að e-m*, fond of, very attached to.

elta (i) *v.t.* chase, pursue; run after; follow.

en *conj.* but; (more) than; *áður en*, before.

enda (a) *v.t.* end, finish, conclude; *v.i.* come to an end.

endi *m.* end, finish; *vera á enda*, be at an end.

endilega *adv.* finally; at last; ultimately.

endur- *prefix* re-.

endursenda (i) *v.t.* send back.

endurskína *v.i.* be reflected.

endurspegla (a) *v.t.* reflect.

endurþekkja (i) *v.t.* recognize, pick out.

engill (-s, englar) *m.* angel.

enginn *pron.* no; none; no one.

Englendingur (-s, -ar) *m.* Englishman.

enn *adv.* still; yet; *einu sinni enn*, once more; *enn betri*, even better; *enn þótt*, although, even though.

enni *n.* forehead.

enska *f.* English (language).

enskur *adj.* English.

epli *n.* apple.

er *pron.* who, that, which; *conj.* when; *þegar er*, as soon as.

erfa (i) *v.t.* inherit.

erfiði *n.* work, labour, toil.

erfiður *adj.* hard, difficult; troublesome.

erginn *adj.* irritable; *vera erginn við*, be annoyed with.

erlendis *adv.* abroad.

erlendur *adj.* foreign.

ermi (ermar) *f.* sleeve.

éta (et; át; etinn) *v.i. & t.* eat.

Evrópa *f.* Europe.

evrópskur *adj.* European.

Evrópumaður *m.* European (inhabitant).

ey (-jar) *f.* island, isle.

eyða (i) *v.t. with dat.* destroy; spend, waste, squander.

eyðilegur *adj.* desolate; waste; dreary.

eyra *n.* ear; handle (cup, etc.).

eyrir (-is, aurar) *m.* cent; *pl.* money.

Eystrasalt *n.* the Baltic.

F

fá (fæ; fékk, fengum; fenginn) *v.t. & v.i.* get; obtain; receive; cause; *fá ekki náð e-m*, not be able to catch someone; *fá skaða*, suffer loss; *fá að heyra*, *sjá*; (be allowed to) hear, see; *fá e-n til að gera e-ð*, get someone to do something.

faðir (föður, feður) *m.* father.

faðma (a) *v.t.* hug, embrace.

fagna (a) *v.t. with dat.* rejoice; welcome.

fagur (-ran) *adj.* beautiful; fair; fine; bright.

fákænn *adj.* ignorant.

fall *n.* fall; (legal) case.

falla (fell; féll; fallinn) *v.i.* fall; be defeated, beaten; *falla frá*, die; *falla saman*, cave in, collapse; *falla í stafi*, be amazed.

fallegur *adj.* pretty.

fang *n.* grip, grasp, hold; armful; *fá fang á e-m*, get hold of; *pl.* (*föng*) provisions; means; *hafa (ekki) föng á því*, (not) be able to afford it; *eftir föngum*, to the best of one's ability.

fangi *m.* prisoner; captive.

fánýtur *adj.* worthless.

far *n.* passage (on ship); track, trace; print; conduct; manners; drift (in the sky).

fár *adj.* few, cold, reserved.

fara (fer; fór; farinn) *v.i. & t.* go; travel; start, leave, set out; *fara villur vega*, go astray; *það er farið að dimma*, it's getting dark; *fara af stað*, set off, leave; *fara fram*, be going on; *fara í fötin*, dress; *fara úr fötum*, undress; *fara með e-m*, accompany; *fara úr landi*, leave the country; *fara utan*, go abroad (from Iceland); *vera farinn að gera e-ð*, to be just doing something.

farast *v. reflex.* die; perish; be drowned.

farinn *p.p.* gone; *farinn að heilsu*, broken in health; *hvernig sem því er farið*, however that may be.

farmur (-s, -ar) *m.* cargo, freight.

fast *adv.* firmly; fast.

fastur *adj.* firm; fast; solid.

fat (*pl.* föt) *m.* article of clothing, garment; *pl.* clothes.

fátækt *n.* poverty.

fátækur *adj.* poor.

fé (*gen.* fjár) *n.* sheep; cattle; *gangandi fé*, livestock.

feginn *adj.* glad; joyful.

fegurð *f.* beauty.

feitur *adj.* fat.

félag *n.* company; society.

félagi *m.* member, associate; partner.

fella (i) *v.t.* fell; kill; fold (clothes); take down (sail); shed (tears); *fella ást til*, (*e-s*), fall in love with (s.o.).

ferð *f.* journey; (sea) voyage; speed; *með fullri ferð*, at full speed.

ferðast (a) *v. reflex.* travel.

ferskur *adj.* fresh; new.

festa (i) *v.t.* fasten; fix; *festa trúnað á*, believe in.

fet *n.* pace, step; (length) foot; *fet fyrir fet*, step by step.

fíll (-s, -ar) *m.* elephant.

fimleikar *m.pl.* gymnastics.

fingur (-rs, fingur) *m.* finger.

finna (finn; fann, fundum; fundinn) *v.t.* find, discover; *finna upp*, invent.

finnast *v. reflex.* meet (one another).

fiskur (-s, -ar) *m.* fish.

fjall *n.* mountain.

fjarlendur *adj.* distant.

fjarri *adv.* far off.

fjörður (fjarðar, firðir) *m.* firth; inlet; bay; fjord.

fjörugur *adj.* energetic; lively, active; brisk.

flaska *f.* bottle.

flatur *adj.* flat; level; *koma flatt upp á*, take by surprise.

fleiri *comp.* more.

flesk *n.* pork; ham; bacon.

flestur *adj.* most.

fleyta (i) *v.t. with dat.* float, set afloat.

fljótt *adv.* quickly, rapidly, fast; soon; *sem fljótast*, as soon as possible, at the earliest possible moment.

fljótur *adj.* quick, fast, rapid, speedy; *fljótur á sér*, rash.

fljúga (**flýg; flaug, flugum; floginn**) *v.i.* fly.

fló (*pl.* **flær**) *f.* flea.

flóð *n.* flood tide; *það er flóð*, the tide is coming in.

flói *m.* bight, bay; marsh.

flokkur (**-s, -ar**) *m.* class (of things); body (of men); party; company.

fluga *f.* fly.

flug- *prefix* very.

flugvél (**-ar**) *f.* aeroplane.

flýta (**i**) *v.t. with dat.* hasten; *flýta sér*, make haste, hurry (up).

flytja (**flyt; flutti; fluttur**) *v.t.* carry; convey, transport; move; *flytja ræðu*, deliver a speech; *flytja sig*, move (house); *flytja vörur út* (*inn*), export, (import).

forlag *n.* publishing house.

formáli *m.* preface.

forn *adj.* ancient, old.

fórn *f.* sacrifice, offering.

fornafn *n.* pronoun.

forseti *m.* president; chairman.

forsetning (**-ar**) *f.* preposition.

forsvara (**a**) *v.t.* defend.

foss (*pl.* **-ar**) *m.* waterfall.

fótur (**fótar, fætur**) *m.* foot; leg; *vera á fótum*, be up (and about); *fara á fætur*, get up; *taka til fótanna*, take to one's heels.

frá *prep. with dat.* from; of; etc.

frakki *m.* coat.

Frakkland *n.* France.

fráleitur *adj.* absurd, ridiculous.

fram *adv.* forward; ·on/wards; *fram yfir*, beyond.

framan *adv.* from the front; *framan af*, in the beginning of; *fyrir framan*, in front of.

framfylgja *v.t. with dat.* execute, carry out; accomplish.

framtakslaus *adj.* lazy, idle.

framvegis *adv.* in future; *og svo framvegis* (*o.s. frv.*) and so on.

franska *f.* French (language).

franskur *adj.* French.

fráverandi *adj.* absent.

fregn *f.* news, information.

freista (**a**) *v.t. with gen.* tempt.

frekna *f.* freckle.

frelsa (**a**) *v.t.* free, liberate; save.

frétt *f.* news.

friður (**-ar**) *m.* peace; *láta e-n vera í friði*, leave someone in peace.

frímerki *n.* (postage) stamp.

frjáls *adj.* free, independent.

frjósa (**frýs; fraus, frusum; frosinn**) *v.i.* freeze.

frjósamur *adj.* fertile.

fróður *adj.* learned.

Frón *n.* Iceland.

frú (**-ar, -r**) *f.* lady; madam; Mrs.

frum- *prefix*, first.

fræði *f.* learning, knowledge.

frændi *m.* cousin; relative.

fugl (**-s, -ar**) *m.* bird.

fullorðinn *p.p.* adult; grown up; fully grown.

fullur *adj.* full; drunk; *fullt tungl*, full moon.

fullvissa (**a**) *v.t.* assure.

fylgja (**i**) *v.t. with dat.* follow; accompany, go with; belong to; *fylgjast með tímanum*, keep up with the times.

fylla (**i**) *v.t.* fill.

fyr *adv.* sooner; previously, before; *fyr en*, sooner than.

fyrir *prep. with dat. and acc.* for; in front of, before, etc.

fyrirgefning (**-ar**) *f.* forgiveness, pardon; *ég bið yður fyrirgefningar*, I beg your pardon.

fyrst *num.* first; *sem fyrst*, as soon as possible; *fyrst og fremst*, first and foremost.

fæða (**i**) *v.t.* give birth to; feed; *fæða e-n upp*, bring up.

fæðast *v. reflex.* be born.
fæði *n.* food; *fæði og húsnæði,* board and lodging.
fær *adj.* capable, able; competent.
færa (i) *v.t.* bring.
færi *n.* chance, opportunity; range; *á stuttu færi,* at short range; *vera í færum um e-ð,* be able to do something.
för (**farar, farir**) *f.* journey; (sea) voyage.
föstudagur *m.* Friday; *föstudagurinn langi,* Good Friday.

G

gáfa *f.* gift, talent, flair; *pl.* natural endowments.
gagn *n.* use; avail; *vera e-m að gagni,* be of use to someone *pl.* (*gögn*) evidence, proof; revenue.
gagnsamur *adj.* useful; beneficial.
gamall *adj.* old; *fimm ára gamal?,* five years old.
gaman *n.* fun, pleasure, enjoyment; *þykja gaman að e-u,* think something is fun; *í gamni,* as a joke, in fun.
ganga (**geng; gekk, gengum; genginn**) *v.i.* walk; go; (cattle) graze; *ganga vel til fara,* be well dressed; *v. impers. e-m gengur e-ð vel,* someone gets on well with, makes progress with; *ganga á móti e-m,* walk towards s.o.; *ganga á milli,* go between; *ganga af,* be left over; *ganga af sér,* fall off, fall into disrepair; (wind) veer (*til suðurs,* to the south); *ganga undir,* (sun) set; (exam.) take, sit for; *ganga um,* walk about.
garður (**-s, -ar**) *m.* garden; courtyard; fence; cottage; *í garð,* set up.
gata *f.* street, road; way.
gáta *f.* puzzle, riddle.
gátt *f.* doorway.
gefa (**gef; gaf, gáfum; gefinn**) *v.t.* give; present; deal (cards); *gefa ráð,* give advice; *gefa sig við e-u,* attend to something; *gefa af sér,* produce; *gefa út,* publish; *v. impers. það gefur öllum að skilja,* it's self-evident.
gefast *v. reflex. gefast vel (illa),* turn out well (badly); *gefast upp,* surrender; be exhausted.
gegn *prep. with dat.* against; *adv.* (*í gegn*) through.
gegna (i) *v.t. with dat.* obey; answer; mean; *gegna skyldu sinni,* do one's duty.
gegnum *prep. with acc.* through (*í gegnum*).
gegnvotur *adj.* soaking wet, wet through.
geigur (**-s**) *m.* fear; danger, peril.
geigvænn *adj.* dangerous, risky.
geisli *m.* ray.
geispa (a) *v.i.* yawn.
geit (**-ar, -ur**) *f.* goat; coward.
gelta (a) *v.i.* bark.
gera (i) *v.t.* make; do; send; *gera gys að e-m,* make a fool of someone; *ég gat ekki að því gert,* I couldn't help it; *gera upp reikning,* settle the bill.
gerast *v. reflex.* become; happen.
gestur (**-s, -ir**) *m.* guest; visitor.
geta (**get; gat, gátum; getað**) *v.t.* be able, can (followed by the supine).
geta (**get; gat, gátum; getinn**) *v.t.* get, *with gen.* guess; mention.
gifta (i) *v.t.* marry; wed.
giftast *v. reflex.* be (get) married.
gizka (a) *gizka á e-ð,* guess at something.
gjald *n.* payment; *pl.* expenses; reward.
gjalda (**geld; galt, guldum; goldinn**) *v.t. gjalda e-m e-ð,* pay (repay) someone s.t.; *gjalda líku líkt,* pay back in like coin.

gjarna/n *adv.* willingly.

gjöf (gjafar, -ir) *f.* gift, present.

glaður *adj.* glad, cheerful, happy, merry; *glaða sólskin*, bright sunshine.

glas *n.* glass, tumbler.

gleðja (gleð; gladdi; gladdur) *v.t.* gladden, please.

gleðjast *v. reflex.* be glad, rejoice.

gler *n.* glass

gleyma (i) *v.t. with dat.* forget.

gleymska *f.* forgetfulness.

glíma *f.* wrestling.

gluggi *m.* window.

glæpamaður *m.* criminal; crook.

glæpur (-s, -ir) *m.* crime; *fremja glæp*, commit a crime.

glær (-s) *m.* sea; *kasta e-u á glæ*, throw s.t. into the sea, waste.

glöggur *adj.* clear, distinct.

góður *adj.* good; kind; honest; fine (weather).

gólf *n.* floor.

gorta (a) *v.i.* boast.

grafa (gref; gróf; grafinn) *v.t.* dig; bury; carve.

gramur *adj.* angry.

grand *n.* harm, hurt, injury; *ekki grand*, not a bit.

grandi *m.* isthmus.

granni *m.* neighbour.

grannur *adj.* thin; slim, slender.

grár *adj.* grey.

gras *n.* grass.

grasafræði *f.* botany.

gráta (græt; grét; grátinn) *v.i.* cry, weep; *fara að gráta*, burst into tears.

greiða (i) *v.t.* disentangle, straighten out; get ready, prepare; *greiða sér*, comb one's hair; *v.i. greiða fyrir e-m*, help; *greiða úr e-u*, straighten out.

greiðlegur *adj.* ready; prompt; quick.

grein (*pl.* **-ir** or **-ar**) *f.* branch, bough; sentence, paragraph; subject, branch; *taka e-ð til*

greina, take into consideration; *koma ekki til greina*, be out of the question.

greina (i) *v.t.* divide; distinguish; explain.

greind *f.* common sense; discernment.

greindarlegur *adj.* sensible; intelligent; bright.

grimmur *adj.* cruel; fierce.

grípa (gríp; greip, grípum; gripinn) *v.t.* seize, grasp.

grobba (a) *v.i.* boast.

gróa (græ; greri; gróinn) *v.i.* grow (up); heal.

gróði *m.* profit.

grunn/ur *adj.* shallow; *á grunn*, aground.

grænn *adj.* green.

grön (granar, granir) *f.* upper lip.

guð (-s, -ir) *m.* God; *guði sé lof*, praise be to God.

guðlasta (a) *v.t.* blaspheme.

gufa *f.* steam.

gull *n.* gold; *barnagull*, toys.

gulur *adj.* yellow.

gæfa *f.* good luck; *bera gæfu til að gera e-ð*, be lucky enough to do something.

gæfur *adj.* gentle, mild.

gær *adv. í gær*, yesterday.

gæs *f.* goose; *grípa gæs meðan hún gefst*, make hay while the sun shines.

gæta (i) *v.t. with gen.* take care of; notice, observe, watch; pay attention to, heed.

H

haf *n.* sea; ocean; *í hafi*, in the open sea.

hafa (hef/i; hafði; hafður) *v.t. & i.* have; *hafa upp á e-u*, find out; *hafa hægt um sig*, keep quiet.

haffær *adj.* seaworthy.

hafjafni *m.* water-level, sea-level.

hafnarbær *m.* seaport.

hafrek *n.* jetsam.

hafrót *n.* surf; swell.
haga (a) *v.t. with dat.* arrange, manage; *haga e-u svo til, að* . . ., arrange things in such a way that . . .; *haga sér*, behave.
hagfræði *f.* political economy.
hagl *n.* hail.
hagur (-s, -ir) *m.* state, condition; *pl.* affairs; profit, benefit, advantage; *i hag e-m*, to the advantage of . . .
haka (höku, hökur) *f.* chin.
haki *m.* hook; *láta e-ð sitja á hakanum*, neglect, put on the shelf.
hald *n.* hold; grasp; arrest; opinion, view.
halda (held; hélt, héldum; haldinn) *v.i. & v.t. with dat.* hold; keep; think, consider *halda*; *sér i e-ð*, cling to, hold on to; *halda niðri i sér andanum*, hold one's breath; *halda áfram*, keep on, go on, continue doing something; *halda e-u við*, maintain; *v.i. halda kyrru fyrir*, remain quiet; *halda upp á e-n*, be fond of; *isinn heldur ekki*, the ice does not hold; *with acc. halda ræðu*, deliver a speech; *halda orð sín*, keep one's word; *halda vörð*, keep watch.
hálfur *adj.* half; *með hálfum hug*, hesitantly; *hálft annað ár*, a year and a half.
háll *adj.* slippery.
halla *v.t. with dat.* turn sideways, lean; tilt; sway; *halla sér upp að e-u*, lean against s.t.; *halla sér út af*, lie down to sleep; *v. reflex.* (*hallast*) lean; incline; slope; *ég hallast að yðar skoðan*, I incline to your opinion.
háls (pl. -ar) *m.* neck; throat; hill; bow (ship); *liggja e-m á hálsi fyrir e-ð*, put the blame on s.o. for s.t.
haltur *adj.* lame.

hamingja *f.* good luck; *það má hamingjan vita*, goodness knows.
hams *m.* skin; *hitna í hamsi*, to become angry.
handleggur *m.* arm.
handlæknir *m.* surgeon.
hani *m.* cock; tap; stop-cock.
hann *pron.* he.
hanzki *m.* glove.
hár *n.* hair.
hár *adj.* high; tall; lofty; loud (noise).
harðlegur *adj.* hard, severe.
harður *adj.* hard, severe, stern; hardy; *hörð orð*, harsh words.
hárfagur *adj.* fair-haired.
harmur (-s, -ar) *m.* sorrow; grief; sadness.
hartnær *adv.* nearly, almost.
háseti *m.* seaman, sailor.
háskóli *m.* university.
hata (a) *v.t.* hate, detest.
hátíð *f.* festival.
hátta (a) *v.t. with dat.* arrange, set out; *v.i.* go to bed, undress.
háttalag *n.* behaviour; conduct; method; *pl.* (*-lög*), bed-time.
hattur (-s, -ar) *m.* hat.
háttur (-ar, hættir) *m.* way of life, habit; conduct; manner; bed-time; *fara i háttinn*, go to bed; *mikils (lítils) háttar*, important (unimportant); *á engan hátt*, by no means; *á allan hátt*, in every respect.
haukur (-s, -ar) *m.* hawk.
haust *n.* autumn; *á haustin*, in autumn.
hávaxinn *p.p.* tall.
hefja (hef; hóf; hafinn) *v.t.* lift, raise; heave; begin; *hefja upp*, lift up.
heilagur *adj.* holy; sacred; *heilagur andi*, the Holy Ghost.
heilbrigði *f.* health.
heili *m.* brain.
heill *adj.* whole, entire; sound; *betra er heilt en vel gróið*, pre-

vention is better than cure; *heill og sæll*, welcome.

heilsa (a) *v.t. with dat.* greet, be remembered to.

heilsa *f.* health; *góð (veik) heilsa*, good (poor) health.

heim *adv.* home; *bjóða e-m heim*, invite s.o. home; *heima*, at home; *eiga heima*, live; *sitja heima*, stay at home.

heimilis- *prefix* family-, home-.

heimska *f.* foolishness.

heimskur *adj.* foolish, silly; stupid.

heimur (-s, -ar) *m.* world.

heita (heiti; hét; heitinn) *v.t.* name, call; *heita á e-n*, call on s.o.; *v.i.* be called; *ég heiti X*, my name is X; *with dat.* promise.

heitur *adj.* hot; warm.

heldur *adv.* rather; on the contrary; *heldur en*, rather than; *ekki heldur*, neither; *vilja heldur*, prefer; *miklu heldur*, far sooner.

helgidagur *m.* holiday; holy day.

helzt *adv.* most; soonest; especially; rather.

henda (i) *v.t.* take in the hand; *henda gaman að e-m*, make fun of s.o.; *e-ð hendir e-n*, something happens to someone; *with dat.*, throw, fling; *v.i.* happen, occur.

heppinn *adj.* lucky, fortunate.

her (hers, herir) *m.* army.

hér *adv.* here.

herbergi *n.* room, lodgings.

herðar *f.pl.* shoulders.

herra *m.* gentleman; master, lord; (title) sir; (address) Mr.

hestur (-s, -ar) *m.* horse.

hey *n.* hay.

heyra (i) *v.t.* hear; *heyra á e-ð*, listen to s.t.; *heyra e-m til*, belong to.

himinn (-s, himnar) *m.* heaven; sky; *undir berum himni*, in the open air.

hingað *adv.* here, hither; *hingað til*, so far, till now; *hingað og þangað*, hither and thither.

hinn (hin, hið) *def. art.* the.

hinn (hin, hitt) *pron.* that; the other one; *pl. (hinir)* the others, rest.

hitta (i) *v.t.* meet (with; come across; *hit, hitta e-n heima*, find someone at home; *v. reflex. (hittast)*, meet (one another); *það hittist svo á, að hann . . .*, he happened to . . .

hjá *prep. with dat. & adv.* near, close to, nearby; beside; in comparison with; *fara hjá*, go by.

hjálp *f.* help.

hjálpa (a) *v.t. with dat.* help.

hjarta (*pl.* hjörtu) *n.* heart; mind.

hjartagóður *adj.* kind-hearted.

hjól *n.* wheel; bicycle.

hjóla (a) *v.i.* to cycle.

hlaða (hleð; hlóð; hlaðinn) *v.t.* load; pile up; build; *with dat.* fell; *hlaða seglum*, take in (furl, stow) the sails; *v. impers. snjónum hleður niður*, the snow is coming down heavily.

hlátur (-rs or -rar) *m.* laugh, laughter; *reka upp hlátur*, burst out laughing.

hlaupa (hleyp; hljóp; hlupum; hlaupinn) *v.i.* jump; leap; run; shrink; *hlaupa á sig*, make a mistake, blunder; *hlaupa upp*, jump up.

hleypa (i) *v.t. with dat. hleypa brúnum*, frown; *hleypa út*, let out, turn out; *hleypa á land*, run ashore.

hlið (-ar) *f.* side; *á báðar (allar) hliðar*, on both (all) sides.

hlíð (-ar) *f.* hillside, slope, mountain side.

hlíta (i) *v.t. with dat.* depend on, rely on.

hlé *n.* shelter; lee; leeside; *á hléborða*, to leeward.

hljóð *n.* voice; sound.

hljóðlegur adj. silent, noiseless.
hlusta (a) v.i. listen; hlusta á e-ð, til e-s, listen to something.
hluti m. part; share, portion.
hlutur (-ar, -ir) m. thing; matter, subject; share, portion, part.
hlýða (i) v.t. with dat. obey.
hlýðinn adj. obedient.
hlæja (hlæ; hló, hlógum; hlegið) v.i. laugh (að e-u, at); hlæja hátt, laugh out loud.
hnappur (-s, -ar) m. button.
hné n. knee.
hnífur (-s, -ar) m. knife.
hnútur (-s, -ar) m. knot.
hnýta (i) v.t. knot, tie (in a knot); hnýta hnút, tie a knot.
hóf n. moderation; temperance; í hófi, in moderation.
hóglegur adj. calm; mild, gentle.
hold n. flesh; vera í góðum holdum, be in good condition.
horfa (i) v.i. look; turn, be turned; horfa á e-ð, look at, watch; horfa út um gluggann, look out of the window.
hósta (a) v.i. cough.
hóta (a) v.t. with dat. threaten.
hraða (a) v.t. with dat. hasten; hraða sér, hurry, make haste.
hraðlega adv. quickly, swiftly.
hraðritun f. shorthand.
hraður adj. quick, fast, swift.
hrafn (-s, -ar) m. raven.
hratt adv. fast.
hreinn adj. clean, clear (voice, etc.)
hreinsa (a) v.t. clean, cleanse.
hrekja (hrek; hrakti; hrakinn) v.t. to refute; worry; knock about.
hreppur (-s, -ar) m. parish, district.
hrífa (hríf; hreif, hrifum; hrifinn) v.t. to catch; affect, concern; touch (emotionally).
hringur (-s, -ar) m. ring; circle; link (of chain).
hrista (i) v.t. shake; hrista e-ð af sér, shake something off.

hróp n. shout, call, cry.
hross n. horse.
hræða (i) v.t. frighten, scare; terrify.
hræðast v. reflex. be afraid of.
hræddur adj. afraid (við, of).
hræðsla f. fear.
hrökkva (hrekk; hrökk, hrukkum; hrokkinn), v.i. fall back; curl (hair); be sufficient; hrökkva fyrir e-m, give way to; hrökkva til, suffice.
hugsa (a) v.t. think; hugsa til e-s, look forward to; hugsa um, think about.
hugur (-ar, -ir) m. mind; mood; desire, wish; mér kemur e-ð í hug, something occurs to me; hafa e-ð í hug, have something in mind, intend; hugur ræður hálfum sigri, a stout heart is half the battle.
hún pers. pron. she.
hundrað n. hundred.
hundur (-s, -ar) m. dog.
hungra (a) v. impers. mig hungrar, I'm hungry.
hurð f. door.
hús n. house.
húsgögn n.pl. furniture.
hvað pron. what; hvað sem, whatever.
hvaða pron. which, what?.
hvaðan adv. where from.
hvalur (-s, -ir) m. whale.
hvar adv. where; hvar sem, wherever; hér og hvar, here and there; víða hvar, in most places.
hvass adj. sharp; pointed; keen.
hveiti n. wheat.
hvenær adv. when; hvenær sem, whenever.
hver pron. interr. who, which; pron. indef. each, every.
hverfa (hverf; hvarf, hurfum; horfinn) v.i. turn round; disappear; hverfa aftur, turn back, return; hverfa frá e-u, leave off, stop.
hvergi adv. nowhere.

hvernig *adv.* how, in what way.

hvert *adv.* where (to), whither; *hvert sem*, wherever.

hvíla (i) *v.t. & v.i.* rest; *hvíla sig*, have a rest.

hvískra (a) *v.i.* whisper.

hvítur *adj.* white.

hvolfa (i) *v.t. with dat.* overturn; *þegar öllu er á botninn hvolft*, when all's said and done.

hvorki *adv.* neither (*né, nor*).

hvort *conj.* whether, if.

hygginn *adj.* clever, prudent.

hyggja (hygg; hugði; hugað) *v.i. & v.t.* think, believe; intend; mean to; *eftir á að hyggja*, on second thoughts; *hyggja af e-u*, forget; *hyggja á e-ð*, think of.

hyggjast *v. reflex.* think, fancy, imagine.

hylja (hyl; huldi; hulinn) *v.t.* hide, conceal, cover.

hyskinn *adj.* idle, lazy.

hæð *f.* height; hill.

hæfa (i) *v.t.* hit; with *dat.* be fit, suitable.

hæfur *adj.* fit, proper; suitable.

hægð *f.* ease; calmness; *með hægð*, easily.

hægri *adj.* right; *til hægri handar*, on the right hand.

hægt *adv.* slowly; gently; in a leisurely way.

hælinn *adj.* boastful.

hæll (-s, -ar) *m.* heel; *um hæl*, immediately.

hæna *f.* hen.

hætta (i) *v.t. with dat.* risk; stop, leave off (*að, . . . ing*).

hætta *f.* danger; risk; *leggja á hættu*, run a risk; *eiga mikið í hættu*, have much at stake.

hættulegur *adj.* dangerous, risky.

hættur *þ.þ.* having left off, stopped.

höfn (hafnar, hafnir) *f.* harbour; port; haven.

höfuð (-s) *n.* head; *leggjast e-ð undir höfuð*, put something on

the shelf, neglect; *yfir höfuð*, on the whole.

högg *n.* blow; stroke; cut.

hönd (handar, hendur) *f.* hand; arm and hand; handwriting; *taka í hönd e-m*, to shake hands with s.o.; *allra handa*, all sorts of.

hörund *n.* skin; flesh (of human).

I

í *prep.* with *acc.* and *dat.* in, etc.

íbúð *f.* flat, apartment; suite of rooms.

íbúðarhús *n.* dwelling-house.

íbúi *m.* inhabitant.

iðja *f.* work, job; business; task.

iðka (a) *v.t.* cultivate; study; practise.

iðn *f.* trade, profession, occupation.

illa *adv.* badly; *fara illa með e-n*, treat s.o. badly.

illur *adj.* bad; evil, wicked; *í illu skapi*, in a bad mood.

inn *adv.* in; *ganga inn*, go in; *inn í*, into.

innan *adv.* from inside, within; *prep. with gen.*, within.

inni *adv.* indoors, in; within.

ís (-s, -ar) *m.* ice.

ísbjörn *m.* polar bear.

Ísland *n.* Iceland.

Íslendingur (-s, -ar) *m.* Icelander.

íslenzka *f.* Icelandic (language).

íslenzkur *adj.* Icelandic.

íþrótt *f.* sport.

íþróttamaður *m.* sportsman, athlete.

J

já *adv.* yes.

jafn *adj.* even; steady, uniform; equal.

jafnan *adv.* always, constantly.

jafnstór *adj.* of equal size, as big.

jakki *m.* jacket.

jákvæða (i) *v.t. with dat.* say yes to, assent to.

janúar (-rs) *m.* January.

jarða (a) *v.t.* bury.
jarðepli *n.* potato.
járn *n.* iron.
járnbraut *f.* railway.
játa (a) *v.t. with dat.* say yes to, assent to; *with acc.*, confess; acknowledge.
jeg *v. ég.*
jeta *v. éta.*
jól *n.pl.* Christmas; *jóladagur*, Christmas Day; *jólatré*, Christmas tree.
jú *adv.* yes (after a negative question).
jökull (-s, jöklar) *m.* glacier.
jörð (jarðar, jarðir) *f.* earth; ground, soil; farm.
jötunn (-s, jötnar) *m.* giant.

K

kaffi *n.* coffee.
kafinn *p.p. önnumkafinn*, busy.
kafli *m.* chapter; section; *með köflum*, now and then.
kaka (köku, kökur) *f.* cake.
kál *n.* cabbage.
kala (kell or **kelur; kól; kalið)** *v.* *impers.* freeze.
kaldi *m.* slight breeze.
kaldur *adj.* cold.
kálfur (-s, -ar) *m.* calf; dolt.
kalla (a) *v.t.* & *v.i.* call, shout, cry; *kalla á hjálp*, call for help.
kambur (-s, -ar) *m.* comb.
kapp *n.* eagerness; ardour, zeal; contention.
kappsamur *adj.* eager, energetic.
karlmannlegur *adj.* manly.
kartafla *f.* potato.
kast *n.* throw; chance; fit; *komast í kast við e-n*, come up against.
kasta (a) *v.t. with dat.* throw; fling; cast; *kasta akkerum*, drop anchor; *kasta mæðinni*, gasp for breath.
kaup *n.* purchase; bargain; wages, pay.
kaupa (kaupi; keypti; keyptur) *v.t.* buy, purchase.

kaupmaður *m.* merchant, trader, dealer; shopkeeper; tradesman.
Kaupmannahöfn *f.* Copenhagen.
keðja *f.* chain.
keimur (-s) *m.* flavour, taste.
kemba (i) sér *v. reflex.* comb o.s., comb one's hair.
kenna (i) *v.t.* know; recognize; notice; feel; *það er honum að kenna*, it is his fault; *with gen.* feel; *kenna grunns*, touch bottom.
kenna (i) *v.t.* teach.
kennari *m.* teacher, schoolmaster.
kerling (-ar) *f.* old woman.
kerti *n.* candle.
ketill (-s, katlar) *m.* kettle; *mér féll allur ketill í eld*, I was greatly taken aback.
kind (-ar, -ur) *f.* sheep; wench.
kinka (a) *v.t.* with dat. *kinka kolli*, nod (the head).
kinn (-ar) *f.* cheek.
kirkja *(gen. pl. kirkna)* *f.* church.
kista *f.* trunk.
kitla (a) *v.t.* tickle.
kjáni *m.* fool, dolt, idiot.
kjarkur (-s) *m.* energy, vigour; heart, spirit.
kjóll (-s, -ar) *m.* frock, dress; tail-coat.
kjósa (kýs; kaus, kusum; kosinn or **kjörinn)** *v.t.* choose, select; elect.
kjölur (kjalar, kilir) *m.* keel.
kjöt *n.* meat; flesh.
klettur (-s, -ar) *m.* rock; cliff.
klóra (a) *v.t.* scratch.
klukka *f.* bell; clock; *hvað er klukkan?* what time is it?
klútur (-s, -ar) *m.* handkerchief.
klæða (i) sig *v. reflex.* dress, put on one's clothes.
klæði *n.* cloth; *pl.* clothes.
kné *n.* knee.
knöttur (knattar, knettir) *m.* ball.
koddi *m.* pillow; cushion.

kol *n.pl.* coal.
koli *m.* plaice.
kollur (**-s, -ar**) *m.* head; top; *velta e-u um koll*, overturn.
kólna (**a**) *v.i.* cool (off), become cold.
koma (**kem; kom; kominn**) *v.i. & v.t. with dat.* come, arrive; turn up; *koma fram*, come up, appear; *koma fyrir*, happen, occur; *koma fyrir ekki*, come to nothing; *koma með e-ð*, bring something; *koma út*, appear, be published; *v.t. with dat.* bring, carry; *koma e-m til að hlæja*, make someone laugh; *koma e-u fyrir sig*, call something to mind; *enn sem komið er*, so far, as yet.
komast *v. reflex.* get, reach; come to an end; *komast af stað*, get away; *komast af án e-s*, get along without something; *komast undan*, escape.
kona (*gen. pl.* **kvenna**) *f.* woman; wife.
konar (*gen. sing.*) *allskonar*, all sorts of; *hverskonar*, all sorts of, every kind of, *einskonar*, a sort of; *þesskonar*, that sort of.
konungur (**-s, -ar**) *m.* king.
kopar (**-rs**) *m.* copper.
kosta (**a**) *v.i. & v.t.* cost; *hvað kostar það?* what does that cost?; *v.t.* damage, hurt; bruise.
kostnaður (**-ar**) *m.* cost; expense/s; *á minn kostnað*, at my expense.
kostur (**-ar, -ir**) *m.* condition; opportunity; chance; choice; *eiga kost á að gera e-ð*, be allowed to do s.t.; *alls kostar*, altogether, in every respect.
krabbi *m.* crab.
kraftur (**-s** or **-ar, -ar**) *m.* strength, power; *pl.* strength.
kragi *m.* collar.

kráka *f.* crow; *betri er ein kráka í hendi en tvær í skógi*, a bird in the hand is worth two in the bush.
krani *m.* tap.
krappur *adj.* narrow.
krefja (**kref; krafði; krafinn**) *v.t.* claim, demand.
Kristur (**-s**) *m.* Christ.
krókur (**-s, -ar**) *m.* hook.
króna *f.* crown.
kroppur (**-s, -ar**) *m.* body.
kuldi *m.* cold; coldness; *pl.* (*kuldar*) cold weather.
kunna (**kann; kunni; kunnað**) *v.t.* know; understand; *kunna e-m þökk*, be obliged to someone; *kunna vel við e-n*, be pleased with.
kveða (**kveð; kvað; kváðum; kveðinn**) *v.t.* say; recite.
kveðja (**kveð; kvaddi; kvaddur**) *v.t.* say goodbye; request, call for.
kvisa (**a**) *v.i.* gossip.
kvistur (**-ar, -ir**) *m.* twig; small branch.
kvittun (**-anir**) *f.* receipt.
kvæði *n.* poem; piece of poetry; song.
kvöld *n.* evening; night; *í kvöld*, this evening, tonight; *annað kvöld*, tomorrow evening; *á kvöldin*, in the evening.
kyn *n.* kin, kindred; kind, sort; gender; *alls kyns*, all sorts of.
kynna (**i**) *v.t. with dat. kynna sér e-ð*, study, make o.s. acquainted with.
kynnast *v. reflex. kynnast e-u, kynnast við e-n*, get acquainted with.
kýr (*gen.* **kýr**, *pl.* **kýr**) *f.* cow.
kyrr *adj.* quiet, still; *halda kyrru fyrir*, stay, remain.
Kyrrahaf *n.* the Pacific Ocean.
kyssa (**i**) *v.t.* kiss.
kærleikur (**-s, -ar**) *m.* love.
köttur (**kattar, kettir**) *m.* cat.

L

lag *n.* layer; chance, opportunity; air, melody; *úr lagi*, out of gear, out of order; *í fyrsta lagi*, firstly; *allt í lagi*, all right, o.k.

laga (a) *v.t.* arrange, mend, see to, put right.

lágur *adj.* low; short (height).

lak *n.* sheet.

lampi *m.* lamp.

lán *n.* loan; good luck; *fá e-ð að láni*, get on credit, on loan.

lána (a) *v.t. lána e-m e-ð*, lend s.t. to s.o.

land *n.* land; country; shore; *ganga á land*, go ashore.

landhelgi *f.* territorial waters.

langa (a) *v. impers. mig langar til að*, I long to.

langt *adv.* far; *langt í burtu*, far away.

langur *adj.* long.

lánsamur *adj.* lucky, fortunate.

lás (-s, -ar) *m.* lock.

láta (læt; lét; látinn) *v.t.* put; let; lose; give up; *láta gera e-ð*, have s.t. done; *láta af e-u*, leave off; *láta aftur dyrnar*, shut the door.

látinn *p.p.* dead; *vel látinn*, popular, well-liked.

latur *adj.* lazy.

lauf *n.* leaf.

laugardagur *m.* Saturday.

laukur (-s, -ar) *m.* onion.

laun *n.pl.* reward; salary, pay.

laus *adj.* loose; free.

lax *(pl. -ar)* *m.* salmon.

leður *n.* leather.

leggja (legg; lagði; lagður) *v.t. & v.i.* put, place, lay; *leggja peninga fyrir*, save money, put money on one side; *leggja saman*, add up; *leggja fram* set out; *leggja út*, translate; *leggja í haf*, to put to sea.

leggjast *v. reflex.* lie down; *leggjast*

fyrir, take a rest; *leggjast til svefns*, go to sleep.

leggur (-jar, -ir) *m.* leg.

leið *f.* way, road, route; *vísa e-m leið*, show s.o. the way; *um leið*, at the same time; *á þá leið*, as follows; *koma e-u til leiðar*, cause, bring about.

leiða (i) *v.t.* lead.

leika (leik; lék; leikinn) *v.t. & v.i.* play; act, perform; *leika sér*, play; *mér leikur hugur á e-u*, I have a good mind to.

leikari *m.* actor.

leikfimi *f.* gymnastics.

leikkona *f.* actress.

leikni *f.* skill.

leikur (-s, -ar or **-ir)** *m.* game, sport.

leit *f.* search.

leita (a) *v.t. & v.i.* search, look for.

lengd *f.* length; *í bráð og lengd*, now and for ever; *þegar til lengdar lætur*, in the long run.

lengi (lengur, lengst) *adv.* for a long time, long; *svo lengi sem*, while, as long as.

lesa (les; las, lásum; lesinn) *v.t.* read.

lest *f.* train.

lesta (i) *v.t.* damage; injure.

leyfa (i) *v.t.* allow, permit, let.

leyna (i) *v.t.* hide.

leyndardómsfullur *adj.* mysterious.

leysa (i) *v.t. & v.i.* loosen; untie, undo; *leysa e-ð af hendi*, do, perform, execute.

leyti *n.* part; time; *að mestu leyti*, mostly; *að svo miklu leyti sem*, as far as; *að öðru leyti*, in other respects; *ég fyrir mitt leyti*, for my part.

líða (líð; leið, liðum; liðinn) *v.i.* pass (away), elapse; suffer.

líf *n.* life; waist; *á lífi*, alive.

lifa (lifi; lifði; lifað) *v.t. & v.i.* live; be alive.

liggja (ligg; lá, lágum; legið) *v.i.*
lie; be situated.
líka *adv.* also; too; as well.
líkami *m.* body.
líkur *adj.* like; similar; likely,
probable.
líta (lít; leit, litum; litinn) *v.t. &*
v.i. see; look; *líta á e-ð,* look at;
líta aftur, look back; *líta út*
(eins og), look (like).
lítill *adj.* little, small.
lítt *adv.* little.
litur (-ar, -ir) *m.* colour; dye;
grænn að lit, green in colour
léttur *adj.* light; easy; mild.
ljós *n.* light; *koma í ljós,* appear.
ljósmynd *f.* photograph.
ljótur *adj.* ugly.
ljúga (lýg; laug, lugum; loginn)
v.i. & v.t. with dat. lie, tell a
lie.
ljúka (lýk; lauk, lukum; lokinn)
v.t. with dat. ljúka e-u, finish,
bring to an end, conclude;
ljúka e-u aftur (upp), shut
(open).
lof *n.* praise; leave, permission.
lofa (a) *v.t.* praise; *with dat.*
allow, let, permit; promise.
loft *n.* air; sky; atmosphere;
liggja upp í loft, lie on the
back; loft; ceiling; storey,
floor.
logi *m.* flame.
lok *n.* lid, cover, top; *að lokum,*
at last.
loka (a) *v.t. with dat.* shut, close.
lúða *f.* halibut.
lúinn *p.p.* exhausted, worn out,
fagged out.
lundi *m.* puffin.
Lundúnir *f.pl.* London.
lyfta (i) *v.t. with dat.* lift, raise.
lygi (*pl.* lygar) *f.* lie.
lykill (-s, -lyklar) *m.* key.
lykt *f.* smell.
lymskur *adj.* sly, cunning.
lýsa (i) *v.t.* light up, illuminate;
with dat. show; describe.

læknir (læknis, læknar) *m.*
doctor.
læra (i) *v.t.* learn; teach.
lög *n.pl.* law; act, statute; *brjóta*
lög, break the law.
löggæzla *f.* police.
löggæzlulið *n.* police.
löglegur *adj.* legal, lawful.
lögreglumaður *m.* policeman.
lögregluþjónn *m.* policeman.
Lögrétta *f.* former Icelandic
Legislative Assembly.

M

maður (manns, menn) *m.* man;
person; husband.
magi *m.* stomach.
mál *n.* speech; language; legal
action, case; affair; matter;
taka e-ð í mál, take into consideration; *það er mál manna,*
it is said; measure; time, high
time; mealtime; *í fyrramálið,*
tomorrow morning.
mala (a) *v.t.* grind.
mála (a) *v.t.* paint.
málari *m.* artist, painter.
mannsaldur *m.* generation, age.
mánuður (mánaðar, mánuðir) *m.*
month.
mara *f.* nightmare.
marg- *prefix* much-, many-,
very, varied.
margur *adj.* many; *margt,* many
things.
mark *n.* sign; target; object, aim;
til marks um e-ð, in token of
s.t.
marka (a) *v.t.* mark (out); note,
take notice of.
mata (a) *v.t.* feed, give food to.
matsalur *m.* dining-room.
máttugur *adj.* strong, powerful.
máttur (-ar, mættir) *m.* strength.
mátulegur *adj.* suitable, proper,
fitting.
matur (-ar, -ar) *m.* food.
með *prep. with,* etc.
meðal *prep. with gen.* among.

meðal- *prefix* average, middle, mean.

meðan *conj.* while.

meðfram *adv.* at the same time.

mega (má; mátti; mátt) *v.t. & v.i.* be permitted, be allowed; may.

megin- *prefix* main, principal, chief.

meinsamur *adj.* evil, malicious.

meiri *adj. compar.* more; larger, bigger; greater.

ment *f.* art; skill.

mestur *adj. superl.* greatest; largest; most.

mey (-jar, -jar) *f.* maiden; virgin.

miður (mið; mitt) *adj.* middle; mid-.

miðvikudagur *m.* Wednesday.

mikill *(neut.* **mikið)** *adj.* great; large, big; much.

milli *prep.* with *gen.* between.

minn *pron. poss.* my; mine.

minni *n.* memory; *í manna minnum,* within living memory.

missa (i) *v.t.* lose; *missa e-ð niður,* drop; *with gen.* miss, not hit; be without.

mistök *n.pl.* mistake, error, slip, slip-up.

misþykkja *f.* disagreement.

mjólk (gen. -ur) *f.* milk.

mjór *adj.* thin; slim, slender; narrow.

mjúkur *adj.* soft; mild.

mjög *adv.* very; greatly, very much.

mjöl *n.* flour; meal.

móðir (móður, mæður) *f.* mother.

monta (a) *v.i.* boast; *montinn,* boastful; snobbish.

morð *n.* murder.

morgun (-s, morgnar) *m.* morning; *frá morgni til kvölds,* from morning to night; *á morgun,* tomorrow.

morkna (a) *v.i.* rot.

mót *n.* meeting; mould; model; manner, way; *með því móti,* in

that way; *með því móti, að . . .,* on condition that.

mót, móti *adv.* against, opposite; *prep. with dat.* opposite, against, contrary to.

mótmæla (a) *v.t. with dat.* object to, protest against.

muna (man; mundi; munað) *v.t. & v.i.* remember, recollect; *muna eftir e-u,* bear in mind, remember; *ef ég man rétt,* if I remember aright.

muna (a) *v. impers.* differ, vary; *það munar miklu,* that makes quite a big difference.

mund (pl. -ir) *n.* time; *í sama mund,* at the same time.

munnur (-s, -ar) *m.* mouth.

munu (mun; mundi; mundu) *v. aux.* shall, will.

munur (-ar, -ir) *m.* difference; importance; *fyrir hvern mun,* by all means.

mý *n.* mosquitoes, midges.

mynd *f.* shape; image; photo; illustration.

myrkur *n.* dark, darkness; *í myrkri,* in the dark.

mæða (i) *v.t.* weary; tire, exhaust; bother.

mæla (mæli; mælti; mæltur) *v.t. & v.i.* speak; *mæla við e-n,* speak to.

mæla (mæli; mældi; mældur) *v.t.* measure.

mæli *n.* voice.

mær (meyjar, meyjar) *f.* maiden, girl.

N

ná (næ and nái; náði; náður) *v.t. with dat. & v.i.* get; reach; attain; catch; *ná að gera e-ð,* manage to do s.t.; *ná í e-ð,* get hold of.

náð *f.* mercy; *pl.* rest.

náða (a) *v.t.* pardon.

nafn *n.* name; *af nafni,* by name.

nakinn *adj.* bare, naked.

nákvæmur *adj.* exact, accurate, precise.
nálgast (a) *v.t. reflex.* come near to, approach.
nálægur *adj.* near.
nám *n.* study; science; learning.
náttúra *f.* nature; supernatural power.
nauð *f.* need, distress.
nauðga (a) *v.t. with dat.* force, compel; rape.
nauðsynlegur *adj.* necessary.
nauðugur *adj.* unwilling, reluctant.
nauðulega *adv.* with difficulty, narrowly, only just.
neðan *adv.* below; *fyrir neðan (with acc.)* below.
nef *(gen. pl.* nefja) *n.* nose; beak, bill.
nefna (i) *v.t.* name, call; mention.
nefnd *f.* board; committee.
nei *adv.* no.
neinn *pron. indef.* any, anybody; *ekki neinn,* no one.
neita (a) *v.t. with dat.* refuse; deny.
nema (nem; nam, numdi, námum, numdum; numinn) *v.t.* take; hear; *nema staður,* stop.
nema *conj.* except, but; unless.
niður *adv.* down; *detta niður,* fall down.
nízkur *adj.* mean, stingy.
né *conj.* nor; *hvorki . . . né . . .,* neither . . . nor.
njóta (nýt; naut, nutum; notið) *v.t. with gen.* enjoy; use; get advantage from.
nóg *adv.* enough.
nógur *adj.* enough; sufficient.
nokkur *pron. indef.* some; somebody; any; anybody; *maður nokkur,* a (certain) man.
nokkurstaðar *adv.* anywhere.
Norðmaður *m.* Norwegian.
norður *n.* north; *adv.* north, to the north.
Norðurálfa *f.* Europe.
norska *f.* Norwegian.
norskur *adj.* Norwegian.

Noregur (-s) *m.* Norway.
nota (a) *v.t.* to use.
nótt *(gen.* nætur, *pl.* nætur) *f.* night; *í nótt,* tonight, last night.
nú, núna *adv.* now; at present.
nýr *adj.* new; fresh; *nýtt tungl,* new moon.
nægð *f.* plenty.
nægilegur *adj.* sufficient.
nær *adv.* almost, nearly; *compar.* nearer.
nærri *adv.* near; *prep. with dat.* near.

O

ó- *prefix* un-, in-, dis-.
oddur (-s, -ar) *m.* point; tip; nib.
ódýr *adj.* cheap.
of *adv.* too; too much.
ofan *adv.* down, from above; *detta ofan af,* fall down from.
ófanginn *adj.* unprejudiced.
oflátungur (-s, -ar) *m.* dandy, show-off.
ofn (-s, -ar) *m.* oven; stove.
ófriður (-ar) *m.* war.
oft *adv.* often.
og *conj.* and; *bæði . . . og,* both . . . and.
ógn *f.* terror; dread; *pl.* threats.
óhagur (-s) *m.* disadvantage.
óhappalegur *adj.* unfortunate.
óhægur *adj.* hard, difficult.
ójafn *adj.* uneven; unequal.
okkar *pron. poss.* our, ours.
ólag *n.* disorder; *í ólagi,* out of order.
olía *f.* oil; petrol.
ólæs *adj.* unable to read.
ónýtur *adj.* useless.
opinbera (a) *v.t.* reveal.
opinn *adj.* open.
opna (a) *v.t.* open; *v. reflex. (opnast),* open, be opened.
óráð *n.* bad advice; delirium; *tala í óráði,* rave.
orð *n.* word.
orðabók *f.* dictionary.
orðrétt *adv.* literally.

óreglulegur adj. irregular.

orka (a) v.t. with dat. manage to do, have the strength to do.

ormur (-s, -ar) m. snake.

óróa (a) v.t. alarm, upset, make uneasy.

orsaka (a) v.t. cause, lead to, bring about.

orsök (orsakar, orsakir) f. cause, reason (til, of, for).

orusta f. battle; fight; (naval) action.

ósk f. wish.

óska (a) v.t. with dat. & gen. óska e-m e-s, wish s.o. s.t.

ostur (-s, -ar) m. cheese.

óteljandi adj. countless.

ótt adv. rapidly, quickly; óðara en, hardly . . . when.

óttast (a) v. reflex. be afraid of, fear, dread.

óveður n. bad weather, storm.

óvinur (-ar, -ir) m. enemy, foe.

óvís adj. doubtful.

óþol n. impatience.

óþökk f. displeasure.

P

pappír (-rs) m. paper.

par n. pair.

páskar m.pl. Easter.

passa (a) v.t. mind, look after, take care of.

peningur (-s, -ar) m. coin; pl. money.

peysa f. jersey; jacket.

piltur (-s, -ar) m. lad, boy.

plægja (i) v.t. plough.

poki m. bag, sack.

pósthús n. post office.

prestur (-s, -ar) m. clergyman; minister, priest.

prjóna (a) v.t. knit.

próf n. examination; taka próf, take an exam., sit for one's degree.

pukur n. mysteriousness; í pukri, secretly, on the sly.

puti m. finger (colloquial).

pylsa f. sausage.

R

ráð n. advice; means, way; plan.

ráða (ræð; réð; ráðinn) v.t. advise; recommend; ráða e-m að gera e-ð, advise s.o. to do s.t.; with dat. rule, govern; ráða sér sjálfur, be independent; ráða draum, interpret a dream; ráða e-m frá e-u, persuade s.o. not to do s.t., dissuade; ráða í e-ð, guess at; ráða við e-ð, manage.

rafljós n. electric light.

ragnarök n.pl. -rökkur, doomsday; the twilight of the gods.

rang- prefix wrongly, falsely, mis-.

rangur adj. wrong; incorrect.

rannsaka (a) v.t. investigate, search, look into.

rauður adj. red.

raun f. trial; experiment; pl. troubles, sufferings.

refur (-s or -ar, -ir) m. fox.

regn n. rain.

reið (-ar) f. ride; vehicle.

reiðast (i) v. reflex. get angry.

reiði f. anger.

reiður adj. angry; ready.

reikna (a) v.t. count, reckon; reikna rangt, miscalculate.

reisa (i) v.t. raise; build; reisa bú, set up house.

reistur p.p. erect.

reita (i) v.t. irritate, tease.

reka (rek; rak; rákum; rekinn) v.t. drive; follow, pursue; do, perform; with gen. reka e-n aftur, drive s.o. back.

rekkja f. bed.

renna (renn; rann, runnum; runninn) v.i. run.

renna (i) v.t. with dat. run, let out; renna augum yfir, glance over.

reykur (-jar, -ir) m. smoke; steam.

reyna (i) v.t. & v.i. try; reyna að gera e-ð, try to do s.t.

reynast v. *reflex.* prove; turn out to be.

reynd f. experience; *í reyndinni*, in effect, in reality.

ríða (ríð; reið, riðum; riðinn) v.t. & v.i. ride; *with dat. ríða hesti*, ride a horse.

rífa (ríf; reif, rifum; rifinn) v.t. tear; pull down; scratch.

rigna (i) v. *impers.* rain.

ríki n. kingdom; *koma til ríkis*, come to the throne.

ríkur adj. rich; strong, powerful.

rísa (rís; reis, risum; risinn) v.i. rise, get up.

rita (a) v.t. write.

ritstjóri m. editor.

ritvél f. typewriter.

rétt adv. straight; rightly, correctly; *rétt bráðum*, at once, directly.

réttur adj. straight; right, correct; just; *með réttu*, justly.

réttur (-ar, -ir) m. law; right; claim.

réttvís, adj. just.

ró f. rest; quiet; *sofa í ró*, sleep soundly; *gefa ró reiði sinni*, let off steam.

rómur (-s) m. voice.

rót (pl. rætur) f. root; foot (of mountain); cause.

rúm n. bed; space.

rúma (a) v.t. hold, contain, have room for.

ræða (i) v.t. & v.i. speak; debate.

röð (raðar, raðir) f. row; series, succession.

rödd (raddar, raddir) f. voice.

rök n.pl. reasons.

rökkur n. twilight, dusk.

S

sá pron. *dem.* that; *sá sem*, he who.

saga (sögu, sögur) f. story, tale, saga.

sagnorð n. verb.

sakir (pl. of sök) prep. *with gen.* on account of.

saklaus adj. innocent.

sakna (a) v.t. *with gen.* miss, feel the lack of.

sala f. sale; *til sölu*, for sale.

saman adv. together; *smám saman*, gradually, little by little.

sam- *prefix* together, co-, like-.

samt conj. still, yet; *samt sem áður*, however.

samtal n. conversation.

samtíðis adv. at the same time.

samur adj. same; *í sama augnabliki*, at the same moment; *hinn sami . . . sem (og)*, the same . . . as (that).

samþykkja (i) v.t. consent to, agree to.

sannleikur (-s, -ar) m. truth.

sannur adj. true; *segja satt*, tell the truth.

sápa f. soap.

sár n. wound.

sauður (-ar, -ir) m. sheep.

segja (segi; sagði; sagður) v.t. say; tell; *segja frá e-u*, tell, relate

segl n. sail; *setja upp segl*, set sail.

seigur adj. tough.

seinn adj. slow; late.

seint adv. slowly; *betra er seint en aldrei*, better late than never.

selja (sel; seldi; seldur) v.t. sell.

sem conj. as; as if; *pron. rel.* who, that, which.

semja (sem; samdi; saminn) v.t. write; settle.

senda (i) v.t. send; dispatch; throw.

sendiherra m. ambassador, minister.

sennilegur adj. probable, likely.

setja (set; setti; settur) v.t. put, place, set; *setja skip út*, launch a ship.

síða f. side.

síðan adv. since; then.

síðast adv. last.

síður (-ar, -ir) m. custom, usage; religion.

sig pron. reflex. oneself, himself, herself, themselves.

sigla (i) v.i. sail.

sigra (a) v.i. win, be victorious; v.t. beat.

sigur (-rs, -rar) m. victory.

síld f. herring.

silki n. silk; úr silki, of silk, silk.

síma (a) v.t. with dat. & v.i. telegraph, wire, cable.

sími m. telephone; telegraph, wire, cable.

sinn pron. poss. his, her, hers, its, one's, their, theirs; sitt hvað, different things.

sinn n. time; eitt sinn, once, once upon a time; tveim sinnum, twice; í annað sinn, for the second time; öðru sinni, on another occasion; fyrst um sinn, for the time being.

sitja (sit; sat, sátum; setinn) v.t. & v.i. sit.

sízt adv. superl. least; síðast, en ekki sízt, last but not least.

sjá (sé; sá; séður, sénn) v.t. & v.i. see; look; sjá fram á, look forward to; sjá um e-ð, take care of.

sjaldan adv. seldom.

sjálfsagt adv. naturally, no doubt, of course.

sjálfsdáðir f.pl. free will; gera e-ð af sjálfsdáðum, do s.t. of one's own accord.

sjálfur pron. dem. self.

sjávar- prefix sea-.

sérstaklegur adj. special.

sjóða (sýð; sauð, suðum; soðinn) v.t. & v.i. boil; seethe; cook.

sjó- prefix sea-, marine-.

sjón f. sight; missa sjónina, lose one's sight; missa sjónar á e-u, lose sight of s.t.; þekkja e-n í sjón, know by sight.

sjónvarp n. television.

sjór (gen. sjóar) m. sea; sea-water,

salt-water; við sjóinn, by the seaside.

sjúkur adj. sick.

skaða (a) v.t. hurt; injure; harm, do harm; það skaðar ekki, it does no harm.

skák f. chess; tefla skák, play chess; skák, check.

skaka (skek; skók; skekinn) v.t. shake.

skakkur adj. crooked, distorted, wry.

skál (-ar) f. bowl; basin; drekka skál e-s, drink a toast to someone.

skáld n. poet; bard.

skammur adj. short; brief; fyrir skömmu, just now; innan skamms, shortly.

skap n. mood, disposition, mind; góður (illur) í skapi, good- (bad-) tempered; í góðu skapi, in high spirits.

skarpur adj. sharp.

skattur (-s, -ar) m. tax; duty; tribute.

ske (skeður; skeði; skeð) v.i. happen, occur.

skegg n. beard.

skeið (-ar) f. spoon.

skeið n. race; course; space of time; um það skeið, about that time.

skellur (-s, -ir) m. crash; smack; mishap.

skemta (i) v.t. with dat. amuse; entertain; skemta sér, amuse oneself, enjoy oneself.

skemtilegur adj. pleasant, entertaining; interesting.

sker (gen. pl. skerja) n. rock; reef; skerry; sigla milli skers og báru, sail between Scylla and Charybdis.

skera (sker; skar, skárum; skorinn) v.t. cut; carve; skera sig í fingurinn, cut one's finger; skera e-ð af, cut s.t. off; skera úr e-u, settle something.

skifta (i) v.t. with dat. divide,

part; distribute; change, shift; *skifta litum,* change colour; *skifta sér af e-u,* interfere in, meddle; *v. impers. það skiftir engu,* it makes no odds; *hann skiftir engu,* it makes no difference to him; *skifta um föt,* change clothes.

skifti *n.* division; time; *eitt skifti,* once; *til skiftis,* by turns; *fá í skiftum,* get in exchange.

skilja (skil; skildi; skilinn) *v.t.* understand; divide, separate; *v.i.* part, part company; be divorced; *skilja e-ð eftir,* leave behind; *skilja e-ð undan,* except; *skilja við e-n,* part from; *skilja við,* die; *v. impers. þar skildi vegina,* there the roads parted.

skiljast *v. reflex.* separate; *láta sér e-ð skiljast,* realize; *skiljast við e-n,* leave, part from.

skína (skín; skein, skinum; skinið) *v.i.* shine.

skinn *n.* skin; hide; leather; fur.

skip *n.* ship.

skipa (a) *v.t. with dat.* command, order; arrange, put straight; *skipa upp vörum,* unload goods.

skítugur *adj.* dirty.

skjálfa (skelf; skalf, skulfum; skolfið) *v.i.* tremble, shake; shiver.

skjóta (skýt; skaut, skutum; skotinn) *v.t. & v.i.* shoot; fire; *skjóta á e-n,* shoot at s.o.; *skjóta e-u á frest,* delay, put off.

skjöldur (skjaldar, skildir) *m.* shield.

skoða (a) *v.t.* see, view; examine, look over; *skoða e-ð í krók og kring,* make a thorough examination of.

skoðun (-anir) *f.* opinion, point of view, view; *ég er á þeirri skoðun, að . . .,* it is my opinion that . . .; *skipta um skoðun,* change one's mind.

skógar- *prefix* forest-, wood-.

skógur (-ar, -ar) *m.* wood; forest.

skóla- *prefix* school-.

skóli *m.* school; *fara í skóla,* go to school; *fara úr skóla,* leave school.

skolli *m.* fox; the devil; *adv. það er skolli kalt,* it is devilish cold.

skozkur *adj.* Scottish, Scotch.

skrá (-ar or **-r, -r)** *f.* list, catalogue; register; lock.

skrautlegur *adj.* splendid, magnificent.

skrefa (a) *v.i.* walk, stride.

skrifa (a) *v.t.* write.

skrín *n.* box; case.

skruma (a) *v.i.* boast.

skrumari *m.* braggart.

skrumsamur *adj.* boastful.

skrökva (a) *v.t. with dat.* fabricate, invent falsehoods; *v.i.* lie.

skuggi *m.* shadow; shade.

skuld *f.* debt; *gjalda skuld,* pay a debt.

skulu (skal; skyldi) *v. aux.* shall, will; must.

ský *n.* cloud.

skynda (i) *v.t. with dat.* hasten.

skynja (a) *v.t.* make out, perceive.

skynlaus *adj.* senseless.

skýr *adj.* clear, plain, evident; distinct; bright, clever.

skýring (-ar) *f.* explanation.

skýrlegur *adj.* bright, clever, intelligent.

skyrta *f.* shirt.

skömm (skammar, skammir) *f.* shame; disgrace; *pl.* abuse; *gera e-m skömm,* put to shame.

skör (skarar, skarir) *f.* edge, rim; hair.

slá (slæ; sló, slógum; sleginn) *v.t. & v.i.* hit, strike; beat; cut, mow; *with dat. slá e-u á frest,* postpone, put off; *slá eldi í,* set fire to; *slá til e-s,* hit, strike at.

slag *n.* blow; stroke.

sláttur (-ar, slættir) *m.* haymaking; harvest-time.

sleggja *f.* sledge-hammer; *vera*

milli steins og sleggju, be between the devil and the deep blue sea.

sleppa (slepp; slapp, sluppum; sloppinn) *v.i.* escape, get off; *sleppa undan e-m*, escape from.

sleppa (i) *v.t. with dat.* let go, leave go; *sleppa sér*, go off the deep end, lose control of oneself.

slíkur *adj.* such; *slíkir menn*, such people; *slíkur sem*, such as; *slíkt*, such a thing.

slíta (slít; sleit, slitum; slitinn) *v.t.* break; tear; *with dat.* break off, break up; wear out; *slíta e-ð í sundur*, tear up, break.

slokna (a) *v.i.* go out, become extinguished.

slys *n.* accident; *verða fyrir slysi*, have an accident.

slökkva (i) *v.t.* put out, extinguish; quench.

smá- *prefix* small.

smakka (a) *v.t. & v.i.* taste.

smár *adj.* little, small; *smám saman*, little by little

smíða (a) *v.i.* do woodwork, do metalwork; forge; *v.t.* make, build; forge.

smjör *n.* butter.

snarráður *adj.* resourceful.

snemma *adv.* early.

sníða (sníð; sneið, sniðum; sniðinn) *v.t.* cut; *sníða föt*, cut out clothes.

snjór (-s or **-var, -ar** or **-var)** *m.* snow.

snúa (sný; sneri, snerum; snúinn) *v.t. with dat. & v.i.* turn; change; translate, render; face, look towards; *snúa sér við*, turn round; *snúa aftur*, turn back.

snæri *n.* string, line.

snöggur *adj.* sudden.

sofa (sef; svaf; sofið) *v.i.* sleep; *sofa eins og steinn*, sleep like a log; *fara að sofa*, go to sleep.

sokkur (-s, -ar) *m.* stocking; sock.

sókn *f.* attack, offensive; fight; prosecution; parish; application.

sól *f.* sun.

sonur (-ar, synir) *m.* son.

sorg *f.* grief, sorrow.

sótt *f.* illness, complaint, sickness; fever; epidemic.

spegill (-s, speglar) *m.* mirror.

spila (a) *v.i.* play.

spjalla (a) *v.t.* talk, chat.

spor *n.* footprint; *ef ég væri í yðar sporum*, if I were in your shoes.

spraka *f.* halibut.

springa (spring; sprakk, sprungum; sprunginn) *v.i.* blow up, explode, burst.

spurning (-ar) *f.* question.

spýja (spý; spjó; spúinn) *v.i. & v.t. with dat.* vomit, be sick, spew.

spyrja (spyr; spurði; spurður) *v.t.* ask, inquire; hear, be told.

staddur *p.p.* situated; present.

staðfesta (i) *v.t.* confirm; establish.

staður (-ar, -ir) *m.* place, spot; town; *pl. parts*; *fara af stað*, set out, leave; *í staðinn fyrir e-n*, instead of; *í annan stað*, secondly.

standa (stend; stóð; staðinn) *v.i.* stand; be situated; last; be valid, be in force; *impers. nú sem stendur*, at present; *meðan á . . . stóð*, while the . . . lasted; *mér stendur á sama*, it's all the same to me; *standa eftir*, be left, remain; *standa við e-ð*, stand by.

starf *n.* work; job; employment; business.

starfa (a) *v.t. & v.i.* work; *starfa að e-u*, work at s.t.

starfsamur *adj.* hard-working, active, industrious.

steinn (-s, -ar) *m.* stone.

stela (stel; stal; stálum; stolinn) *v.t. with dat.* steal.

sterkur *adj.* strong.

stig *n.* step; degree; *pl.* lineage; *á þessu stigi málsins,* at this stage of the matter.

stíga (stíg; steig, stigum; stiginn) *v.i.* step, tread; *stíga á land,* land; *stíga á skip,* go aboard.

stígvél *n.* boot.

stinga (sting; stakk, stungum; stunginn) *v.t. & v.i.* prick; sting; *with dat.,* put, stick.

stirður *adj.* stiff; rigid; heavy.

stjórn *f.* government; management; steerage; committee, board (of directors).

stjörnu- *prefix* star-.

stóll (-s, -ar) *m.* chair; seat.

stór *adj.* great; large, big.

stormur (-s, -ar) *m.* storm; gale.

strand- *prefix* coast-, coastal.

straumur (-s, -ar) *m.* tide; current.

strönd (strandar, strendur or strandir) *f.* coast; shore; beach.

stúlka *f.* girl.

stund *f.* while, time; hour.

stundvís *adj.* punctual.

stuttur *adj.* short; brief; *í stuttu máli,* in a few words.

stöðugt *adv.* constantly, steadily.

suður *n.* the south.

súkkulaði *n.* chocolate.

sumar *n.* summer; *í sumar,* this summer; *að sumri,* next summer.

sumir *adj. pl.,* some (people).

sund *n.* swimming; strait, sound; passage.

sundföt, *n.pl.* bathing costume.

sunnan *adv.* from the south; on the south side; *fyrir sunnan,* in the south.

súr *adj.* sour; sharp, acid; surly.

svalur *adj.* cool.

svangur *adj.* hungry.

svanur (-s, -ir) *m.* swan.

svar *n.* reply, answer.

svara (a) *v.t. with dat.* answer, reply.

svartur *adj.* black.

svefn (-s) *m.* sleep.

sveit *f.* country; rural district; parish.

sverð *n.* sword.

sverja (sver; sór; svarinn) *v.t. & v.i.* swear.

Svíþjóð *f.* Sweden.

svíkja (svík; sveik, svikum; svikinn) *v.t.* deceive, cheat; betray; let down.

sviksamlegur *adj.* deceitful.

svipur (-s, -ir) *m.* look; face; likeness; *í þessum svip,* at this moment; *í svip,* for a moment.

svo *adv.* so; thus; then; *svo lengi sem,* as long as; *conj. (svo að),* so that.

svona *adv.* in this way, thus.

sykur (-rs) *m. & n.* sugar.

sýn *f.* sight; appearance; vision; *horfinn sýn,* lost from sight.

sýna (i) *v.t.* show.

synd *f.* sin.

synda (i) *v.i.* swim.

syngja (syng; söng, sungum; sunginn) *v.t.* sing.

sýsl *n.* business, occupation, line, job.

sýsla (a) *v.t. & v.i.* be busy with.

sýslun (-anir) *f.* job, employment.

systir (-ur, -ur) *f.* sister.

sæ- *prefix* sea-, marine-.

sæll *adj.* happy; *sælir verið þér,* welcome.

sæng (-ur, -ur) *f.* bed, eiderdown.

sænskur *adj.* Swedish.

sætur *adj.* sweet.

sögn (sagnar, sagnir) *f.* tale; statement; report.

sök (sakar, sakir) *f.* suit, action; charge; cause, reason.

sökkva (sökk or sekk; sökk, sukkum; sokkinn) *v.i.* sink, go down.

sökkva (i) *v.t. with dat.* submerge, sink.

sökum *prep. with gen,* on account of.

söngur (-s, -var) *m.* song, singing.

T

tá (táar, tær) *f.* toe; *standa á tánum,* stand on tiptoe.

tafl *n.* chess; *leika að tafli,* play chess.

tak *n.* grasp, grip; hold; *vera til taks,* to be ready, be at hand; *hafa margt í takinu,* have many irons in the fire.

taka (tek; tók; tekinn) *v.t. & v.i.* grasp, grip, seize, take hold of; begin to; *taka próf,* pass an examination; *taka málstað e-s,* take someone's part; *with dat. take e-m vel,* receive s.o. kindly; *taka framförum,* make progress; *taka bótum,* improve; *taka mark á e-u,* note, take notice of; *taka e-ð á sig,* take on, undertake; *taka eftir e-u,* take notice of, observe; *taka e-ð fram yfir e-ð,* prefer s.t. to; *taka í hönd e-m,* shake hands with s.o.; *taka sig saman,* pull oneself together; *taka til máls,* start speaking; *taka e-ð upp,* pick up.

tal *n.* talk; conversation; language; number; list, series; *eiga tal við e-n,* talk with.

tala *f.* speech; number, figure; bead, button; *halda tölu,* make a speech; *vera að tölu,* number.

tala (a) *v.t. & v.i.* speak, talk; *tala við e-n,* speak to s.o.; *tala um e-ð,* speak about s.t.; *tala ensku,* speak English; *tala af sér,* speak out of turn; *v. reflex. talast við,* speak together.

tapa (a) *v.t. with dat.* lose.

tár *n.* tear.

taska (tösku, töskur) *f.* handbag, bag; wallet.

taug (-ar) *f.* rope; string; nerve.

telja (tel; taldi; talinn) *v.t.* count; reckon; number; consider, deem; *telja á e-n,* tell off, reprimand; *telja að e-u,* blame, find fault with; *telja e-ð með,* include, count in.

tíð *f.* time; season; weather; tense; *áður á tíðum,* in former times.

tíður *adj.* usual; frequent; *hvað er títt,* what's new?

til *prep. with gen.* to; towards; till, until, etc.

tilbaka *adv.* back; *fara tilbaka,* go back.

tilgangslaus *adj.* without purpose, aimless.

tillit *n.* look; glance; respect, esteem; *taka tillit til,* take into consideration.

tilviljun (-anir) *f.* chance; *af tilviljun,* by chance, accidentally.

tími *m.* time; hour; *í þann tíma,* at that time.

togari *m.* trawler; tug.

tollur (-s, -ar) *m.* customs; duty; toll; *gjalda toll af e-u,* pay duty on.

tómur *adj.* empty.

tor- *prefix* difficult; slow.

traust *n.* trust; confidence.

tré *n.* tree; wood.

trú *f.* belief; faith; religion.

trúa (trúi; trúði; trúað) *v.t. with dat.* believe; credit.

trúnaður (-ar) *m.* faithfulness; loyalty; fidelity; faith; *segja e-m e-ð í trúnaði,* tell someone something in confidence.

trúr *adj.* faithful; safe.

tryggja (i) *v.t.* make safe; secure; guarantee; insure; *tryggja líf sitt,* insure one's life.

tröll *n.* troll; ogre.

túlka (a) *v.t.* interpret.

tún *n.* field; homefield.

tunga *f.* tongue; language.

tungl *n.* moon.

tvennur *adj.* two; double; *höggva í tvent,* cut in two; *tvenns konar,* two kinds of.

tví- *prefix* double, two.

tvisvar *adv.* twice.

tæki *n.pl.* gear, implements; means.

tækifæri *n.* opportunity, chance.

tönn (tannar, tennur) *f.* tooth.

tötrugur *adj.* torn, tattered, ragged.

U, Ú

ugga (uggi; ugði; uggað) *v.t.* fear; be apprehensive about; *v. impers. mig uggir að* . . ., I fear that. . . .

úlfur (-s, -ar) *m.* wolf.

ull *f.* wool.

ullar- *prefix* wool; woollen.

um *prep.* of, about, etc.

umbreyta (i) *v.t. with dat.* change.

umbuna (a) *v.t. with dat.* reward; recompense.

umbylta (i) *v.t. with dat.* overturn; revolutionize.

umfram *prep. with acc.* above; beyond; *adv.* besides.

umhverfa (i) *v.t. with dat.* overturn; turn upside down.

umhverfis *prep. with acc.* (and *adv.*) around.

umkringja (i) *v.t.* surround.

umræða *f.* discussion.

umtalsefni *n.* topic, subject of conversation.

umturna (a) *v.t. with dat.* overthrow; upset.

una (uni; undi; unað) *v.t. with dat. & v.i. una e-u, una við e-ð,* be content with; *una e-u illa,* be dissatisfied with.

undan *prep. with dat.* (and *adv.*) from underneath; away from, off, from; *á undan e-m,* before, ahead of; *líta undan,* look away; *komast undan,* escape.

undarlegur *adj.* strange; odd; funny; extraordinary.

undir *prep. with dat. and acc.* under, below, underneath, beneath.

undir eins *adv.* at once, directly,

straight away; *undir eins og,* as soon as, hardly . . . when.

undra (a) *v.t.* wonder at; *v. impers. mig undrar e-ð,* I am amazed by.

ungfrú *f.* young lady; Miss.

ungur *adj.* young.

unna (ann; unni; unnað or unt) *v.t. with dat.* love; *unna e-m e-s,* grant; not grudge s.o. s.t.; *unna e-m alls góðs,* wish s.o. every success.

unnusti *m.* sweetheart; fiancé.

unz *conj.* till, until.

upp *adv.* up; *taka upp,* pick up; *búa upp rúm,* make a bed; *upp á við,* up, upwards; *gera e-ð upp aftur,* do s.t. again; *upp frá því,* ever since; *upp úr,* out of.

uppáhalds- *prefix* favourite; pet-.

uppfylla (i) *v.t.* fulfil.

uppgefinn *p.p.* exhausted, fagged out; spent.

upphaf *n.* origin, beginnings.

uppi *adv.* up, upstairs; above; *vera uppi,* be all up, be at an end; living.

uppkominn *p.p.* grown-up.

uppljóstra (a) *v.t. with dat.* disclose; show; report.

upplyfta (i) *v.t. with dat.* raise.

upplýsa (i) *v.t.* illuminate, light up.

upplýsing (-ar) *f.* information; education.

uppnám *n.* confusion.

upprunalegur *adj.* original.

upptök *n.pl.* beginning; origin; source; initiative.

úr *n.* watch.

úr *prep. with dat.* from, out of; *fara úr landi,* leave the country; *fara úr fötunum,* undress; *úr gulli,* gold, of gold; *úr hófi,* excessively; *úr því að,* since, as.

úrræði *n.* expedient, way out (of a difficulty).

úrval *n.* selection.

út adv. out; *út um gluggann*, out of the window.

utan adv. from the outside; on the outside; abroad; *utan á*, on the outside of; *utan um*, round; *utan við sig*, absent-minded; *utan yfir*, over; *conj.* except; *prep. with gen.* outside; *prep. with acc. fyrir utan*, outside.

utanbókar adv. *læra (kunna) utanbókar*, learn (know) by heart.

utanhúss adv. out of doors.

utanlands adv. abroad.

utanríkisráðherra m. Foreign Minister.

útbýta (i) v.t. *with dat.* distribute.

útdeila (i) v.t. *with dat.* deal out, give out, distribute.

útfluttur p.p. exported; *útfluttar vörur*, exports.

útgáfa f. edition; issue.

úti adv. out, out of doors; out-doors; abroad; finished, over.

útlendingur (-s, -ar) m. foreigner.

útlendur adj. foreign.

útlista (a) v.t. explain.

útskýra (i) v.t. explain, elucidate.

útslitinn p.p. worn out.

útvarp n. radio, wireless.

útvegur m. way out; means; expedient.

útvelja v.t. select.

uxi m. ox, bull.

V

vaða (veð; óð; vaðinn) v.t. & v.i. wade; ford; *vaða á súðum*, babble, gabble.

vafalaust adv. beyond doubt, without a doubt.

vagn (-s, -ar) m. carriage; wagon; cart; cartload.

vaka (vaki; vakti; vakað) v.i. be awake; *vaka yfir e-u*, watch over.

vakna (a) v.i. wake up.

val n. choice.

vald n. power; authority; *hafa vald til e-s*, have a right to; *með valdi*, by force.

valda (veld; olli; valdið) v.t. with dat. occasion, create, give rise to, cause.

vandi m. difficulty; difficult task; responsibility; *i vanda staddur*, in an awkward situation; custom, habit; *að vanda*, as usual; *eiga vanda til e-s*, be inclined or liable to.

vandlegur adj. careful.

vandur adj. difficult; delicate.

vani m. custom, habit; *af gömlum vana*, by force of habit.

vanta (a) v. impers. *e-n vantar e-ð*, lack or be in need of s.t.; *klukkuna vantar fimm mínútur í fimm*, it's five to five.

var adj. aware; wary; cautious; *verða var við e-ð*, notice s.t.

vara (vöru, vörur) f. article, commodity; *pl.* goods.

vara (a) v.t. warn; *vara e-n við því að gera e-ð*, warn s.o. not to do s.t.

vara- prefix vice-, deputy-.

varða (a) v.t. defend, protect; guard; v. impers. *mig varðar litlu*, it is of little concern to me.

varfær adj. cautious, careful.

vargur (-s, -ar) m. wolf.

varla adv. scarcely, hardly, barely.

varmur adj. warm.

vatn n. water; lake; river.

vaxa (vex; óx, uxum; vaxinn) v.i. grow; increase; *vaxa upp*, grow up.

veðja (a) v.i. & v.t. with dat. bet; *veðja við e-n um*, bet s.o. s.t.

veður n. weather; wind; *ef veður leyfir*, weather permitting.

vega (veg; vó, (v)ógum; veginn) v.t. & v.i. weigh; kill.

veggur (-s or -jar, -ir) m. wall.

vegna prep. with gen. on account of; *þess vegna*, therefore; *hvers vegna?* why?

vegur (-s or **-ar, -ar, -ir)** *m.* road; way; direction; manner; *einhvern veginn,* in some way; *hins vegar,* on the other hand.

veiði- *prefix* fishing, hunting.

veikur *adj.* weak; ill; sick.

veita (i) *v.t.* grant, give; treat (with); *veita e-m,* aid s.o.; *veita hjálp,* give assistance.

vekja (vek; vakti; vakinn) *v.t.* wake up, awake, rouse, call.

vel *adv.* well; *gerið svo vel að;* please, be good enough to; *þakka e-ð vel,* thank very much; *vel mikill,* rather too large; *gott og vel,* well.

vél (-ar) *f.* machine; engine; device.

veldi *n.* power; empire.

velja (vel; valdi; valinn) *v.t.* pick out, choose.

venja (ven; vandi; vaninn) *v.t.* accustom; *reflex. (venjast),* get used to *(við).*

venjulegur *adj.* usual, customary.

vera (er; var, vorum; verið) *v. aux.* be; *vera til,* exist; *vera að gera e-ð,* be doing s.t.; *til eru menn, sem . . .,* there are people who . . .

verð *n.* price; value; worth.

verða (verð; varð, urðum; orð-, inn) *v. aux.* become, get, be; grow, turn; happen; *verða reiður,* get angry; *verða veikur,* fall ill; *ég verð að fara,* I must go; *verða eftir,* be left behind.

verður *adj.* worth.

verja (ver; varði; varinn) *v.t.* defend, guard; *(peningum, tíma)* spend.

verk *n.* work, business; deed.

verka (a) *v.i.* act, work; *verka á e-ð,* have an effect on, influence.

verkfall *n.* strike; *gera verkfall,* go on strike.

verkja (a) *v. impers.* ache, hurt; *mig verkjar í augun,* my eyes ache.

verulegur *adj.* real, actual; essential.

verzlun (-anir) *f.* trade, commerce.

verzlunarferð *f.* business trip.

veröld (-aldar, -aldir) *f.* world.

vestan *adv.* from the west; *fyrir vestan,* in the west.

vestur *n.* west; *adv.* towards the west.

Vesturheimur *m.* America.

vetrarlegur *adj.* wintry.

vetur (-rar, vetur) *m.* winter; *í vetur,* this winter; *að vetri,* next winter.

við *prep. with acc. & dat.* at, by, with, etc.

við *pron. pers.* we.

viðburðaríkur *adj.* eventful; exciting.

viðstöðulaus *adj.* uninterrupted, continuous, non-stop.

víður *adj.* wide; large.

viðurkenna (i) *v.t.* acknowledge; admit.

viðvíkjandi *prep. with dat.* re, concerning, regarding, about.

víg *n.* killing, manslaughter; battle, fight.

vigt *f.* weight; *eftir vigt,* by weight.

vík (-ur, -ur) *f.* inlet; creek; bay.

vika *f.* week.

víkja (vík; veik or **vék; vikum; vikinn)** *v.i.* yield, give way; move, turn, turn aside; *víkja á e-ð,* refer to, mention; *víkja burt,* go away; *v.t. with dat.* turn; *víkja sér að e-m,* address oneself to.

vilja (vil; vildi; viljað) *v.t. & v.i.* want; wish; be willing; *ég vil,* I will; *vilja gjarna gera e-ð,* be quite willing to do s.t.; *with dat. vilja e-m til,* happen to s.o.

villi- *prefix* wild.

vindur (-s, -ar) *m.* wind.

vinna *f.* work; job, employment; *vera að vinnu,* be at work.

vinna (vinn; vann, unnum;

unninn) *v.t. & v.i.* work; do perform; win, obtain, gain; *vinna e-ð upp aftur,* make up for.

vinningur (-s, -ar) *m.* profit; prize.

vinsæld *f.* popularity.

vinur (-ar, -ir) *m.* friend.

virði *n.* value, worth.

vís *adj.* certain; wise; *víst er um það,* to be sure.

vísa (a) *v.t.* show, point out; direct; *vísa e-m veg,* show the way.

vissulegur *adj.* certain.

vit *n.* sense, reason; intelligence; *tala af viti,* talk sense.

vita (veit; vissi; vitað) *v.t. & v.i.* know; be aware of; *fá að vita,* get to know, learn; *láta e-n vita,* inform, let know; *vita af e-u,* know of; *vita til e-s,* know of, be aware of.

víxl *n.* alternation; *á víxl,* alternately.

víxla (a) *v.t. with dat.* change, exchange.

voga (a) *v.t. with dat.* dare, venture.

von *f.* hope; expectation; *eiga von á e-u,* expect; *í von um,* in expectation of.

vona (a) *v.t. & v.i.* hope.

vondur *adj.* bad; wicked; angry.

vopn *n.* weapon.

vor *pron. poss.* our; ours; *pron. pers. (gen. pl.) til vor,* to us.

vor *n.* spring; *í vor,* this spring.

votur *adj.* wet.

völlur (vallar, vellir) *m.* field.

vöxtur (vaxtar, vextir) *m.* growth; *pl.* interest.

Y, Ý

yðar *pron. pers. (gen. pl.) til yðar,* to you; *pron. poss.* your, yours.

yfir *prep. with acc. & dat.* over, above; *with acc.* across, over.

yfirgefa *v.t.* abandon, forsake; leave.

yfirheyra (i) *v.t.* hear, examine.

yfirvararskegg *n.* moustache.

ykkar *pron. pers. (gen.) til ykkar,* to you; your, yours.

ymis *adj.* various; *pl. (ymsir, ymsar, ymis, yms)* several, various.

ysa *f.* haddock.

Þ

þá *adv.* then; *conj. þá er,* when.

þaðan *adv.* from there; thence.

þak *n.* roof.

þakka (a) *v.t.* thank; *þakka e-m fyrir e-ð,* thank s.o. for s.t.

þangað *adv.* there, to that place; *hingað og þangað,* hither and thither.

þar *adv.* there; *conj.* as, since, whereas; *þar til,* till then.

þáverandi *adj.* then, of that time.

þegar *adv.* already; at once; *conj.* when.

þegja (þegi; þagði; þagað) *v.i.* be silent, remain silent.

þekkja (i) *v.t.* know; *þekkja aftur,* recognize.

þerra (a) *v.t.* dry.

þessi *pron. dem.* this, that *(neut. þetta).*

þing *n.* parliament; assembly; meeting; thing, object.

þingmaður *m.* Member of Parliament.

þinn *pron. poss.* your; yours.

þjóð *f.* people, folk, nation.

þjóð– *prefix* national, social, public.

þjófur (-s, -ar) *m.* thief.

þjónn (-s, -ar) *m.* servant.

þó *adv.* yet, still, however; *conj.* although, though.

þoka *f.* mist; fog.

þola (þoli; þoldi; þolað) *v.t.* bear, suffer, stand.

þora (þori; þorði; þorað) *v.t.* dare.

þorskur (-s, -ar) *m.* cod.

þótt *conj.* although.

þrátt *adv.* frequently; *þrátt fyrir, prep. with acc.* in spite of.

þreyttur *p.p.* tired.
þrí- *prefix* three-, tri-.
þruma (a) *v.i.* thunder.
þröngur *adj.* narrow; tight; close; crowded.
þungur *adj.* heavy; hard, difficult.
þunnur *adj.* thin.
þurr *adj.* dry.
þurrka (a) *v.t.* dry.
þver- cross-, wrong-.
því *adv.* therefore, thus, consequently; *conj.* for, as.
þvo (þvæ; þó, þógum; þveginn) *v.t.* wash.
þýða (i) *v.t.* explain; interpret; mean, translate.
þykja (þyki; þótti; þótt) *v.i.* seem to be, appear to be, be thought to be; *v. impers.* with *dat.* *mér þykir það ótrúlegt*, it seems incredible to me; *mér þykir gaman að e-u*, I enjoy s.t.; *mér þykir fyrir því*, I'm sorry.
þyngd *f.* weight; *að þyngd*, in weight.
þyrsta (i) *v. impers. mig þyrstir*, I am thirsty.
þýzkur *adj.* German.
þökk (þakkar, þakkir) *f.* thanks; *kunna e-m þakkir fyrir e-ð*, be grateful for; *með þökkum*, with thanks, gratefully.
þörf (þarfar, þarfir) *f.* need, use; *þörf er á e-u*, s.t. is wanted; *eftir þörfum*, according to requirements.

Æ

æði *n.* nature; character, disposition.

æði *adv.* very, rather.
æfa (i) *v.t.* practise.
æfi *f.* age, time; life, lifetime.
æfinlegur *adj.* eternal, everlasting.
æfisaga *f.* biography.
æsa (i) *v.t.* excite; stir up.
æsing (-ar) *f.* excitement.
æstur *adj.* excited.
ætíð *adv.* forever, always.
ætla (a) *v.t.* be going to; intend; think, suppose; mean; *þeir ætla að fara*, they are going to go.
ætt *f.* family; extraction, stock.

Ö

öðruvísi *adv.* otherwise, differently.
öfund *f.* envy.
öfunda (a) *v.t.* envy; grudge.
öfundarfullur *adj.* envious.
ökli *m.* ankle.
öl *n.* beer, ale.
öld (aldar, aldir) *f.* age; *um aldir alda*, for ever and ever.
ölvaður *adj.* intoxicated; drunk, tight.
önd (andar, andir or endur) *f.* duck; breath; soul; life.
önn (annar, annir) *f.* business, work; occupation; *vera í önnum*, be busy.
ör *n.* scar, arrow.
örn (arnar, ernir) *m.* eagle.
öruggur *adj.* fearless; safe; trustworthy.
örvun (-anir) *f.* encouragement.
örvænta (i) *v.i. örvænta um e-ð*, despair of s.t.
öxl (axlar, axlir) *f.* shoulder.